Joseph Edkins

China's Place in Philology

An Attempt to Show that the Languages of Europe and Asia Have a Common Origin

Joseph Edkins

China's Place in Philology
An Attempt to Show that the Languages of Europe and Asia Have a Common Origin

ISBN/EAN: 9783744760737

Printed in Europe, USA, Canada, Australia, Japan

Cover: Foto ©Thomas Meinert / pixelio.de

More available books at **www.hansebooks.com**

CHINA'S PLACE IN PHILOLOGY:

AN ATTEMPT
TO SHOW THAT THE LANGUAGES
OF
EUROPE AND ASIA
HAVE A COMMON ORIGIN.

BY

JOSEPH EDKINS, B.A.,

of the London Missionary Society, Peking;
Honorary Member of the Asiatic Societies of London and Shanghai, and of the Ethnological Society of France.

LONDON:
TRÜBNER & CO., 8 AND 60, PATERNOSTER ROW.
1871.
All rights reserved.
G

TO THE DIRECTORS

OF THE

LONDON MISSIONARY SOCIETY,

IN RECOGNITION OF

THE AID THEY HAVE RENDERED TO RELIGION AND USEFUL LEARNING,

BY

THE RESEARCHES OF THEIR MISSIONARIES

INTO THE

LANGUAGES, PHILOSOPHY, CUSTOMS, AND RELIGIOUS BELIEFS,

OF VARIOUS HEATHEN NATIONS,

ESPECIALLY

IN AFRICA, POLYNESIA, INDIA, AND CHINA,

THIS WORK IS

RESPECTFULLY DEDICATED.

CONTENTS.

	PAGE
INTRODUCTION.	xi

CHAPTER I.—Introductory.—Comparison between the ancient Chinese civilization and that of the Babylonians and Egyptians.—Resemblance in genius and early inventions implies consanguinity in race.—Chronology.—Climatic conditions.—Agriculture.—Altars.—Government.—Arts.—The kings were priests.—Tombs.—Causes of the permanence of Chinese institutions. 1

CHAPTER II.—Comparison with Western Asia continued.—Resemblances in philosophy and religion.—Numerical philosophy.—The nine categories of the Hung Fan.—Measures.—Practical genius.—Astrology.—Cycles.—Early religion of the world.—Monotheism and burnt sacrifices in Genesis, Job, and the Shu King.—Sabeanism.—Angels.—Evil spirits.—Chinese burnt offerings to Shang Ti.—Worship of spirits and of visible nature.—These customs were brought from the west.—Worship of ancestors in temples. 13

CHAPTER III.—Geographical areas of languages.—Chinese and Eastern Himalaic—Japanese—Corean—Mongol and Turkish—Manchu—Tibetan—Tamul—Indo-European—Semitic.—Effect of geographical contiguity. 31

CHAPTER IV.—On the primeval language.—It was monosyllabic.—Examples.—Pronouns.—Laws of position.—Laws of rhythmus.—Pronominal roots also verbs.—Closed syllables a proof of man's continental origin.—Early use of final *m*.—Names of animals.—Divine origin of language. 51

CHAPTER V.—The Chinese probably Hamites.—Chronology of the Deluge.—Genealogies in Genesis. — Ancient Semite occupation of Persia.—Semitic impress on the Himalaic race.—The Chinese moved eastward before the Confusion of Tongues.—The Chinese ancient syllabary recoverable from the phonetics.—Six final consonants.—The surd initials derived from the sonants.—Tones.—Syntax. 67

CHAPTER VI.—The Semitic system older than the Turanian; younger than the Chinese.—Triliteral roots.—Insertions.—Suffixes.—Prefixes.—Growth of inflexions.—Sex.—Personifications.—Syntax.—The verb placed first.—Post-position of adjective and of genitive. — Post-position of genitive borrowed by European languages.—Semitic relative and European relative compared with the Chinese and Turanian equivalent. 92

CHAPTER VII.—The Himalaic languages younger than the Chinese; older than the Turanian.—Eastern Himalaic branch.—Siamese phonal system.--Cochin-Chinese tones.—Chinese natural tones. —Vocabulary.—Syntax.—Western Himalaic branch.—Tibetan phonal system.—Tibetan and Hebrew common words.—Tibetan tones.—Post-position of case particles.—Derivatives.—Tibetan verb.—Antiquity of the Tibetan type. 111

CHAPTER VIII.—First division of the Turanian system.—Japanese branch.—The triple-branched Turanian family: Japanese, Dravidian, and Tartar.—First, the Japanese.—Japanese syllabic alphabet.—Common roots in Japanese.—Formation of compounds.—Case particles. 139

CHAPTER IX.—Second division of the Turanian system.—The Dravidian languages.—Proof that this family is truly Turanian. —Common words.—Common laws of sound.—Surds and sonants. —Deficiency in sibilants.—Abundance of liquids.—Syllables usually open.—Derivation.—Comparative list of words.—The passive.—Negation.—Tense formation.—Dravidian syntax. . . . 168

CHAPTER X.—Third division of the Turanian system.—Mongol as a type of Tartar languages.—An old Turania in Western Asia.—The Tartar Turanians come nearest to the Indo-Europeans. —System of sound.—S and j for sh and d.—Ch for s.—Final ng dropped.—No f.—The seven vowels.—Tone.—Accidence.—

Substantive verb and first personal pronoun.—Mongol declension. —Pronouns.—The Mongol verb.—Conjugation.—Adverbial suffixes.—Mongol syntax. 204

CHAPTER XI.—Malayo-Polynesian.—The Malay the type of a distinct family.—Alphabet and syllable.—Polynesian syllable based on the old Chinese syllable.—Effect of marine climate on the Malayo-Polynesian syllable.—Continental origin of the Polynesians.—Connexion of Siamese and Malay.—Post-position of the adjective and genitive.—Pronouns.—Case particles.—Semitic principles.—Chinese influence on Polynesia.—Pronouns.—Verbal directives.—Comparison.—Arithmetic.—American languages do not possess an exclusively Turanian or Polynesian type.—The more civilized were mainly Polynesian.—Semitic and Hindoo traditions in America.—Legends of the Deluge descended from Noah. 247

CHAPTER XII.—The Sanscrit language.—Sanscrit richness in forms. Its principles of development based on older systems.—Alphabet. —Syllable.—Prefix of *s*.—Insertion of *r* and *l*.—Polysyllabic word.—Declension.—Case suffixes.—Plural.—Gender.—Comparison of adjectives.—Pronouns.—Derivative verbs.—Personal endings.—Tense marks.—Potential and conditional mood.— Infinitive.—Participle.—Auxiliary verbs.—Adverbial suffixes.— Prepositions.—Compounds.—Laws of position.—Zend Syntax. . 274

CHAPTER XIII.—European languages.—Latest and grandest development of language.—The alphabet.—Common radical syllabary of Chinese and European languages.—European radical syllabary. —The European word.—Semite influence seen in conjugational vowel changes, in doubled consonants, in masculine and feminine terminations, and in dual and plural numbers.—Turanian influence seen in moods and tenses, and in compounds.—European syntax.—Chinese element.—Semitic and Turanian elements.— Greek.—Tones in Chinese are accents in Greek.—Common words in Greek and Mongol.—Latin.—Resemblance of Latin gerund and supine to those of Tartar languages.—List of roots common to Latin, Chinese, and Mongol.—Latin syntax more Turanian than the Greek.—Roman family relationships suggestive of connexion with eastern ideas.—Resemblance between Roman and old Chinese religious beliefs.—Russian: The best new type of

b

the Sclavonic family.—Full alphabet.—Abounds in prefixes to roots.—Examples of syntax.—Anglo-Saxon.—The syntax Turanian.—Anglo-Saxon and German have more of the Turanian element than is seen in the English.—English returns to Chinese and primeval syntax.—Cause of these variations.—Resemblance of Anglo-Saxon poetry to that of the Mongols.—Alliteration: exchanged for rhyme; cause of this change.—English.—List of common words, Chinese and English. 318

CHAPTER XIV.—Conclusion.—Primeval Aryan civilization as known from language.—The common civilization of Aryans and Chinese may be known from language in the same way.—Activity of the third millennium B.C.—Ethnology of Genesis x. compared with the modern distribution of races.—Characteristics of families: the Chinese, *order;* the Semitic, *life;* the Himalaic, *quietness;* the Turanian, *extension;* the Malayo-Polynesian, *softness;* the Indo-European, *elevation;* all of one blood.—Proof from Polynesian and American traditions.—Résumé.—Duty of Christians to Asia, ... 385

INTRODUCTION.

To show that the languages of Europe and Asia may be conveniently referred to one origin in the Mesopotamian and Armenian region, is the aim of the present work. Sanscrit philologists, entranced with admiration of the treasure they discovered south of the Himalayan chain, forgot to look north of that mighty barrier. Limiting their researches to the regions traversed by Alexander the Great, they allowed themselves to assume that there was no accessible path by which the linguistic investigator could legitimately reach the vast area existing beyond their adopted boundary.

The result of this abstinence on the part of Bopp and other scholars of high fame has been that the idea of comparing Chinese, Mongol, and Japanese with our own mother-tongue appears to some chimerical, hopeless, and uncalled for.

Yet Scripture, speaking with an authoritative voice and from an immense antiquity, asserts the unity of the human race, traces the most general features of the primeval planting of nations, and declares that all men once spoke a common language. The most revered and most ancient of human books, in making these statements, sheds a bright and steady light on the obscurity of history, and at the same time reveals the imperfection of those views held by some modern thinkers and writers who deny that the languages of the world had one origin and that its races came of one stock.

Alike for the vindication of Scripture and the progress of knowledge, the comparison of the eastern Asiatic languages with the western is a task which must be undertaken, by whatever prescription it may seem to be forbidden. It is indeed not a little surprising that this inviting field of scientific research has been hitherto so little cultivated.

Among the causes which have operated on the modern school of comparative philology to prevent the advance of inquiry in this direction is the neglect of syntax. By Sanscrit scholars it has been too much taken for granted that this subject is unimportant. At least, Bopp, in his great work on the Comparative Grammar of nine Indo-European languages, has entirely passed it by. As there is no language in the world in which the order of words is not controlled by fixed laws, the omission of these laws from any book on grammar leaves it incomplete in a most vital part. Probably Bopp, seeing that Zend and Sanscrit, while they were sisters in all other respects, had in syntax the most singular disparity, allowed himself to conclude that difference in the order of words in a sentence is a mere matter of rhetoric, emphasis, and agreeable effect. The tendency of Greek and Latin studies is to produce this feeling.

One of the commonest effects of the juxtaposition of languages is the disjunction of syntax and roots. Every one who has visited China knows something about the grotesque dialect called Canton-English. It consists of English words arranged in a Chinese order. Sons of Cantonese traders procure a manuscript vocabulary of English words and contribute the syntax from their own language. A brief time of study qualifies them to become commercial agents, who can make themselves sufficiently well understood to gain profitable employment. In a Semitized country a like phenomenon would occur on a larger and more permanent scale, if it were conquered by a people of a strange language. The new words introduced would be arranged in the order familiar to the old population. Persia, for example, would retain Semite syntax when it received an Aryan immigration; and India would retain Turanian syntax after being conquered by the speakers of Sanscrit. It seems reasonable to account in this way for the resemblance existing between the Dravidian and Sanscrit syntax.

Another cause of the extensive belief in the impassable nature of the chasm between Indo-European and Turanian languages, is the assumption that the inflexional principle in the formation of compound words is something entirely distinct from the agglutinative. Yet in fact, as explained by Professor Max Müller and others, they are but different stages of the same process. Inflexion was at first agglutination, and agglutination can in many instances not be distinguished from what is called inflexion. The distinction, however, really exists, as is indicated by the circumstance that the writing of the Eastern Asiatic languages is always syllabic, while that of the Indo-European is alphabetic. Children are in the far east taught to read in syllables, rather than by letters. Where the inflexional stage of language prevails, the finer analysis of alphabetic writing also exists. If a sufficient deduction be made for the different aspect of languages as they are written syllabically and alphabetically, and if, further, the inflexional elements added to roots in Europe can be identified with those added by agglutination in Tartary, South India, and Japan, the supposed chasm will vanish from view.

The remaining cause for the want of attention to the

claims of the Chinese and other eastern languages for recognition as genuine sisters, coming from the common ancestry, like Hebrew, Sanscrit, and Greek, is unbelief in the identity of the roots. Klaproth and other authors, whose studies have led them to make wide comparisons of words in languages of widely separated families, had a conviction that the roots are originally one. This is eminently true of Gesenius. If Semitic scholars have a more thorough confidence in the original identity of the Hebrew and Indo-European vocabularies than is shown by philologists of the Sanscrit school, it is probably because they have had the advantage of knowing both the vocabularies more thoroughly. The dissyllabic character of the Semitic roots has been a serious bar to progress in comparing them with those of families which are, like the Indo-European and Turanian, based on the monosyllable. But this should not be viewed as proof of different origin. It is only to be taken as evidence of contemporaneous development. Branching from the same trunk, the Chinese, Semitic, Turanian, and Indo-European systems grew up together, each with its own laws, and in early times powerfully influenced by each other. If the Semites, as their first step in change, chose to prefix or append another consonant to their roots, and found that which satisfied their love of what is fitting in this widening of the radical base, we need not be deterred by this circumstance from the attempt to reduce the word thus altered to its original form. Take the word Shebet, *sceptre, rod,* to pieces by removing the sibilant excrescence. The remaining *bet* is our *beat* and *bat,* the Latin *batuo,* and the Chinese *fa* or *bat,* "to strike," "punish," or "chop down." So the verbs *kamah,* "to be consumed with desire," and *kamar,* "to burn with love," are identical with the Sanscrit *kam,* "to desire," the Persian *kam,* "love," the Chinese *kam,* "sweet," "to love." There is every reason to hope for the most solid and interesting results from a careful comparison of all the roots in the Eastern and Western families of languages, as has been done with those of the constituent members of the Indo-European group.

Since the time of William von Humboldt, the reference of language to a plurality of origins has been in Germany not uncommon; and Pott, Steinthal, and F. Müller hold this view still, against the opinions of F. Schlegel, Bunsen, and Max Müller. Should it be proved that the Chinese and Turanian families are certainly akin in syllabary, roots, and syntax to the Semitic and Indo-European languages, the area on which this battle can be fought will be very much diminished. To many minds the difference between Chinese and English will appear as great as that which could be found between any two languages whatever. To such minds what is proved in regard to Chinese will be admitted at once with regard to others. But should further processes of proof be demanded, it may be shown that the languages of the Pacific Ocean are firmly linked to those of the south-east of Asia in syntax, in roots, and in inflexional growth. Polynesian speech being thus shown to have branched off from the common trunk of Asiatic language, the defender of the doctrine of human unity in origin and in language may proceed to America. There is good reason to believe that the languages of that continent can be explained on the principles of the Polynesian and Turanian systems combined. If grammatical processes common in South-Sea speech are found in America, its partial colonization by way of the South Seas and Sandwich Islands must be conceded. The meeting of Turanian peculiarities, introduced from Greenland and Kamschatka, with those of south-eastern Asia, entering America by the tropics across the ocean, will be recognized as having made the languages of that continent what they now are. In the same way in Africa a Malay element would enter from Madagascar and a Turanian element by the Straits of Gibraltar; and the languages of colonies thus introduced may be expected to have exercised an important influence on the original Hamitic stock of that continent.

When to the strictly philological proof are added such evidences as may be derived from history, traditions, mythology, the arts, and special habits of grouping the objects of thought, the argument is powerfully increased. For example, in Polynesia, as in Eastern Asia, it is common to have two words for "brother," one for those older than the speaker, and another for those younger. The Mexican and Peruvian civilizations bear a strong likeness to that of Southern Asia. There seem to be none of the religious usages of those races which cannot be furnished with a prototype from the older locality first inhabited by the human family.

All these things taken together tend to confirm, with overwhelming certainty, the impression common to mankind in all countries, that all are of one original parentage. This was felt by Terence when he wrote the famous line:

"Homo sum, humani nil a me alienum puto."

Confucius believed that men are all of one ancestry when he said, "Si hai chi nui kiai hiung ti ye," *All within the four seas are brethren*, or more literally, *are elder and younger brothers*, for here we have an example of the principle referred to in the last paragraph. The Buddhists had a deep conviction of the same kind when they taught the vanity of caste distinctions, and the equality, before Buddha's law, of Sudra and Pariah with the most high-born Brahman. They also put in practice this article of their faith when they crossed seas and mountains to proselyte the Javanese islander, the Chinese, and the Tartar, to the cosmopolitan religion of their founder. But having only Hindoo legends as a basis of faith, they could not teach a reasonable account of the origin of man or of language, and the monstrous fictions of their national mythology shut out from their view the perfect God and eternal Creator.

It was reserved for Christianity to make known the true commencement of history and of language in the narrative of the creation of Adam. The triple unity of God, of the race of man, and of human speech, are taught in the sacred books of the Jews, and the first two of these are re-asserted with the strongest emphasis in the New Testament. Imbued with this faith, it is impossible for the Christian missionary not to feel an ineradicable conviction that the heathen tribes to whom he proclaims the Gospel are at one in origin with those civilized races that have been long blessed with the light of Christian truth. He sees among the islanders of Polynesia and Madagascar the descendants of the common Adam, who have, through want of instruction and long-continued isolation, lost the knowledge they once possessed, but retain in their traditions, mental structure, habits of thought, and peculiarities of speech, more or less clear traces of their original oneness with the more civilized nations.

Such also has been the opinion of men in all ages. Even the claim of the black-skinned African to recognition by the white man as "a man and a brother" is admitted instinctively by the common human conscience, as it is required definitively by the Christian law. It was reserved for modern science to propose for the first time the hitherto unknown hypothesis of a plurality of origins for the human species and for language. That this has been done without an attempt to compare the Chinese ancient language with the Indo-European is an indication of rashness on the part of the promoters of this novel hypothesis. It is hoped that in the following chapters there will be found a sufficient number of new and incontestable facts bearing on the subject to justify the re-opening of the whole question.

After a careful sifting of recent discoveries by the geologists on the antiquity of man, it will be the duty of the Christian theologian to examine afresh the question of early Biblical chronology. All new light brought upon this subject from unexpected quarters must be cheerfully accepted, so that difficulties in the current scheme may be as far as possible removed, and the claims of the older portions of the Bible to our intelligent faith may be shown to be as satisfactory as those of the more recent.

It only remains to mention the steps by which the hypothesis contained in this work respecting the connexion of languages assumed the form in which it now appears.

Commencing the study of the Chinese language under the auspices of the London Missionary Society, in 1847, and arriving at Shanghai the following year, I early sought to learn the laws of connexion between the dialects of that vast country. These, with the examination of the phonetic element in the Chinese characters, led me to see in 1854 that a rich mine of information regarding the ancient state of the Chinese syllabary and language lies concealed in the characters themselves, as written 4,000 years ago, and that the dialects furnish the key to it. The use of the Chinese mode of writing began to spread into Japan, Corea, and Cochin-China 2,000 years since, and the transcriptions then and subsequently made of Chinese sounds contain valuable information on the contemporary state of the Chinese language. These have been made available by various useful works, published by the deceased missionary, Dr. W. H. Medhurst, who spent forty years in the East, on Corean and Japanese; by Dr. Hepburn, American missionary-physician, at Yokohama, on Japanese; and by Father Morrone, of the Roman Catholic missions, on Cochin-Chinese. From these works and a study of the Chinese transcriptions of Sanscrit words found in Buddhist works, made 1,500 years since by the Hindoo missionaries of Buddhism in China, I derived new light on the history of the Chinese language. The examination of this subject has been greatly aided by the work of M. Stanislas Julien.

Sent to Peking in 1863, to join the missionary-physician, Mr. Lockhart, in commencing a mission there, I also studied Mongol; it being the Society's intention to begin afresh the diffusion of Christian light among the tribes of Tartary, a benevolent enterprise which for more than twenty years had been necessarily intermitted. This gave me the opportunity of tracing the connexion between Chinese and that language, and of examining how far it may be regarded as a missing link between Chinese and the polysyllabic speech of western nations.

Feeling convinced, on consideration, that Tartar agglutination and European inflexion are essentially one, I came to the conclusion that the apparently accidental likeness in some Latin and Manchu words, signalized by Herr Von der Gabelentz in his Grammar of the latter language, are examples in some instances of real identity. Such, too, appeared to be the case with Klaproth's list in Asia Polyglotta of what he calls Antediluvian words.

The present publication is an imperfect attempt to embody the views thus arrived at.

Residing in Peking, I have been unable to consult Mr. Hunter's work on the languages of India and Tartary, and many other valuable books, old and new. Very useful in these inquiries would be examples of old Turanian words from the Turanian cuneiform inscriptions, but these I have no means of obtaining.

I have been specially indebted to Dr. Karl von Scherzer for the use of some excellent works executed at the Imperial printing-press at Vienna, the names of which occur in the following pages.

PEKING, *September 23rd,* 1870.

CHINA'S PLACE IN PHILOLOGY.

CHAPTER I.

INTRODUCTORY.—COMPARISON BETWEEN THE ANCIENT CHINESE CIVILIZATION AND THAT OF THE BABYLONIANS AND EGYPTIANS.—RESEMBLANCE IN GENIUS AND EARLY INVENTIONS IMPLIES CONSANGUINITY IN RACE.—CHRONOLOGY.—CLIMATIC CONDITIONS.—AGRICULTURE.—ALTARS.—GOVERNMENT.—ARTS.—THE KINGS WERE PRIESTS.—TOMBS.—CAUSES OF THE PERMANENCE OF CHINESE INSTITUTIONS.

THE resemblance existing between the old Chinese civilization and that of the Hamite race long ago developed on the banks of the Nile and Euphrates is very remarkable. The two races made a common progress in agriculture, astronomy, and the arts of weaving and building. They also achieved the invention of an available mode of writing. The Babylonians impressed their characters on bricks when in a soft state; the Egyptians cut them on stone; and the Chinese painted them on tablets of bamboo or other kinds of wood. The first books in China consisted of bundles of these tablets strung together. In the west, the first books were made either of the papyrus, or of sheepskin sewed piece by piece into long rolls. So close a similarity in genius between the descendants of Cush and Mizraim, who founded the first arts of the west, and the Chinese, who on the east of the Indo-European area have always reigned supreme in intellect and manual ingenuity, argues a probable connexion of race.

Living in a latitude of 30° to 40° north of the equator,[1] the early Chinese possessed a climate which during the predominance of the Hamite and the Shemite intellect proved most favourable to progress in science and the arts. They probably came into the noble country assigned them by Providence for an inheritance, with an adequate knowledge of the Babylonian agriculture and astronomy. Their most ancient writings record the names of stars, an approximate length of the year, and the use of the intercalary month. As the Pleiades and other stars were, according to the native account, observed by means of an armillary sphere 2,000 years before Christ at the times of the solstices and equinoxes, we can test the general accuracy of their chronology. Making use of the correction required by the law of the precession of the equinoxes, we learn, for example, that the Pleiades were 4,000 years ago 60° behind their present position. This is in agreement with the Chinese ancient account.

[1] The Egyptian Thebes was in 26°, Memphis in 30°. Babylon was in 33°, and Nineveh in 36°. The old Chinese capital was in 35°.

We may therefore rely upon the history, so far as these old astronomical fragments are concerned, as generally trustworthy.

It has been suggested that the Chinese brought these observations at the solstices and equinoxes with them from the west,[1] and preserved by tradition the old positions of the stars. That they brought with them the rudiments of the arts and sciences seems to be unquestionable. But the fact that they brought them is evidence that they were able to make the described observations of celestial phenomena, and we gain nothing by shortening the national chronology.

If it had been at a date less than 2,000 years before the Christian era that the earliest Chinese came into their country, the difficulty of the historical problem would be increased. For how are we to explain the physical changes that have made the Chinese type of man what he now is if our chronological scheme is to be curtailed? It would not be wise to shorten the time of the separation of the Chinese from the men of the west, to whom they once stood, as will be shown, in the brotherhood of a common ancestry. Alterations in the language are of such a nature as to demand that we should allow for the Chinese occupation of North-western China a period certainly not less than that which is now usually assigned for the Hindoo occupation of India, or about 4,000 years.

[1] Legge's Chinese Classics. Chalmers' Origin of the Chinese.

As it happened to the Babylonians, so was it with the Chinese; their agricultural, settled life was affected by the geological changes proceeding in their time. The Yellow River[1] abandoned what appears to have been its old direction from the Ordos country eastward by Peking to the sea, and turned abruptly southward between Shansi and Shensi to the province of Honan. Here it flowed east, wound its way afterwards north-east, and reached the sea at Tientsin, near its former mouth.

The great central plateau of Asia has always been rising since and for ages before the commencement of history. The communication of the Caspian with the Polar Sea has long been dried up, and has become the bountiful inheritance of a Sclavonic population. The north coast-line of Siberia is still going out to sea at a rapid rate, viz.: at one degree of latitude in a century.[2] The Yellow Sea becomes each year more shallow, and the coast which was a few centuries ago at Tientsin is now forty miles away from it to the eastward. New alluvial islands spring up in the mouth of the Yang Tsz Kiang through the gradual elevation of the sea-bottom, and, covered with fertile alluvium from the river, become populous and wealthy farming districts. Teng cheu fu, in Shantung, used to be a port for native

---

[1] Pumpelly in Publications of the Smithsonian Institution, Washington.
[2] Arago, " Natural History of Human Species.' Quoted in *Princeton Review*.

vessels of large burden. Now they cannot anchor there. The old port is left high and dry, and the native shipping proceeds to Chefu, sixty miles eastward. In Babylonia the coast-line advances at the common mouth of the Euphrates and Tigris one mile in from thirty to seventy years.[1] These facts seem to point to the conclusion that the whole of Eastern Asia is constantly rising. In particular, the Yellow River has been subject, through subterranean forces causing oscillation,[2] to perpetual changes in its course, and it has entered the sea sometimes to the south of the Shantung promontory and at other times to the north. The necessity of protecting the fields from inundation proved a powerful stimulus to the emperor Yü and his contemporaries (as afterwards to the Chinese of each dynasty), and taught them to erect embankments and cut canals, just as it happened to the ancient Babylonians, that they were obliged to make provision against the overflow of the Euphrates by an extensive system of artificial watercourses.

The ancient Chinese also erected large square altars and high terraces of earth, stone, and brick. The sacred altars in Peking, on which imperial sacrifices are offered, are usually square earthen terraces about sixty yards in circuit, and from four to six feet high. There is a flight of wide marble steps in the centre of each side. The emperor, or his substitute, worships on

[1] P. Smith's "History of the World."   [2] Pumpelly

the altar, and on it are placed also the offerings, and the wooden tablet which represents the object worshipped. The terrace for the worship of heaven, 天壇 *T'ien t'an*, is round, is in three stages, and is ascended by twenty-seven steps. The paving-stones and carved balustrades of this altar are all of marble. When we keep in mind that the ancient Chinese have always been accustomed to erect lofty terraces for astronomical purposes,—such as the Observatory terrace now in Peking; that most of their terrace altars were for the worship of Heaven, or rather of God under that name, and of the powers of nature; and that the Cushites, who invented Cuneiform writing, erected in maritime Babylonia, for the worship of their divinities, terrace towers in stages still remaining; we cannot but imagine consanguinity between these races as probable.[1]

Let the inquirer take into account also the ancient government of the Chinese. They had feudal barons in five grades, Kung, heu, pe, tsz, nan, in subordination to a lord paramount. The oldest national traditions speak sometimes of the Hwang, and at other times of the Ti, as the lord paramount of the state, and recognize no period when such a personage was wanting. The Chinese, therefore, must be supposed to have entered

---

[1] The tower of Borsippa had seven stages, each dedicated to one of the seven heavenly powers, and distinguished by an appropriate colour. At the top was the Moon, silver, area twenty square feet. Then came, 2, Mercury, blue; 3, Venus, yellow; 4, Sun, golden; 5, Mars, red; 6, Jupiter, orange; and, 7, Saturn, black. Area at base, 272 square feet.

their present country with the idea of an absolute and wise ruler, as essential to the notion of a state. They have also always regarded him as entitled to his position by the choice of Heaven, communicated through successful war, the consent of the people, and the personal display of imperial virtues. We also know, by the Biblical history of Nimrod, that imperialism was one of the ideas of the Cushites. They with the Chinese were the first imperialists of whom history speaks.

Many ancient customs point to a connexion once existing between Western Asia and China. The use of magic, of music, of war chariots, and of religious usages, are in many respects parallel. In Layard's "Nineveh," three horses are seen harnessed abreast, in a bas-relief, to a two-wheeled chariot without covering, and occupied by warriors with bows. It is a curious fact that in native engravings, such as the Chinese love to make in illustration of their classics, ancient two-wheeled chariots without covering should be drawn with four horses abreast, while the emperor sits in the carriage protected from the sun by an umbrella which is held over him by an officer. At present in North China horses are not harnessed abreast. The farther we go back, the nearer are the resemblances.

Sorcerers are mentioned under the name *Mo* 巫 in the Shu king, in the second reign of the Shang dynasty, which commenced B.C. 1765. They are there spoken of in a disparaging manner, according to the invariable custom of the stern moralists who in China have been the makers of history.[1] The Chinese word *Mo*, "sorcerer," "witch," points historically and in its etymology to "brandishing the arms," "rubbing," and "handling." The ancient magicians wrought charms with their hands in India, Persia, and China. The Latin *manus*, "hand," and Greek μάω, "to rub," "handle," are from the same root, and it appears in Chinese as *Ma*, "to handle," "touch," and *Mo*, "to brandish the arms." This therefore is the most probable explanation of the word *Magi*, the common appellation of the Persian magicians.

In the same ancient Chinese records the arts of weaving and of working in metals are mentioned. The "Tribute of Yu"[2] says of Tsing cheu in Shantung, "Its articles of tribute were salt, fine grass-cloth, and the productions of the sea of various kinds, with silk, fine hemp, lead, pine-wood, and strange stones. The Lai barbarians are shepherds. They brought in their baskets silk from the mountain mulberry." They seem at that early period to have been acquainted with all the ordinary metals. The date of the "Tribute of Yu" is given by the Chinese B.C. 2205. From South-eastern and Western China came, as tribute to the emperor of that time, gold, silver, copper, iron, tusks,

[1] Perhaps this tone of disparagement may be taken as an indication of later composition. It occurs in a long speech attributed to the sage Yi Yin.
[2] Legge's "Shoo king," Part I., p. 102, slightly altered.

hides, feathers, cinnabar, timber, and various fabrics of flax, hemp, and hair. In the time of Joshua, B.C. 1450, Babylonish garments were conveyed to Judæa (Josh. vii.). The Persian race in Persia Proper, and as colonists in Turkestan, have always manufactured elegant woollen carpets. The Chinese ordinary word to "weave" is 織 *Chï*, old sound *Tek;* Latin, *texo*, "weave." To "build" is 築 *Chu*, old sound *Tok*. Its being placed under the bamboo-class symbol suggests that it was the custom to make bamboo hedges. They interlaced thin bamboo stems and used stouter ones as posts. The same word was applied to brick, earthen, and stone walls : for instance, the walls of cities. The Greeks called a carpenter τέκτων.

It is highly probable that the kings of Nineveh acted as priests. "As in Egypt, they may have been regarded as the representatives on earth of the deity, receiving their power directly from the gods, and being the organ of communication between them and their subjects."[1] In China there is no doubt on the point that the emperor has always borne a sacred character, and acted as a priest between God and the people, praying for them in times of distress, and acknowledging guilt on his own and their behalf.

The tombs of the Chinese emperors are remarkable. They are vast conical mounds of earth from a quarter of a mile to a mile in circuit. A long arched passage

[1] Layard's "Nineveh."

through brick-work leads up to the mound door. Over the passage is the monument inscribed with the title of the emperor. The hall in front, where worship is performed, is magnificent in size and appearance. Before this is another smaller hall. The tomb entrance, halls, courts, gates, and boundary walls are all on a large and complete scale. The tombs of the Lydian kings were something of the same kind. "The remains of that of Alyattes still stand near Sardis. The sepulchral chamber is surmounted by a lofty pile, and so far it is like the pyramids, but as the pile is a mound it is more like the tumuli or barrows of the western world. The basement consists of immense blocks of stone, above which is a heap of earth, surmounted by five pillars carved with inscriptions. The ground plan is a circle three-quarters of a mile round, a little larger than the great pyramid. The sepulchral chamber in the centre of the tumulus is eleven feet long, by eight feet broad, and seven feet high." See Rawlinson, quoted in P. Smith's History. Several of the ancient Chinese emperors, fabulous and historic, have funeral mounds assigned to them by tradition. That of Yu, the great engineering emperor, is near Ningpo. That of Fu hi is near Kai feng fu. The tomb of Yau is in Shansi, and that of Shau hau in Shantung. The identification of the tombs of these ancient princes cannot be relied upon without excavations. But the custom of burying the emperors in vast sepulchral mounds of earth is thus shown to be a custom as old as that of erecting large terrace altars for sacrifices, as already described.

To suppose that the Chinese originated independently the arts and usages to which allusion has now been made, is to assign two beginnings to a many-branched civilization which is one in its main features. At this stage of archæological inquiry in Europe it is preferable, when we accept the conclusion now generally arrived at, that it was the Cushites, the brothers of the Egyptians, who commenced and developed the Babylonian civilization, to proceed to class the Chinese with them. The likeness found to exist in practical bent, in the arts of life, and in all the solid elements of the old-world *régime* is sufficient to justify this step. If the Chinese did not bring with them to their new country all the arts mentioned, at least they came away with the same sort of mind and the same instinctive impulses. With a perseverance and enthusiasm which insured success, they laboured triumphantly for science and for the arts. More fortunate than the inhabitants of Babylon and Thebes, they have never seen the wreck of their institutions or the extinction of their national existence. In this they were favoured by their isolated position and the compact mass of their immense population. No Indo-European races approached them. The aborigines they found in the country, and the races that occupied Tartary, Tibet, and the Birmese peninsula, have always been inferior to themselves. When vanquished and subdued by Tartar races, they taught their conquerors the Chinese civilization, and when they became enervated by it, easily drove them back to their native wilds. With a wise foresight, two centuries before the Christian era, they abandoned feudalism, and adopted the centralization system of government, which they have ever since retained. When merchants brought them paper, and probably ink, of Greek manufacture from the West in the Han dynasty, they at once began to make them for themselves. The cumbersome bamboo tablets and coarse paint which were formerly used, they exchanged for wolf's-hair pencils and Indian ink, the modern implements of writing. They gave up war chariots, as did our ancestors, and commenced the use of cannon in place of catapults and battering rams. They discovered the properties of the loadstone, and probably applied it to navigation in the Indian Ocean several centuries before the mariner's compass was thought of in Europe. It was by these and such like improvements on their old institutions that the Chinese have kept pace with the ages, and prevented the fabric of their ancestral civilization from crumbling to irremediable decay.

CHAPTER II.

Comparison with Western Asia continued. — Resemblances in Philosophy and Religion. — Numerical Philosophy. — The Nine Categories of the Hung Fan.—Measures.—Practical Genius.—Astrolggy.—Cycles.— Early Religion of the World. —Monotheism and Burnt Sacrifices in Genesis, Job, and the Shu King. — Sabeanism. — Angels. — Evil Spirits. — Chinese Burnt Offerings to Shang Ti.—Worship of Spirits and of Visible Nature.—These Customs were brought from the West.—Worship of Ancestors in Temples.

THE numerous and very remarkable resemblances found to exist between the ancient Chinese philosophy and religion and those of Western Asia constitute a powerful proof of early connexion. There are many and very detailed allusions in the Chinese "Shu king," the most important of the classics, to the philosophy and religion current among the people in the second millennium before the Christian era.

The philosophy was in one aspect numerical. The five elements are alluded to as the five energies. *Hing* (old sound, *Gang*), "to walk," "to act," may be translated "elemental activities." They are water, fire, metal, wood, and earth, or the five powers supposed to inhere in these substances. Then we meet with the five relationships, namely, those of prince and subject, father and son, husband and wife, elder and younger brother, and the bond of friendship. The following extract, somewhat altered, from Legge's "Shoo king," p. 79, will illustrate the usage of the numbers four and five, etc., in common phrases:—

"The emperor Shun said to Yu, You, my ministers, are my legs and arms, my eyes and ears. I wish to help and protect my people. You assist me. I wish to proclaim the powerful efficacy of my government through the four quarters. You act for me. I wish to see the emblematic figures of the ancients : the sun, moon, and stars (illumination), the mountains (security), dragons (variety), and pheasants (beauty), painted on the upper garment, the tiger of the ancestral temple (filial piety), the aquatic grass (purity), fire (brightness), rice (the support of life), the hatchet (legal decision), and the symbol of discrimination, consisting of two representations of the character 己 *ki*, placed back to back, thus, 叝 embroidered on the lower garment. They should be figured with five colours, splendidly distributed among the five colours for the imperial robes. It is for you to adjust them plainly. I wish to hear the six pipes, the five sounds, the eight kinds of musical instruments, and the seven beginnings, in order that poems, made according to the scale of five sounds, may go forth from the Court and be brought in from the people. Hear this."

In the Hung Fan[1] is found the most comprehensive statement on the old numerical philosophy to be met with in any ancient book. It is said to have been received by Wu wang, B.C. 1100, from Ki tsze, who informed him that Heaven gave it to Ta yu, B.C. 2200, as a reward for his success in subduing the inundations of the rivers, and that the orderly arrangement of the moralities and social relations might thereby be completed.

THE NINE CATEGORIES OF THE HUNG FAN.

I. *Five Elemental Energies.*

water	moistens and goes down	salt
fire	blazes and ascends	bitter
wood	crooked and straight	sour
metal	obeys and changes	acrid
earth	sowing and reaping	sweet

II. *Five Human Actions.*

expression	respectful	venerable qualities
speaking	persuasive	order
seeing	clear	prudence
hearing	intelligent	deliberation
thinking	profound	wisdom

III. *Eight Departments of Government.*

food	commodities	sacrifices	works	instruction
	crime	guests	the army	

IV. *Five Registers of Time.*

years	months	days	stars	calendar

V. The emperor's perfection in virtue, or himself attaining the summit of virtue

---

[1] Legge's "Shoo king," p. 320.

VI. *The Three Virtues.*

uprightness	times of peace	
prevailing by firmness	times of violence and resistance	for the reserved and retiring
prevailing by mildness	times of harmony and compliance	for the lofty and intelligent

VII. *Investigation of Doubts by the Tortoise and Diviner's grass.*

Tortoise (*Chan*), *Tam*.	Five marks: rain, fine weather, clouds, connexion, crossing.
Diviner's grass (*Pu*), *Pok*.	Two marks: solidity, repentance.

VIII. *Five Natural Indications.*

rain   sunshine   warmth   cold   times

IX. *Five Kinds of Happiness and Six of Misery.*

long life   riches   health and peace   love of virtue   submissively accomplishing to the end the will of heaven

accidental death   sickness   grief   poverty   wickedness   weakness.

The Pa kwa, or system of whole and broken strokes in groups of three, arranged octangularly, was a set of symbols intended to represent a very ancient philosophy, consisting partly of physics, partly of morality, and partly of divination. It is the basis of the "Book of Changes," the time-honoured text-book of the masculine and feminine or dual philosophy. There are two other schemes of strokes and lines, called the "Ho t'u" and the "Lo shu," maps fabled to have come, the one out of the Yellow River, and the other, the Lo, one of its Honan tributaries. But none of these can be compared in value with the Nine Categories of the Hung Fan, if it be desired to see at one view the forms of ancient Chinese thought.

In the sphere of *physics*, the sages of this nation saw

five powers moving through heaven and earth without ever resting, giving variety to the forms of matter, imparting a natural constitution to all things, and causing the multifarious distinctions of colour, taste, and sound.

In the field of *human action* they remarked the *fivefold qualities of the sage* corresponding numerically to the activities of the senses and the thinking power.

In the government of the empire they had the idea from the first of an imperial head, under whom there was a division of departments, embracing agriculture, trade, religious ceremonies, works, education, judicial decisions, court ceremonial, and war.

Their next field of investigation was astronomy and astrology, which were always regarded as important enough to constitute a distinct branch of study for the sage.

Occupying the centre of this logical scheme, and the summit of the social pyramid, appeared to these ancient thinkers the ideal emperor, the priest, the ruler, and the example in his own person of all the virtues. It was the duty of the conscientious statesman to keep constantly before the view of the reigning prince, especially in his youth, the rounded and stainless image of moral perfection, that he might never forget the obligation to reflect it from himself.

The sixth division in the scale of thought was occupied by the discussion and inculcation of the qualities necessary to a ruler, consisting, when stated most briefly, of strict integrity, firmness, and mildness.

The seventh was divination for the foretelling of future events. For this purpose, so essential, as was thought, in agriculture, war, and politics, the aged forms of the same wise men, who during the long ages of the past gradually shaped out the Chinese civilization, must be imagined bending over the boiled or scorched shell of the tortoise and the forty-nine stalks of the diviner's grass. They desired to know what they indicated in regard to rain, wind, success in battle, and the suitableness of political measures.

The eighth department was that of the examination of natural phenomena to know if the emperor was acting wisely and well. Heat and cold coming in due proportion and at proper times indicate that Heaven is pleased with him and with the people. Particular stars foretell wind and rain, and also indicate the existence of certain virtues and vices among princes and their people. This was the people's divination, as that of the tortoise and the forty-nine stalks of grass was the emperor's.

Lastly, the sages studied human life in its varying fortunes and the inequalities existing in regard to length of life, riches, health of body, virtuous dispositions of mind, and moral strength and feebleness; in other words, the doctrine of *retribution*, visiting men always on moral grounds and by the direct agency of the Supreme Ruler.

In this sketch of the ancient philosophy of the

Chinese, coming from a time five centuries earlier than Confucius, we see the predominance of the numerical idea. Fixed categories of thought were constructed by them and by the Babylonians from a cursory observation of mental and natural analogies. The number of the fingers on the human hand and of the months of the year furnished them with sufficient ground for making five, ten, and twelve the bases of their cycles. The cardinal points, discovered by mankind in the infancy of language, as shown by the grammatical terms for direction existing in the speech of all races, combined with the succession of the four seasons, gave rise to the categories of four and eight. The category of three came from the observation of heaven, earth, and man, or of heaven, earth, and water, as the three provinces of being. The old category of two was originated by the observation of light and darkness eternally succeeding each other as day and night. There is a striking contrast here observable between the ancient dual philosophy of China and Persia resting on physical and moral distinctions, as light and darkness, or good and evil, and that of modern western philosophy, which turns its eye inward, and sees only in the world of existence the antithesis of the *ego* and the *non ego*.

This numerical philosophy was naturally accompanied by measures and measuring instruments both in China and among the Babylonians. Both races had measures of length and capacity, which they afterwards communicated to surrounding nations. Our own weights and measures and divisions of time came originally, it is agreed, from Babylon. The genius of the Babylonians and Chinese was so similar that, in both cases studying nature synthetically, they were contented with those useful and simple applications to common life and the service of the state which were in accordance with the practical bent of their minds. The more striking and profound discoveries of the analytical faculty they left to the Indo-Europeans, among whom thought was destined to soar with a bolder flight, and wing its way to loftier regions.

In the astronomy of Babylon and of China there was a common tendency to astrology. As to the numerical philosopher heaven and earth constituted one world, controlled by like laws, and those laws for ever unalterable, human events, he believed, can be foretold by reading aright celestial phenomena. For what reason do the stars grow bright and pale, and shine with a different coloured light? They are surely indications of the dispositions of the heavenly powers towards mankind. The same feeling which at a scientific epoch inclines an ardent mind, when gazing on the always mysterious, always wonderful, scenery of the starry sky, to wish to know the laws of motion, light, and mutual influence which there dominate, inspired in the childhood of science a mind of like aspirations with a longing to become an astrologer. But there was this difference. The aspirant after astronomical knowledge wishes to arrive at correct views of the laws of the physical universe, and to add to the ever-accumulating stores of science. The astrologer, on the other hand, aimed to acquire the key of destiny, and to wield it as a power over his fellow-men.

It appears to me more consonant with the facts of the case to trace the Chinese philosophy ultimately to Babylonia than to any other source, because, from its predominantly numerical and cyclical characteristics, it seems to have been founded very much on astronomy. The land which originated the numerical science of the Greeks, and of the Hindoos probably at a still earlier time, gave the Chinese the germs of their astronomy and philosophy,

The many striking similarities existing between the Babylonian and Chinese civilization warrant the expectation that the faith and usages of the religion of Enoch, Noah, and Abraham may be found among the ancient Chinese. Belus and Merodach were names unknown when the ancient connexion here contended for existed. It was the time described in the book of Job and the early parts of the book of Genesis, when the monotheistic faith prevailed in Western Asia, contemporaneously with the brick-building, metallurgy, music, cloth-weaving, writing, and other primitive arts, for which the people of that region were famed.

Babylonia and Mesopotamia were the theatre of the earliest revelation, and it was there that the historic muse first commenced the record of the events of time. From thence, also, China derived her earliest ideas. The inspired men of that early period led the march of the ages, and were the instructors who communicated the knowledge of the Supreme God, with worship by prayer and burnt sacrifices, to the ancestors of the Indo-Europeans,[1] the Chinese, and all races that have preserved the monotheistic tradition.

I will here place in succession the argument from the book of Genesis, the book of Job, and the Chinese Shu king. Faith in one God and worship by animal sacrifices (Gen. iv. 4, and viii. 20), with the general duties of morality and religion, taught by the father of the family, who acted as priest and instructor, constituted, according to the book of Genesis, the faith of mankind, first in the region of the Mesopotamian rivers, and afterwards, when the history becomes limited in its scope, in Canaan. The separation of the early nations is described, but nothing is said of their mythologies, which we are left to infer all sprang up subsequently. In India, for example, the Brahmanical religion began with monotheism; then it merged into a

[1] The Greeks in Homer's day used language which shows plainly that they had still the monotheistic tradition. Θεὸς τὸ μὲν δώσει τὸ δ' ἐάσει ... "For God will grant and permit whatever has pleased him, for he can do all things."—Od. xiv., 444, 445. See Max Müller's "Lectures on Language," second series.

mythology consisting of a mixed hero-worship and polytheism; then in the fifth century before Christ it passed into the Buddhistic atheism, substituting an image-worship of ideas for that of mythological personages; and subsequently went back to polytheism. In Genesis, the first man tilled the ground, and he and his wife were clothed in skins by divine direction. The discovery of the metals soon followed, and the ear of primitive men was pleased with the concord of musical sounds. They dwelt either in tents or in cities, and it is curious that cities should be mentioned first, as agriculture is mentioned before the keeping of sheep. The first animal sacrifice, that offered by Abel, we are left to suppose was burnt by fire from heaven, for we are not told in what way God signified his acceptance of it. Of Noah it is expressly stated that he offered burnt offerings on an altar, and this is the first mention of an altar.

One of the most impressive facts in the book of Job is that while he knew the names of stars, was able to describe the process of mining for silver, had an extensive acquaintance with natural history, and was himself an agriculturist and owner of extensive flocks and herds, he knew nothing of any pagan mythology. He was acquainted with the turning of the clay to the seal, and the graving of the pen upon the rock, with the productions of Egypt, with the government of kings upon their thrones, the pawing of the war-horse, the thunder of the captains, and the shouting of battle; but he had heard of no God beside Elohim and Shaddai, and to him he offered burnt offerings, as Noah had done before.

Though there is an allusion (chap. xxxi. 26) to the Sabean and old Persian worship of the sun and moon, which is condemned as contrary to the monotheistic doctrine, there is no reference to Babylonian or Syrian mythology; but there is distinct evidence of belief in the existence of good and evil angels. The enemy of mankind, appearing in Genesis in the form of a serpent, here comes upon the scene as a fallen angel.

The ancient Chinese emperors, as the Shu king teaches us, offered from time immemorial burnt sacrifices to Shang Ti, the Supreme Ruler, and the custom has been retained till the present time of burning an entire bullock, which must be without blemish, and, with the other bullocks which are offered unroasted, is previously kept in the park of the altar of Heaven. The entire bullock is at the present time roasted to ashes in a large furnace built of green glazed bricks, and set fire to from beneath. It stands on the southeast side of the great altar, on which are placed the tablet of Shang Ti and the offerings which are not consumed by fire. The emperor kneels and offers his prayer on the large altar, on the centre stone, having the unburnt victims and the tablets before him on the north. The furnace of the burnt offering is nine feet high and seven feet wide, and is ascended by nine steps on the south, east, and west sides. The fire is kindled from below on the north side. In several points it differs from the altars of burnt offering in the Old Testament, which were made of earth or of unhewn stones, and at a later period covered with brass. The burning took place among the Jews and other Western nations on the platform of the altar, and such was the ancient custom of the Chinese. The great altar proper, on which the emperor worships, occupies the place of the Jewish Holy of Holies, which contained the ark, and where the high priest offered prayer. Pursuing this comparison, the Chinese furnace of burnt offering is behind the imperial pontifex as he worships, and in front of the tablet, which is the visible symbol of the divine presence, and before which the emperor kneels. The more ancient custom was to have for the burnt sacrifices (as we learn from the Li ki, or Book of Rites, the fourth of the five classics) a second altar, T'ai t'an, to the south of "the round hillock." When the emperor knelt on the round hillock this altar of burnt sacrifice was behind him. The furnace is a modern invention, and its position to the south-east is a novelty. With regard to the object of the burnt sacrifice, the Chinese state it to be to attract the attention of the Spirit of Heaven.

This they also represent as the intention of the music which has, in ancient and modern times, always accompanied the sacrifices. Special odes are composed for these occasions, adapted to certain melodies, which constitute a sort of sacred music. They are introduced at fixed times during the progress of the ceremony, and much in the same way as at the setting up of the golden image by Nebuchadnezzar in the plain of Dura.

The want of acknowledgment of sin and of substitutionary punishment in the Chinese burnt sacrifices distinguish them from those of Genesis, the book of Job, and the Old Testament generally. They are now different, but they were one originally. Forgetting certain essential ideas, the Chinese have retained some features of undoubted antiquity which link them with the beginnings of human history in Southwestern Asia, and with the age of the first divine revelations.

To the original monotheism taught by the first inspired men succeeded, when they ceased to guide human thought, the nature-worship of the Turanians and Persians, the polytheism of the Hindoos and Babylonians, the animal-worship of the Egyptians, the Sabeanism of the Arabians. But the primitive age of monotheistic belief is not so far removed, nor has the gnawing tooth of time been so destructive among old-world traditions, as to allow the memory of that early faith to be entirely obliterated in any of the ancient literatures still extant:

It was to 上帝 Shang Ti alone that the burnt sacrifice was offered. This is a name which carries on the surface its own meaning—the Supreme Ruler. Since the Chinese came from South-western Asia (where monotheism originally prevailed), as is shown by a multiplicity of common customs, arts, and beliefs, and that at a time anterior to the change from the worship of one God to polytheism, how can we doubt that the Being they worshipped with burnt sacrifices under this lofty title is the Elohim and El Shaddai of the Old Testament?

The old Chinese records say that the emperor also worshipped the six honoured ones, thought by native critics to be the seasons, cold and heat, the sun, the moon, the stars and drought; after them the rulers of the mountains and rivers, and finally the multitude of spirits. The honoured ones are called 宗 *Tsung*, " the lofty ones." They are to be viewed as the intrusion of nature-worship into the old monotheistic religion. Evidently they mean those nature divinities that are above the earth, for the mountains and rivers and the spirits that occupy the lower regions of the air are referred to separately. The spirits Shen, anciently pronounced Zhin, may be the Jinn of the Arabs and

[1] Legge's "Shoo," p. 34. The name *Luy* 類 old form *Lut*, was probably chosen on account of the roundness of the altar. Other altars were square. *Lut* has, for one of its most prominent meanings, "roundness," as in *lut*, "reed," "pipe," etc.; and *Lu*, old sound *Lut*, "a round stove," "a skull," " a round hut."

Persians, which were fairies or demons. Perhaps they were originally the same as the Beni Elohim, "sons of God," of the book of Job, the ordinary name for angels in that inspired poem.

The deep impress of religious faith on the national mind continues to be apparent throughout the history of the Shu king, terminating B.C. 650. It was during this time also that the Shï king, the invaluable collection of old national poetry, was written; and here the same reverence for the Supreme Ruler, faith in his providential government of the world, and confidence in those traditions which represented him as speaking to Wen wang, the favourite sage and royal founder of the Cheu dynasty, are abundantly manifest. Monotheistic faith only became weakened on the arrival of an age of speculation, in the latter part of the Cheu dynasty.

The emperors were accustomed in their tours of inspection through the empire to offer burnt sacrifices to Shang Ti, on the summit of mountains in the north, south, east, and west provinces. Among the sins of Sheu which caused his death and the overthrow of his dynasty is mentioned his neglecting the annual sacrifice at the Altar of Heaven. The accession of emperors to the throne, and the occurrence of remarkable victories, together with times of drought and other public misfortunes, were always deemed suitable occasions for these sacrifices.

The books of Genesis and Job, with the Shu king,

all depict an age when open altars were used for worship, when one God was adored, when there was no priestly class, when the chief of the family and of the state was its priest, and when the happiness and misery of man were universally believed to be providentially assigned by God in the way of rewards and punishments. The Sabean worship of the heavenly bodies grew up with open altars, and was the cause of Abraham's removal to Canaan. The Chinese brought with them this earliest deviation from a monotheistic creed, and the habit of worshipping and attempting to propitiate those angels, whether well or ill disposed (the Shen and the Kwei), in whose existence they had learned to believe before coming from the west. To this they added the worship of ancestors in temples by means of tablets. This third deviation from the primitive faith of the world corresponds to the honours paid to heroes, and the polytheistic worship of images with human names in Babylon, Syria, Egypt, and India, which were also performed in all cases in temples. The temple is imitated from the house, and was intended originally for the posthumous worship of heroic men and the ancestors of kings. When the Chinese left the west, nearly three thousand years before the Christian era, the germs had scarcely begun to appear of those mighty polytheistic religions which followed monotheism and Sabeanism, and preceded or precede Christianity among the nations of South-western Asia, India, and Europe.

That the early Chinese should, in addition to their monotheism, have become infected with the Sabeanism which Job condemned, and with some other heathen usages found to prevail long after in the countries from which they came and through which they passed, need not be wondered at when we recollect that vestiges of the old monotheism co-existed with the Roman, Greek, Egyptian, and German idolatries. Cicero said, "Dei nutu omnia provisa sunt," "all things are provided beforehand by the will of God." He also says elsewhere, "Haec omnia deorum nutu atque potestate administrari," "that all these things are administered by the will and power of the gods." He speaks in the one case under the influence of the monotheistic faith, which lay beneath the prevalent polytheism, and in the other case under that of the popular faith in the greater and lesser gods. Wilkinson, vol. i., in his chapter on the Religion of the Egyptians, ascribes to the priests an esoteric faith in the Unity of the Deity.

Before the introduction of images and temples there was one religion spread among all the Asiatic races. It was the nature-worship which grew up upon the primeval monotheism, and it assumed different phases, as the professors of it were Persians, Hindoos, Sabeans, Turanians or Chinese.

CHAPTER III.

GEOGRAPHICAL AREAS OF LANGUAGES—CHINESE AND EASTERN HIM-
ALAIC—JAPANESE—COREAN—MONGOL AND TURKISH—MANCHU
—TIBETAN—TAMUL—INDO-EUROPEAN—SEMITIC.—EFFECT OF
GEOGRAPHICAL CONTIGUITY.

THE Chinese probably entered their country, nearly 3000 years B.C., by the usual highway from Mohammedan Tartary, into Kansu and Shensi,[1] founding colonies along the banks of the western tributaries of the Yellow River, where we find the ancestors of the Cheu family. The road by Kia yü kwan and Lan cheu to Si an Fu would bring the first settlers to the south bend of the Yellow River, at the pass called T'ung kwan, so well known in history. Following the river east and north, they would arrive in Honan, where Tang, the founder of the Shang dynasty, had his origin, and in Chili, the north part of which province gave birth to Yau, the first emperor mentioned in the Shu king. Other colonists, crossing the river into Shansi at

[1] Dr. Legge, who, by his translations, has opened to view in the English language the treasures of the Chinese ancient literature with unexampled fullness, is inaccurate when he brings the early settlers by the Yellow River into Shansi, vol. iii. Prolegomena, p. 189. That route would have lengthened very unnecessarily the journey across the desert. The cities of Kansu mark the most practicable route.

T'ung kwan, settled in the rich valleys of that province, where the emperor Shun was afterwards born. Everywhere they found aboriginal inhabitants, whom they pushed before them, the ancestors of the present Miau tribes. By the time of Christ they had reached the south-east coast, for that part of China is then spoken of as well colonized. They also pushed their conquests into Cochin China, which was made a Chinese province.

The languages of the Chinese, the Miau tribes, and of Cochin China are monosyllabic, and marked by the presence of tones. The same characteristics belong to the speech of Tibet, Birmah, Siam, and Cambodia, with all the hill tribes embraced within their boundaries. These languages together constitute the great monosyllabic family of south-eastern Asia.

Of this numerous family the type is the Chinese, which deserves this distinction, not only on account of the unparalleled population that makes use of it, but for its antiquity, its high literary development, and its independence of foreign accessions. It appears from the vocabularies possessed by the Chinese of the Miau dialects that their tribes inhabiting the hill districts in Kweicheu, Kwangsi, Canton and Yünnan are best regarded as a northern extension of the Siamese and Birmese population. They use partially both the Siamese and Birmese writing.[1] The customs of Siam,

[1] See the vocabularies of the Ming Imperial College for Languages, of which Klaproth has made ample use in his "Asia Polyglotta."

its calendar, its costume, are found among them. A few are Buddhists, but most tribes are believers in demons, enchantments, and ancestral worship, and as such must be assigned to the dominion of that old Turanian religion and system of institutions which Logan, speaking of the Tibeto-Burmans, has thus characterized : " The Tibeto-Burmans, where least modified by India and China, preserve all the traits of the ancient race and civilization of Upper and Eastern Asia. They are Turanian or Mongolic in person only; their usages are of archaic Mid-Asian origin, like those of the Tartars and Chinese. Long before the rise of the Egyptian, Semitic, and Iranian civilizations, one well-marked civilization, characterized by a common morality and by peculiar usages, religious, social, and domestic, prevailed almost universally." "In this old system," he continues, "women were slaves, clanship existed, with sorcery, divination, and ordeals. The old, weak, and useless lives were sacrificed when they became burdensome. They believed in one Supreme God, and an immaterial imperishable spirit in man; the spirits of ancestors and relatives were feared and worshipped. To gratify the dead and avert their malice, part of their possessions were burnt or buried with them."[1]

By vocabularies contained in the Hing i fu chi and Kwang si t'ung chi,[2] it appears that the Chung Miau

[1] J. R. Logan's "Journal of the Indian Archipelago," 1858.

[2] 興義府志, 廣西通志

are allied to the Siamese. They reside in the south-west of Kwei cheu province. The Lo lo, a very old and extended tribe, in the north-west of the same province, are connected with the Burmese. The first personal pronoun in these dialects varies between *ye*, *ku*, and *nau*; while the second is very frequently *meu* and *meng*, so that they are cut off from any Indo-European or Tartar connexion.

Logan has conferred a great service on philology by his division of the Himalaic languages into two branches, eastern and western. He states that the eastern or Mon Anam branch has some radical peculiarities in structure, and has been deeply influenced, first, by the Dravidian family, and, secondly, by the Chinese. The area of this branch is Cochin China, Pegu, Siam, and Cambodia. Farther south, at the peninsula of Malacca, it meets the Malay, which constitutes the type of the Australasian and Polynesian languages. The western Himalaic branch retains the same characters in Tibet, India, and Ultra-India, and is more Scythic than the eastern.

Most of the migrations of races have been in the direction of radii from the common centre where the first human pair was created, and where the first generations of their posterity lived. Along one radius came the Dravidian races, and after them the Hindoos, by way of the Punjaub into India. The Eastern and Western Himalaic peoples, after traversing Tibet, passed along the valley of the Brahmaputra into Ultra-India; settling not only in that peninsula, but probably also in Southern China, where the Miau, Lo lo, Nung, Yau, and other tribes are their descendants. The Chinese, taking a more northerly route, came along the lands watered by the Turkestan rivers till they reached the north-western corner of China Proper. They met with the Jung in Western China, the modern Sz c'hwen. These people have left descendants in the Nung, one of the most celebrated branches of the Miau. The equivalent of the Mandarin initial *J* is in old Chinese *N* and *Ni*. In 778 B.C., the Jung were powerful enough to kill an emperor[1] at the capital, which was then in Southern Shen si. They were soon afterwards driven back. At present one of the tribes bordering on Yünnan is called Nu i, or the Nu barbarians. Here the same name occurs, but without the final *ng*. The Chinese also met in their earliest wanderings other sections of the Himalaic migration in Hunan, viz., the three Miau tribes, and the Lai and Nung in North-eastern China. The old names in China of rivers, tribes, and mountains are but one word, and appear to have been all monosyllabic. From this it may be inferred that the various aborigines all spoke monosyllabic languages.

The present spoken language of the Chinese, as used over two-thirds of China, is called *Kwan hwa*, and

[1] Legge's "Shoo king," p. 615.

by Europeans, *the Mandarin dialect*. The term *Mandarin* is of Portuguese origin and means *commander*. Indispensable as it seems, it is a name which cannot be defended, except on the ground of convenience.

The northern Mandarin is spoken in the capital and in the four north-eastern provinces: Chili, Shantung, Shansi, and Honan. It has also spread itself through Manchuria and parts of Mongolia by colonization. The Manchus in Girin and Kwantung form but a tithe of the population, and have long forgotten their native tongue. The northern Mandarin is also spoken partially in Shensi and Hupe.

The western Mandarin is spoken in Kansu and Sz c'hwen, Kweicheu and Yünnan, and partially in Shensi and Hupe. Portions of Kwangsi and Hunan also belong to its area.

In the modern Mandarin language the old sonant initials *g, d, b, v, z,* have disappeared. But they are retained in the dictionaries of the book language. So also the final letters *k, t, p,* once abundant at the end of syllables, have been entirely lost over the whole of Northern and Western China.

The northern and western Mandarin are differentiated principally by the Ju sheng tone class. The immense group of words, amounting to nearly a fourth of the vocabulary, belonging to this tone class are in the northern Mandarin irregularly distributed among the other four classes. In the western, on the other hand, they have all gone to swell the Hia ping class, which has thus come to embrace about a third of the entire vocabulary.

The southern Mandarin, which retains the Ju sheng as a distinct class, prevails at Nanking, in the north part of Kiangsu and Anhwei, and partially in Hunan. Its area is a belt of varying width, extending from the ocean at the mouth of the Yang tsz kiang and the old mouth of the Yellow River to Chang sha in Hunan.

The old middle dialect is spoken at Sucheu, Shanghai, Hangcheu, and Ningpo, and has the distinctive characteristic of possessing the old thirty-six initials and four tones as used in the syllabic spelling. Kanghi's Dictionary and the native tonic dictionaries all register an ancient pronunciation, which, so far as the initials and the medials are concerned, is best represented at present by the old middle dialect. Its area embraces Chekiang and the southern part of Kiangsu. It then proceeds westward through Anhwei and Kiangsi into Hunan, where, near the boundary of Sz c'hwen, it meets the western Mandarin.

This dialect is invaluable for the study of the old Chinese language. A knowledge of its peculiarities renders the syllabic spelling, now eleven or twelve centuries old, perfectly available; and thus the sounds of all characters may be known as they existed before the language underwent that great organic change which produced the Mandarin dialect in its three-fold form.

The assistance derived from the old middle dialect for research into the ancient Chinese language needs to be supplemented by the southern dialects, which are also, especially in regard to their final letters, of great archæological value. The lost finals, *m, k, t, p*, are retained with almost perfect uniformity in the dialects of Canton, Chaucheu, and Amoy. The dialects of Fucheu and Hweicheu, and that called the Hakka, are less valuable in research, being situated on a line of transition. The relation of French to Latin resembles that of Mandarin to the Canton and Amoy dialects. *Am,* "dark," Latin *umbra,* "shade," has become *an* in Mandarin, as *suum,* "his," has become *son*. *Kot,* "to cut," has become *ko* in Mandarin, as *gladius* has become *glaive,* and *traditor, traître*. The root *kot,* "to cut," appears in *gladius,* with the sonants *g* and *d,* instead of the surds *k* and *t*. It is also found in *cædo,* "to cut," *culter,* "a knife," and the English *cut*. The *l* inserted in *gladius* and *culter* is dropped in the French *couteau*. The Japanese call "a sword," *katana*. The Mongols say *hadahu,* "to cut," "to reap." The Tamul-speaking people of Southern India say *katti* for "a knife." The Hebrew word for "to cut off branches" was *gadang,* גָּדַע. In the case of a wide-spread root like this, found in so many families, it is certainly no slight advantage to have the ancient form well preserved in the south-eastern dialects of China.

The Japanese language, spoken and written, is much mixed with Chinese. The Chinese language, literature, and customs were introduced there in or about the first, fifth, and seventh centuries of the Christian era. In addition to many thousand Chinese words, introduced with the contemporary pronunciation and still kept unaltered in the language, the native vocabulary of words is also very extensive. The first Chinese immigration was probably Tauist, and perhaps chiefly intended for the propagation of religious opinions; but it spread also the Confucian literature and morality, and gave the Japanese the alphabet of fifty letters which they still use. The temples and habits of life and thought of the Sinto priesthood resemble those of the ancient Chinese Tauists of the Han dynasty, who did not use images. During four or five centuries before the arrival of the Buddhists, A.D. 400, the influence of China in Japan continued, and this was the period when the Sinto system, with its numerous *Kami*, " spirits " or " gods," became consolidated. From A.D. 400, during the introduction of the *Go won*, " Wei pronunciation," and *To won*, " Tang pronunciation," there was an immigration of Buddhist priests of various Chinese schools. They aided in continuing that powerful impulse which ended in the establishment of a complete system of Chinese instruction throughout Japan, and the universal profession there of the Buddhist faith. From this time every youth learned the language of Confucius at school, and the Colloquial Chinese of the period became mixed with the national language to a most remarkable extent, for the ordinary purposes of life as well as for the exigencies of the scholar.

But in regard to the Japanese native idiom and vocabulary, what is it? It bears a manifest resemblance to the Mongol. The root takes polysyllabic suffixes and vowel prefixes in both languages. The verb is placed at the end of the sentence, and is preceded by its object. The case particles are syllabic suffixes attached to nouns. In *Akari.wo tomoshi*,[1] "to light a lamp or candle," *wo* is the case suffix for the objective case. *Akari*, "a light," is the Mongol *gerel* with a vowel prefix, in Chinese kwang. *Tomoshi* is the Chinese *tiem*, "to light," "kindle," with verbal suffix *oshi*. The Japanese, in regard to pronouns and substantive verbs, is more like the Chinese than the Mongol, but in respect of syntax and polysyllabic derivation, it is manifestly like the Mongol, Manchu, and Turkish. It is then Turanian, but it does not bear so close an appearance of kindred to the Tartar languages as they do to each other. Their having in common the first personal pronoun and substantive verb in *b* and *m*, links these three modes of speech together as first cousins, while the Japanese, Corean, and Tamul languages, from the want of

[1] See Hepburn's "Japanese Dictionary."

these prominent features, are but as second or third cousins.

Hence, for the convenient classification of the Turanian system, three sub-families are required:—

1. The Tartar, comprising Mongol, Manchu, Turkish, etc.

2. The Japanese, embracing Japanese, Aino, and Corean.

3. The Dravidian, including Tamul, Telugu, etc.

That the Corean language should be placed in close family relationship with the Japanese cannot be doubted, when it is remembered that there is in it no trace of the favourite Tartar and Indo-European pronoun and substantive verb in *b* and *m*, and that it resembles the Mongol and Japanese in placing the verb at the end of the sentence, immediately following its object, and in adding to the roots polysyllabic suffixes. For the sentence "this room has two windows," the Coreans say *i k'utul*, "this room," *t'ul c'hang isir*, "two windows has." The pronoun *i*, "this," is in Mongol *ene*, "this," in Chinese *i*, "that." *K'utul* may be the Mongol *ger*, "house," and Chinese *kia, ke*, "home." *T'ul* reminds us of the Persian *du* and English *two*. *C'hang* is borrowed from the Chinese *c'hwang*, "window." *Isir* is probably the Chinese *yeu*, "to have," with suffix *sir*.

The Japanese *ware shiranai*, "I do not know," where *ware* is "I" and *nai* is "not," may be compared with the Corean *na*, "I," *aji*, "know," *mothar*, "not."

Like the Japanese, the Coreans study Chinese literature, and mix Chinese words with their own in the common intercourse of life. An immigration of Chinese Buddhists, continuing for several centuries, communicated to the language a large Chinese element. The introduction of French words like *adieu* into English may be adduced as an example of the same kind of influence on our own language. The Chinese sacred books are read in schools throughout Corea, and the doctrines of Confucius inculcated. The Corean alphabet made for them by the Buddhists on a Tibetan or Sanscrit model, is now used to write the mixed languages as at present spoken.

The Aino language spoken on Yesso has the Japanese polysyllabic formation and laws of position, and is without the substantive verbs and personal pronouns in *m* and *b*. It is therefore a Turanian language, and is to be classed with the Japanese branch.

The best type of the Tartar sub-family of the Turanian languages is apparently the Mongol. The Turks have always been much mixed with the Persians, who early occupied Bactria. That country, indeed, is spoken of in the Zendavesta as the original home of the Arian religion. Though called Turkestan by our geographers, it was Persian before it was Turkish, and its Persian population are the Tadjiks of the present day, and the 大食 *Ta shih*,[1] old sound *Da zhik*, of Chinese historians.

[1] In the Chinese dynastic histories, the Arab conquests are attributed to

They pressed over the passes of the T'sung ling chain, called by the Turks *Mustag*, "Ice Mountains," into Chinese Turkestan; here they became mixed with the Wigur Turks, as at Bokhara with Usbeks, Turcomans, and other races. The result has been that the Turks of Yarkand, Cashgar, and Bokhara, as well as those of Constantinople, have assumed more of the Indo-European appearance than is seen in the Mongols or the Manchus. This is true also of the Mahommedans who have crowded into North China during the Sung, Yuen, and Ming dynasties. This numerous class, coming, as their traditions say, from Bokhara and the other Turkish cities, have very much of the European head and physiognomy—their deep and horizontal eyes, prominent nose, with a tendency to a vertical facial angle, and to the growth of whiskers, bespeak western descent, and help to give them, among the surrounding Chinese, a characteristic and easily recognized physiognomy. This mingling of Turanian and European features of race has affected the Turkish language. The Mahommedan religion has also added many Arabic words which have been adopted into the Turkish, both of Constantinople and of Yarkand, with the other cities of Chinese Turkestan. The word *Adam* for "man," and *ruh* for "spirit," are used in the easternmost Turkish cities. A Bucharian vocabulary, translated by Klaproth from

the Ta shih. This is through an error in their information. They did not learn the true name of the Arabs till more recently.

Chinese, and printed in the Asia Polyglotta, is entirely Persian. It is called in Chinese the language of the Hwei hwei or Mahommedans, who during the Ming dynasty appear to have been identified by the Chinese with the Persians, in regard to language, religion, and race. The Turkish is consequently so permeated by the Persian and the Semitic element introduced by religion, that it can scarcely be considered the best type of the Turanian languages; especially is this true, because the relative pronoun, otherwise foreign to the Turanian family, is found in Turkish in its Persian form, and may best be regarded as borrowed from that language. The Persian influence on Turkish extends even beyond the boundaries of Mahommedanism, into Siberian dialects. In Castren's vocabulary of Turkish dialects in Siberia, *Kudai*, the Persian word for the Supreme Being, often identified with our term *God*, and the German *Gott*, is employed for "heaven" and for "God." Our word *foot* appears as *put* and *but*, which are quite Indo-European, the Persian being *pai*.

The Mongol, therefore, may be viewed as a better Turanian type. It occupies scattered sections of that great belt of land which stretches from near the mouth of the Amoor to the banks of the Volga, and from the Kokonor lake to the Altaï mountains. In its eastern extension it meets with Tungus tribes and Chinese colonies of agriculturists, some of whom, near the banks of the Amoor, learn to speak better Mongol than they do Chinese. The Buriat Mongols, east of the Baikal Sea, are also conterminous in area with Tungus tribes. West of the Gobi Desert the Mongols are mixed with a Turkish population, the descendants of the ancient Wigurs, and with various other tribes of the same race in Turkestan and European Russia. To the south-west they come in contact with the Tibetans, and to the south-east with the Chinese. The Mongol language occupies the centre of the Turanian area so far as Tartary is concerned, and became a written language about five centuries ago, when, in the Yuen dynasty, it was necessary for the fierce nomades of the great central plateau of Asia to accommodate themselves to the usages of civilized countries and commence the formation of a literature. They adopted the alphabet already in use among the Wigur Turks and which had been given them by the Nestorian missionaries. Thus the present Mongol and Manchu alphabet (for the Manchus took theirs from the Mongols) was derived from the Syriac, through the missionary zeal of the Nestorian communities in Western Asia.

The Manchu language is spoken on the lower course of the Amoor by tribes under Chinese and Russian domination. In the Greek church mission, recently established there, the Manchu translation of the New Testament, made at Peking about 1805 by Lipoptsoff, is found to be intelligible and useful. This is the version published by the British and Foreign Bible

Society. In the Chinese province of Hei lung kiang, north of Girin, the Manchu language would seem to have lost ground and to have contributed to the Mongol area, for the Chinese colonists there speak Mongol fluently. In the provinces of Girin and in sea-board Manchuria Chinese is the common speech. If we would look elsewhere for spoken Manchu, it must be among the Tungus tribes of Siberia, found scattered at various localities east of the Baikal. In Peking Manchu is spoken as a Court language, and learnt for that purpose from teachers. It is also extensively written as a documentary language. Numerous helps exist for the study of it in the form of translations, dictionaries, and phrase books, published at Peking. The study of the language is maintained in all the Manchu garrisons in the eighteen provinces of China Proper, and in Mongolia. A syllabary is used of about 1,000 syllables. Where the Mongol writing was deficient in the power of distinguishing sounds, the Manchu has added special marks, so that the mode of writing indicates the pronunciation satisfactorily, which is far from being true of the Mongol.

The Tibetan, perhaps the most convenient type of the Himalaic languages, has been well opened to observation by the Dictionaries and Grammars of Csoma de Körös, Schmidt, and others. These two grammarians have not, however, considered the tones, which in a monosyllabic language become of special importance.

Georgi's notice of the Tibetan tones is only sufficient to show that they are of the same nature as the Chinese. We have not yet any comparative lists of common words in the Anamitic, Siamese, Burmese, Tibetan, and Chinese languages made with reference to their intonations, by help of which the general laws of tones for all this widespread family might be investigated.

The Tibetan language spreads from Ladak, the most northerly of our British Indian possessions, to Sz c'hwen, where it meets the Chinese area. Its eastern member is the Si Fan dialect. The nomade Mongols also occupy Eastern Tibet, and are there mixed irregularly with the Si fans.

Crossing the Himalayas we find the Dravidian area occupying hill districts in Northern India and the plains and mountains of the South. Among the languages of this family, the Tamul is the best to use as a type. It is spoken by ten millions of people, extending on the east coast from Cape Comorin to a point eighty miles north-west of Madras, and on the west coast from Cape Comorin to Trivandrum.[1]

The Dravidian family is cut off from its relatives in Tartary and Tibet by the intrusion of a broad belt of the Indo-European area. The Arian invasion of India is supposed to have taken place about 2,000 years before the Christian era. Those who came into India

[1] Pope's "Tamil Handbook."

at that time spread the Sanscrit tongue, which was followed by the Pracrit, over three-fourths of India, and gave origin to the numerous group of languages known as Bengali, Sindi, Hindustani, Guzarati, Urdu, and Marathi.

The superior energy of the Indo-European race enabled it to conquer wherever it found a home. Europe and Asia Minor, Persia and Bactria, were all subdued and occupied by this powerful branch of the human family.

Their home extended from Samarcand to Lisbon, and from Calcutta to the land of Thor, and the multiplied experiences of so wide a region tended to excite in their intellectual development a proportionate richness and variety.

The gift of imagination was awakened in this race by residence in mountain scenery and around inland seas. They wandered far, they grew up amidst the most beautiful and varying landscapes. Their homes were among the great mountain chains of the world: the Himalayas, the Bolor Tag and Mustag of Bactria, the Caucasus, Mount Taurus, the mountains of Thessaly, and the Alps and Apennines. Their earliest navigators traversed the Black Sea and the Caspian, the Archipelago and the Adriatic. Hence the spirit of freedom and the irrepressible sense of poetry, the tendency to speculation and the keen appetite for science, that have always characterized this race. All other races, except the Semitic, are comparatively wanting in these splendid gifts, which make the Indo-European nations the very flower and crown of humanity.

A natural love for variety of experience, difficult travelling, and new scenes, led the earliest colonies of this favoured race to choose their homes where the eye and the hand, the mind and the body, should be exercised in due proportion, and thus the human species be brought higher up on the ladder of progress. The result we see in the wonderful expansion of philosophy, science, and literature among many nations of this race, ancient and modern, which has made Europe what it now is.

The elder branch of the Caucasian race, the Semitic, occupying Syria, Mesopotamia, Assyria, Babylonia Judæa, and Arabia, was destined to do more for the religious culture of the race than any other linguistic family. The religious, moral, and spiritual impress on the European races had a parallel in the earlier linguistic influence which it appears to have exercised. The superior ease and fluency of European speech, compared with that of Eastern Asia, comes partly from the relative pronoun and partly from the liberty allowed in the construction of sentences. Both the relative, and the freedom used in the position of verbs and words belonging to the other parts of speech, probably come from the influence of Hebrew and its cognate languages. On the Chinese side of the Himalayas, and of the Persian- and Russian-speaking area, the laws of position in sentences are fixed, and there is, properly speaking, no relative pronoun. It was not, then, from this side that the Arians, the youngest of races, derived their freedom in syntax, leading to a beauty and expansion in poetic expression which are inconceivable to the less imaginative races. These characteristics, with the genders of nouns and the voices of verbs, came from the influence exercised by the combined Hamite and Semitic races on the early language of the world. The Semites were always neighbours to the Hellenes and the Persians.

The influence of old Turanian languages on the formation of the Indo-European system was favoured to an equal degree by geographical contiguity. Colonies belonging to this stock were sprinkled over Western Asia in many localities; and in the Persian area, Iran and Turan from the dawn of history stood in close contact to each other and in hostile attitude.

The polysyllabic development of the Arian languages, their case and tense suffixes, together with such vestiges as they retain of a law relegating the verb rigidly to the end of the sentence, are the effect of Turanian influence.

CHAPTER IV.

On the Primeval Language.—It was Monosyllabic.—Examples.—Pronouns.—Laws of Position.—Laws of Rhythmus.—Pronominal Roots also Verbs.—Closed Syllables, a Proof of Man's Continental Origin.—Early Use of the final M.—Names of Animals.—Divine Origin of Language.

WITHOUT venturing to discuss, except very cursorily, the origin of language, I shall here first attempt to mark out some of the common elements existing in the speech of all nations which seem to belong to a primeval language older even than the Chinese and the Egyptian. The mother from whom all existing dialects have been born may possibly be revealed to our view by carefully rejecting all new elements and retaining what appear to be universal.

That it was monosyllabic is deducible from the fact, that in all the families, from the Indo-European upwards, the roots are monosyllables. The words *separation* and *departure*, for example, are traced to the Latin *Part* in *pars, partis*. The *r* is lost sight of in the Sanscrit *bheda*, "dividing," *bhedita*, "divided," *bhinna*, "separated." It occurs in a dissyllabic form in the Hebrew *badak*, "split" (Latin *fidit*), and *badad* and *badal,* "divided," and without a third consonant in the Hebrew *bad,* "separation." The Chinese is *Bit, Pit,* "separate," "other."

Our words *rotation* and *radiation* are traced to *rota,* "a wheel," and *radius,* from the same root, *Rad* or *Rot,* German *rad,* "wheel," Sanscrit *lut,* "roll about." In Tamul we find *urutchi,* "roundness," and *urul,* "a carriage-wheel." The Chinese call "a wheel" *Lun,* and many round things, as "a stove," "a cottage," "a skull," "a reed," are known as *Lu,* where a final *t* has been lost. Musical pipes they call *Lut.* The same idea of roundness is found, more or less remotely, in the English *rod, reed, oar, row, round.* The German *ruder,* "oar," *rudern,* "to row," compared with the Greek *eretmos,* "oar," *eresso,* "row," Latin *remus,* "oar," *remigo,* "row," throw light on the origin of the word *oar,* and enable us to trace it to the same root with the others. The Chinese *Lu,* for *Lut,* is a scull, such as is used in China for propelling a boat by stern action.

When we have arrived in such investigations at the monosyllabic root *Lut, Rad, Rot,* our progress is entirely checked, and we are left to conclude that the primitive speech of man was monosyllabic, and contained in it such widespread roots as the two just given.

Father and *mother* must be admitted without hesitation into the primeval vocabulary of the human family, for though some nations, as the Mongols, appear to want them, nine-tenths of the inhabitants of Europe and Asia agree in their use. Of course they must be accommodated to the necessities of infancy by cutting off the second syllable of the English form and changing the initial *f* into *p*, or, still better, into *b*. The Turks in saying *Baba* for " father " are more primitive than any. The Semites in saying *ab* and *em* for " father " and " mother " gratified a tendency to prefix vowels. In the Chinese *fu, mu,* we have the newest form of what was a few centuries ago *Bo, Mo*.

The claims of *brother* to a place in the primeval vocabulary are quite hopeless. It appears to be unknown in Asia beyond the Indian and Persian area. There is more hope for *sister* than for *brother*. It may perhaps be recognized in the Chinese *Tsie* for an older *Si* or *So,* used in the sense of *elder sister.*

The names of number differ so widely in the various Asiatic languages that they are not to be expected to be very ancient.

Of the pronouns, *a* and *nga* or *ga* for the first person, *u, nu,* and *yu* for the second, and *i, gi, hi* for the third, may claim a very high antiquity; for their widespread use through the linguistic families is a palpable and striking fact.

For the first person we find the old Chinese 我 *nga* and 予 *yo* or *o,* of which the latter, being without an initial consonant, suggests that the *ng* was prefixed afterwards. Another prefix consisting of *a* or *e* made the Sanscrit *aham* and Latin *ego*. The *m* final was a suffix also found in the Chinese 俺 *am*, a dialect form for "*I*." The Hebrews added *nochi, anochi,* "*I*." The Arabs said *ana*, and the Egyptians *anok*. There appear to be very few languages in any part of the world that do not in their pronominal forms betray the presence of this root. The same is not true of the pronoun in *m*, which is almost entirely limited to the Indo-European and Tartar languages. *Bi, men,* "I," and *manai,* "my," are as common in Tartary as *me, mein, meus,* εμος in Europe, but there is not a trace of them to be found in China, Tibet, or Japan. Quite as little are they known in the Dravidian area or in the islands of the Eastern seas. The Mongol riding into Peking on his camel, says, *manai bic'hig,* for "my book," and the Manchu student learns from his instructor, *manai bit-he,* in the same sense, while the German, in a region 100° of longitude further west, says, *mein Buch*. But these words, in their European or Tartar form, are alike foreign to the Chinese ear, and to that of all the races, Arab or Hebrew, Tamul, Corean, Tibetan, Burmese, or Malay. While, therefore, the pronoun *a, nga, kau,* or *go,* for our English *I,* represents the primeval pronoun of the first person with great probability, the root in *m* and *b*, with its correlate substantive verb, *be, bin, futurus, fuisse,* in Mongol, *amoi, bolhu, bolmoi,* can be traced no farther back than the Turanian family in its Tartar branch, from which it has gone over into the last great linguistic formation, the Indo-European.

The structure of sentences in the primeval language, it may be reasonably concluded, was according to the order of nature. The nominative preceded the transitive verb, and the transitive verb preceded its object. The Chinese, the Hebrew, and the English here agree. It is the Turanian family that is chiefly at fault when tested by these laws. The Japanese, the Mongols, the Tamuls, and the speakers of Sanscrit, evidently following an older *usus loquendi* found in the contemporary Turanian speech, resolutely limit the verb to the last place in the sentence, and make the accusative precede it. This is extremely unnatural, and tends to restrict painfully the powers of human speech. Nature first names the actor, then the mode of his action, and finally the person or thing on whom or on which such action is performed. But Turanian speakers avoid this construction. *Ching-gis hagan airiben t'umen k'umun alaba*, "Genghis Khan many ten thousands of men killed." The western branches of the Indo-European family refused to imitate the speakers of Sanscrit in their slavish adherence to this Turanian law, and succeeded in restoring the freedom of nature to our modern European modes of speech.

So again, in placing the adjective before its substantive, the Chinese, English, and Turanian languages have a clear advantage over the Semitic, the eastern

Himalaic, the Malay, and the Polynesian, which invert this order. The adjective naturally precedes the noun, as the mark of the species precedes that of the genus. We know a thing from its qualities. The "Bactrian camel" may be called the "Camel of Bactria," or "le chameau Bactrien." Of these, the first is the most natural, and is favoured by the greatest number of important languages and families. The second form, inverting the position of the words and connecting them by *of, de, von,* etc., adds greatly to the ease and variety of language. But it is almost exclusively European and Semitic.[1] The Sanscrit follows the Turanian and Chinese order in this respect, and thus it is shown that, although she may lay claim to be the model of the European languages in regard to her richly developed system of grammatical inflexions, she cannot be looked to as their mother in syntactical order.

It is to the Semitic family that we must look for the origin of this inversion, and also for the introduction of the relative pronoun.

The third form, "le chameau Bactrien," is not so much a peculiarity of any one family, as of languages occurring here and there in the area of various families. Its introduction has conferred no great advantage on language.

---

[1] I suppose the post-position of the genitive and of the adjective to have been borrowed from the Semitic by the Polynesians, Siamese, and other races.

We have now arrived at several approximate notions of a rudimentary kind with regard to the primeval language.

1. It was monosyllabic, and its syllabary, though containing no double consonants, had probably consonant finals, as *bid* and *lod*.

2. Certain roots, verbal and pronominal, are so widely spread among the various linguistic families of Europe and Asia, that a large portion of the primeval vocabulary may be expected to reveal itself as the reward of careful research.

3. The order of words in sentences was that of nominative and verb, verb and object, adjective and substantive, subject and predicate, species and genus. The common laws of position in the primeval language probably agreed with those of the Chinese, Greek, English, and some other languages in such sentences as *Charles beat William, good man, this man is good*, or *this man good, fir tree*. When two or more verbs occurred, the order was that of time. Our sentence, *went near and killed him*, would be " go near kill," or " go approach kill," and some device would be contrived to represent past time.

4. The primeval language had probably a rudimentary tonic pronunciation. Variety in pitch, even tones, inflexions, pauses, accents, long and short quantity, belong more or less to all the tongues spoken among men. The Greeks inflected the vowels of

certain syllables in their words. The Chinese do the same with their monosyllables, and so do all the neighbouring peoples on the west and south. The Hebrews had an elaborate system of accents. The Greek and Chinese inflexions exist in modern European languages, but without attachment to special words or syllables. Probably this last was the character of the primeval prosody. The speech of modern Europe, struggling for greater freedom, rebelled against the prosodial laws which prevailed in the old Indo-European, Semitic, and Chinese areas, and by a powerful instinct succeeded in recovering the primeval use of inflexions and accents. These aids to a natural, efficient, and graceful elocution should never become dialectic, or be tied to particular words. If language were what it ought to be, all local tones would cease, and those windings of the voice, simple or circumflex, which in England constitute the local habit of dialects, and in China are an element in particular words, would be limited to elocutionary uses. Thus language would be ennobled, the intercourse of men with each other would become refined, and the swiftly changing feelings of the heart would all have a suitable expression.

Among the elements of the primeval language, capable of discovery by comparative philology, I omit the distinction between verbal and pronominal roots. All the pronouns seem to be used as verbs. It was when the eye of primitive man saw action that his hand pointed to the moving object, and if his lips uttered a sound it was an imitation of the natural sound caused by the movement he witnessed. Speech became the instinctive imitation of natural sounds, and words were the names both of objects and actions. How then could the pronouns fail to be also verbs? Thus, *bad*, "divide," "separate," "depart," was also in old Chinese used for "that," "he," and called *pat* or *pit*, 彼 now known as *pi*. *Do*, "to give," is the same word as *that, das*, etc. The Chinese locative case suffix *chung*, "middle," more anciently *tang*, is, when employed as a verb, used in the senses "to strike in the middle," "to strike," "to undertake." As an adjective it means "middle," as in "the Middle Kingdom," and as a substantive it is the name of a "bell."

A further proof is found in the fact that the instrumental case suffixes are like others formed from pronouns, but they must from the nature of the case also be verbs. In fact, post-positions, like prepositions, are all verbs. All case suffixes, as well as case prefixes, may be explained, according to circumstances, either as demonstratives or as verbs. The nominative, possessive, and accusative case suffixes are most conveniently explained as demonstratives. The case suffixes which express instrumentality, motion from, motion to, giving, and locality, are best considered as verbs.

Should it be objected to this view that every verb

would then become a pronoun, it may be answered that, for reasons not difficult to discover, the only verbs used as pronouns would be those that occurred most commonly, such as *giving, going, coming, being, leaving, carrying*. The early forms of such verbs as these by perpetual recurrence established themselves as pronouns; *e.g.*, the pronoun *I*, "he," is probably identical with *I*, "to go." Such verbs as only find their way into conversation now and then would not become pronouns.

It appears to have been an important feature in the primeval language that the syllabary had both open and closed vowels. Many modern languages have no closed syllables. They were rare in Sanscrit and are still more so in Japanese. It is susceptible of proof that the primeval syllabary was not one of this kind. Races occupying areas where enervation is induced by climate are liable to lose the final letters of their syllabaries. Nations that spread themselves over mountainous areas and cultivate hardy habits show less tendency to the disintegration of their roots. The absence of final consonants is the result of phonetic decay, or the addition of vowels through change in climate and in national habits, or through foreign influence, and other causes. Hence man must have been created in a temperate climate and in a continental locality.

On the hypothesis that words were first formed from

the imitation of natural sounds, it may be expected that both kinds of syllables will occur. Sounds ending in vowels and in consonants occur abundantly in nature, as is shown by the spelling of imitative words in our own language, *e.g.*, *peewit, cuckoo, dingdong, hiss, hush*, etc.

There are other reasons why some words should terminate with certain consonants. Words ending in *m* and *p*, are usually expressive in Chinese of combination, closing, holding in the mouth, union, taste, containing, *e.g.*, *gap*, "combine," *kam*, "sweet," *yem*, "salt," *gam*, "hold in the mouth," "contain," *k'am*, "hollow," "deficient." The final letter seems in these and similar examples to indicate that the words where it is found are expressive of actions which are easily represented by the mouth opened or closed. Emptiness or deficiency would be fitly pictured by an open mouth, union by a mouth closing. But the labial letters *m* and *p*, which would be brought into requisition on such occasions, would naturally be used, because the shaping of the lips in forming them was a not unlikely manner of expressing the ideas to be conveyed. In English *gap* and *gape* are nearly alike in sound. The labial *p* with which they terminate may be accounted for in the same way. *Gap* in old Chinese means "to combine," "press under the arms," "narrow," "a narrow pass through mountains," "books fastened together with two boards and straps," "the action of scissors." We may explain the final *p* as expressing the action of the lips, in imitating the act of pressure witnessed by the word-maker, when he first encountered the problem how to describe intelligently to his companion the events he had witnessed. The meaning of the root in English and Chinese coalesces when a narrow opening among mountains is in both languages called *gap*. The initial *g* will then be left to be accounted for on the principle of the imitation of natural sounds.

Should a root once become established in use, the principle of association of ideas would explain the origin of a multitude of connected words. The adverb "back" is to be derived from the substantive "back." The Chinese word for "the back" is *pak*. In Kwan hwa, the modern pronunciation, it is *pei*. It has for derivative meanings "to carry on the back," "to repeat lessons" (because the Chinese pupil always turns his back to the schoolmaster while repeating his tasks), "to turn back," or "run away," "the north," "to disobey," etc. We find the same root in $\beta\alpha\sigma\tau\acute{\alpha}\zeta\omega$, *fero*, *bear*, *porto*, etc. For all these words, with a multitude more, one root *bak*, as we may judge from the Chinese analogy, would be approximately the original form, and it might be the imitation of sound. The finals *k* and *g* occur not seldom in words imitative of sounds, as *flagellation*, *thwack*, *strike*, and the Chinese *p'ak* to "strike gently," which is identical with the root of *flagellum*, *plaga*, $\pi\lambda\acute{\eta}\sigma\sigma\omega$, the *l* being inserted later. The thwack of a whip is to one ear *dak*, and to another *bak*. The twang of a bow to the Chinese is *kong*, to the Greek it was *tok*, and to the speaker of Latin *dok*, which became τόξον and *arcus*, the *d* becoming *r*, and the vowel *a* being prefixed. But to the Teuton *bak* was the sound, as it would appear from the verb *beugen*, bow, and the substantive bow. The Russian *luk*, " bow," is evidently of the same origin as *arcus* and τόξον. So also the Arabic *raka'a*, " to bow."

In the Biblical account of the origin of language, it is said that " God brought " the animals " to Adam to see what he would call them, and whatever Adam called every living creature, that was the name thereof." In accordance with this statement, while it was by divine assistance that primitive man made language, it was not without the active exercise of his own faculties. God placed the animals before him and made him feel that he must give them names. In doing this, he would in many cases imitate the sounds they uttered. The roar of the lion may have originated the words *leo*, *lion*, and *roar*. As *r* and *l* are both derivable very frequently from *d*, the primitive form may have been *ru* or *du*. The Hebrew is *ari* or *arye*. On the supposition, as philologists tell us, that *r* and the sibilants are interchangeable letters within the Semitic area, a word with a sibilant initial might be expected as a name for lion. In fact, in the Persian, which from the most ancient times came under Semitic influence, the word for lion is *shir*. The Chinese word, *shi*, "Lion," seems to be borrowed from the Persian. It occurs first in Chinese literature a little before the Christian era.

Other animals would be named from the noise made by them in flying, as the "Kingfisher," which in old Chinese was called *sut*. Such a combination would as well represent the sound heard when that beautiful bird darts on its prey, as the combination *shoot* does in English and in Chinese the sound of an arrow which has just left the bow. The same root *sut* is used in Chinese to express the "hissing noise of water in extinguishing fire," "to revile people," "to be grieved," and "to be broken to pieces." The modern forms it takes are *t'sui* and *suy*.

The scriptural account is restricted to the naming of animals. This is in harmony with the fact that language was gradually formed. The opinion has been very generally held, that man had extraordinary divine aid in the construction of language. This would probably consist, partly, in a special control and guidance exercised over him, impelling him to the use of the language forming faculties, and partly in the positive communication to him of such parts of the primitive language as were necessary for the carrying on of those interviews which took place between God and himself in Paradise. Enough of language was taught our first parents by revelation to make existence a pleasure, to lead them to understand each other's wants and feelings, the first duties of religion, the requirements of a simple agriculture, the preparation of food, the construction of a suitable habitation. They learned how to make the first rude attempts at clothing and how to take care of domestic animals. Such instruction is implied in the words, "The Lord God made for Adam and his wife coats of skins, and clothed them." Dr. Magee (On the Atonement, Dissert. 53) says, "It is sufficient if we suppose the use of language taught him with respect to such things as were necessary, and that he was then left to the exercise of his own faculties for further improvement upon this foundation."

Revelation was to primitive man what instinct is and always has been to the lower animals. The same paternal wisdom which teaches the bird to build its nest, gave to the first men by direct instruction the necessary knowledge to make life happy, and to give the human race a good start on its long career. Man was created with physical, social, moral, and religious instincts. They were at first called into exercise by suitable teaching. This seems the only reasonable way of accounting for the common notions of morality that prevail among all nations, and the monotheistic tradition which underlies the religious thought of all ancient literatures. Hence the superior antiquity of moral words in language over those specially suited for science and philosophy, which are always of later origin. The moral element inheres in all language, and the fundamental moral ideas remaining there after many millenniums of waste and wear, are vestiges of the primeval revelation granted for their early guidance to our first forefathers. If man had been without reason, instinct would have been a sufficient director; but having also the high endowments of the thinking and language-forming faculty, he needed that special teaching which, according to the Biblical account, he received.

CHAPTER V.

The Chinese probably Hamites.—Chronology of the Deluge.— Genealogies in Genesis. — Ancient Semite Occupation of Persia.—Semitic Impress on the Himalaic Race.—The Chinese moved Eastward before the Confusion of Tongues. — The Chinese Ancient Syllabary recoverable from the Phonetics. —Six Final Consonants.—The Surd Initials derived from the Sonants.—Tones.—Syntax.

THE most remarkable indication of change in the primitive language given in Scripture is at the Confusion of Tongues, which took place, according to the Septuagint chronology, 400 years after the Flood. This might not unreasonably be regarded as a limit for the continuance of the primeval language. Yet colonization must have been rapidly proceeding from the beginning. During the 2,200 years that elapsed between the Creation and the Flood, the speech of each band of emigrants would, after the lapse of a few generations, unconsciously assume a new form. The Scriptural account of the Deluge and of the Confusion of Tongues I suppose to refer particularly to the world according to its dimensions as then understood, the πᾶσα οἰκουμένη of the day. Colonies that went beyond the limits of the Flood of Noah, if there were such, were lost from view. The descendants of Seth were spread perhaps over what afterwards became the Semitic region. The Cainites went more to the east. Whether any of them and the other descendants of Adam passed into Eastern Asia and America during those 2,000 years now so little known, we cannot tell. If they did, they would there be beyond the reach of the Deluge, which science has shown did not extend to the more distant parts of the continent.

Among the Cainites sprang up the arts of music, metallurgy, and the tending of cattle on a large scale. The first two of these features marked the ancient Chinese, but they were never a nomade people given chiefly to the care of flocks and herds. They were more like the Cushites than the Cainites. The art of writing, the idea of universal government, rather mark them out as descendants of Noah. When they came into China, they were not the first emigrants. Others had arrived before them. We therefore can scarcely be wrong in limiting the Chinese emigration to Post-Noachic times, when the arts flourished sufficiently in the Babylonian region to allow of our identifying that locality with the original source of the Chinese civilization.

The Deluge I suppose to have taken place upwards

of 3,000 years before the Christian era. Hales states it at 3,155. Let us allow for it 3,500. The Call of Abraham he states at B.C. 2078. It was about this time that the Hindoo race took possession of North India, driving the Dravidian population before them. At this date also the Chinese were settled on the Yellow River under imperial chiefs, practising astronomy, agriculture, writing, and other ancient arts and sciences. It would be very conformable to the circumstances of the case if we suppose that they came over from the west soon after the Deluge, and yet not too soon to allow scope for the previous development of the Cushite civilization. The Semite occupation of Babylon took place at nearly the same time. The Semites then came into possession of the regions they have held ever since, while the discomfited Cushites either taught their arts to their conquerors, originating the Phœnician alphabet, or carried them elsewhere. It was with an earlier time that the Chinese emigration is with most probability connected, viz., the age and race of Nimrod.

The Christian apologist who desires to see the reconciliation of Science and Scripture made thoroughly clear, must not be dismayed by the chronological difficulties connected with the genealogies given in the Book of Genesis. That the evangelist Matthew omitted three names in the list of the kings of Judah who were ancestors of Jesus is a well-known fact. He wished to aid the memory by recording three fourteens. In the genealogy of the patriarchs before the Deluge, ten generations are given, and in the interval between Noah and Abraham there are also ten names. It is not improbable that some names are omitted. What took place so late as the time of Matthew may have occurred in the period of the early transmission of the Book of Genesis. These accounts of the early world were perhaps translated from the primitive monosyllabic language into Hebrew, soon after the Semite conquest of Babylon, and may have been transmitted orally and by writing from the time of Noah. Moses may have used documents which came from the hands of more ancient inspired men. They would, if this supposition be correct, be among the earliest documents committed to writing.

The Septuagint, Hebrew, and Samaritan copies of the Old Testament all differ in regard to dates and numbers in the early genealogy. Too often has it happened in the history of literature[1] that numbers have been tampered with for controversial purposes. Who shall say now which of these is the most trustworthy? Certainly the Septuagint chronology is the most advantageous for use in ethnological researches. The cramping of the Hebrew chronology is intolerable. There is no room for the development of races and the

[1] The Northern Buddhists state the birth of Buddha about B.C. 1100. The Southern Buddhists give it in about 500, and they are right.

growth of languages between Noah and Abraham, if that scheme be adopted.

Since Elam is mentioned among the sons of Shem, Persia, of which Elam was always one of the names, was probably a Semite country before it entered the Indo-European area on the arrival of the Persians. The cuneiform writing and the Phœnician alphabet were probably spread over the southern cities of that country early enough to allow for the Devanagari alphabet having been derived from a Semitic source. Attention has been recently again drawn forcibly to the strong resemblance existing between the old Sanscrit writing and the ancient Semitic alphabet, by Professor F. Müller of Vienna.[1] Besides, the languages of Persia, from the Zend to the modern Persian, have always possessed more or less a Semitic syntax. There has also been Semite influence operating in the forming of the Himalaic and Dravidian languages. The masculine and feminine suffixes found in them are thus best explained. Further, the post-position of the genitive, for which Semitic grammar is so remarkable, is equally characteristic of the eastern Himalaic and Polynesian languages. I suppose, therefore, that South Persia was strongly Semitized in the third millennium before Christ, and that races which passed that way into India and Tibet derived certain linguistic elements

---

[1] Novara Expedition. Linguistischer Theil, p. 219, ff.

and articles of belief from the Shemite and Cushite inhabitants of the country. Hence the abstinence of the western Himalaic races from the flesh of the hog, and the remarkable religious traditions of the Karens of Burmah.

In the languages of Tartary and China we do not find the same Semite impress. The syntax is not Semite, and masculine and feminine suffixes are unknown. The Chinese and Turanians proper may have come through Persia before it was Semite, or by the north part of the country where the Semite influence was then unknown. Thus it might happen that the Chinese, whose language is of older type, found Eastern and Southern China in the third millennium before Christ already occupied by races partially Semitized in their syntax. These ancient occupants of China were far less civilized than the Chinese, and travelled faster.

That the Chinese have not been under a Semite influence appears clear when the laws of syntax are considered, as it also appears clear that the Eastern Himalayans were influenced by the Semites while they still spoke a monosyllabic language.

It may therefore be not unreasonably supposed that the Chinese, and after them the Japanese and Tartars, leaving North Persia, were first attracted by the country of Bokhara, and, crossing the mountains, proceeded by the Kashgar route eastward, always travelling in a latitude of about 40° north. There are no passes through the Bolor Tag and Tsung ling mountains south of the Cashgar route, till you come to the Khyber Pass into Cashmere and India in about 34° lat. This would be the route of the Himalaic race, who, leaving Affghanistan and penetrating into the beautiful valleys of Cashmere, went eastward into Tibet by Ladak and the upper course of the Indus.

Under these conditions it would seem that the great breaking up of languages at the epoch marked in Scripture by the building of the Tower of Babel took place soon after the departure of the Chinese from Western Asia. The progress made by the Semite and other language systems is what is described as the Confusion of Tongues. The Chinese people may have remained in North Persia long enough to leave traces behind them or acquire a knowledge of the dual philosophy and the worship of angels and the powers of nature. At this time they may have been partially in juxtaposition with the Himalaic races, and those who have since become Malays and Polynesians, as well as with the triple-branched Turanians. Thus, some of the resemblances found in the languages spoken by these races may be accounted for.

At least, we are very much under the necessity of allowing that the Chinese started on their Eastern pilgrimage late enough to bring with them the Baby-

Ionian arts, and early enough to retain the features of the primeval monosyllabic language more distinctly than any other old linguistic family has been able to do. The first great step in the development of human speech was taken in the formation of the Chinese language.

While residing in Persia and Mesopotamia, the ancestors of the Chinese would both give and receive. The philosophy, religion, and language of the times were common. From the moment of separation changes would commence, and in every emigrant band, each new generation would see an advance towards that complete national individuality which it was destined eventually to achieve.

It might be supposed by those who are fresh to the subject, that the task of searching for the old Chinese syllabary of the times of Yau and Shun was hopeless. But it is far from being so. The Chinese had already the knowledge of the art of writing, and the preservation of the phonetic element in the written characters is particularly favourable for investigation. Their use and signification have never been forgotten. We are able to assign, in consequence, definite values to the phonetics without much difficulty, and the syllabary of 4,000 years ago comes out to view in a comparatively clear and trustworthy form. For example, the modern *sin*, "heart," Canton *sem*, Fu kien *sim*, Cochin-Chinese *tim*, Tibetan *sems*, is known to have been *sim* anciently, because it rhymes in all old poetry with words in *m*. But the poetry reaches back to eleven centuries before the Christian era, and earlier, and the characters were made, according to native opinion, B.C. 2300. In this way we are able to reach the conclusion that the final *m* and with it, by similar proofs, its correlates *ng, n, k, t, p,* the six consonant finals of the Chinese rhyming art in all ages, were also the six consonant finals of the earliest Chinese syllabary. The Greek τοξικόν,[1] "poison," resembles accidentally the Chinese 毒 *tu,* old sound *dok.* The upper part of the Chinese character *chu,* "leader," "lord," 主 if we may argue from its use here as a phonetic, was probably once called *tok,* and still earlier *dok.* It is thus brought into agreement with the Latin *duco, dux,* and Greek δείκνυμι, and belongs to the verbal root *dik,* "to point," in Chinese 指 *chï,* and in Latin and English *doceo* and *teach.*

The following example will show the remarkable aid to philology afforded by the phonetics. In Callery's Systema Phoneticum 元 *yuen,* 完 *wan,* 宛 *yuen,* 員 *yuen,* are, as may be shown, equipollent phonetics, with the sounds *wan, an, yuen,* etc., and the meaning,

[1] The drug used for poisoning arrows was called τοξικόν, from τόξον, "a bow." This word, again, was from τυγχάνω ἔτυχον, "to hit," "meet with," Chinese 着 *cho,* old sound *dok,* "to hit," "to be right," "yes," "put on clothing." The etymology cannot be easily traced of the Chinese for "poison."

"roundness," "completion," "origin," "globule," and "circle."

EQUIPOLLENT PHONETICS.	COMPOUND DERIVATIVE CHARACTERS.
元 "origin."	刓 *wan*, "cut out in a round shape."
	頑 *wan*, "rude," "obstinate."[1]
宛 "bend."	箢 *yuen*, "canister," 琬 "name of a sceptre."
	盌 *wan*, "a bowl," 剜 "cut out in a round shape."
	鵷 *yuen*, "king of ducks," Latin *anas*.
	椀 碗, 塊 *wan*, "bowl," 豌 "bean."
完 "complete."	綄 *wan*, "bind round."
.	骩 *wan*, "thigh bone," "that which bends."
員 "round."	圓 *yuen*, "circle," 韻 *yün*, "rhyme,"[2] 隕 "fall."
因 "cause."	姻 *yin*, "marriage," 烟 *yen*, "smoke."

None of these words, nor any of their derivatives, ever take initial consonants or undergo any alteration, except in vowels and an occasional change of the final *n* to its correlate *t*. We therefore conclude that 4,000 years ago these words, and others with the same phonetics, began with a vowel and ended with *n*. The Latin vocabulary furnishes us with *annus*, "a year," *annulus*, "ring," *anima*, "breath," "the soul;" the Greek has *aiών*, "an age," with its equivalent *ævum*.

[1] As *rudis*, "rude," in Chinese 魯 *lu, lud*, comes from *rot*, "round," viewed as unimpressible, so *wan*, "round," in Chinese is taken to mean "dull," "stupid."

[2] Compare in Greek ρυθμός, "rhyme," from *rot*, "round."

The Latin *v* has the force of *w*, as in *vinum*, Greek, οινο. The Russian *v*, written *b*, and pronounced *v*, has in these comparisons of words also the force of *w*. We find *vina*, "cause," *vyenetz*, "crown," "coronet," "cloud of glory," *vyenok*, "garland," *vyenchat*, "to crown." The English *wind*, *wend*, and *wander*, appear to be of the same family. Wind is *anima*, "breath," *ventus*, "wind," Sanscrit, *an*, "blow." The "vine" is that which winds. In Latin it takes *t* for *n*, as in *vitis*. Further, the Mongol has *undus*, "root," "source," and the suffix *dus* may be compared with *nus*, in *annus*, "year," and the *d* in the English wind. The principle of adding syllabic suffixes and cognate letters is the same. In Sanscrit we have *vána*, "pipe," *vanada*, "cloud," *venu*, "bamboo," *vata*, "circle." The letter *v* is in fact *w*. Further, in the Dravidian vocabulary we meet with the Tamul *undei*, "a round thing," "a ball," "pill." In Chinese 緣 *yuen*, signifies "a cause," and 雲 *yün*, "cloud," doubtless the same words originally as 元 *yuen*, "origin," and *yen*, "smoke." The Chinese *yin*, "marriage," when compared with *yuen*, "draw with the hand," suggests the Latin *unio* and our *unite*. In Greek ἔνος, "a year," ἔτος, also "a year," belong to the same family of words, and perhaps ἐν, "in," is the same with the Chinese 因 "cause," "because."

If we take another example with *m* final, the light thrown on the primeval form of the syllabary will be seen still more plainly. The Latin *umbra* consists of the root *um*, and a common suffix *bra*, which may be compared with *ber* in *imber*, "rain," *bræ* in *tenebræ*, *bris* in *salubris*. We have in Hebrew *emesh*, "night," "darkness," where *sh* is a suffix, as in *kafash*, "to cover," "overwhelm," cognate with *kafar*, "to cover," "forgive," Chinese 蓋 *kai*, "cover," old sound, as known from the phonetic, *kap*. The Latin *um*, Hebrew *am*, as it reads without the points, with the sense of "shade," "darkness," "night," are in Chinese 暗 *an*, old sound *am*, "dark," 陰 *yin, om*, "obscure," "the principle of darkness in the dual philosophy," 掩 *yen, am*, "to shade," "cover," 簷 *yin, om*, "eaves." In Chinese buildings the eaves project far enough to make a broad shadow. These coincidences are quite sufficient to show that in the Chinese primeval syllabary *m* was the final letter in this root, and that the initial was a vowel.

We thus by multiplying our researches in all parts of the Chinese vocabulary, always adopting the old pronunciation registered in Kanghi's dictionary and other older lexicographical works, arrive at the fact that the final letters *ng, n, m, k, t, p*, with the vowels, were the final letters of the pronunciation in use when the characters were made. And though they are much disturbed in the Mandarin dialect, they are retained to this day with an approach to faultless regularity in the Canton and Amoy dialects. They are also found in the Tibetan, Cochin-Chinese, and Siamese languages, all belonging to the allied Himalaic family.

Having obtained this solid foundation of knowledge with regard to the final letters of the Chinese syllabary in use 4,000 years ago, we may proceed to inquire into the initials. Of these, the most certain are *g, d, b, ng, n, m, l, z, dz, zh,* and the vowels. Initials of the next stage of probability are the aspirates *k', t', p', t's,* the surds *k, t, p,* and the sibilants *s, ts, sh.* This difference in probability arises from the vestiges existing of an old law of change similar in part to Grimm's law, by which the sonants have always been throwing out words into the surd series. So numerous are the examples of this law, that it is open for consideration whether the surd series is not altogether made up of successive contributions from the sonants.

Before giving examples of the sonant contributions to the surd series, let me premise that in the Amoy and Canton dialects, the surd and sonant series receive the name of upper and lower series, and are identical with the so-called four upper and lower tones. In other words, characters in each division are pronounced with special intonations of the voice, and thus distinguished from the upper or surd division. Thus, 平 *bang,* "even," is at Amoy *pieng* in the lower first tone, while in the syllabic spelling of the dictionaries it is *bang* or *biang* in the first tone. In dialects having eight tones, words in the lower series may be transferred into the system of the dictionaries by changing the surd initials into sonants, and allowing the peculiar intonation to coalesce with that of the upper series.

The word 旁 *bang*, "side," the English "bank," "bench," with its equipollent phonetics 方 *fang*, "square," 邦 *pang*, "state," "kingdom," 平 *bang*, "even," "peaceful," 並 *bang*, "side by side," etc., have together an extensive cluster of derivatives, some of which take *b*, and the rest *p*. The meanings are, "side," "even," "tie together," "tie," "impinge upon," "strike," "wings," "catalogue of names arranged side by side," "square," "anything square in shape," as a "territory," a "seal," etc., "edge," "mountain ridge," etc. Corresponding words in European languages are *impingo*, "strike against," πήγνυμι, "fix," *pax*, "peace," *pack*, *bang*, *fingo*, *fixi*, etc. Two hard things brought into rapid contact caused a sound which primeval man heard as *bang*. Thus the peculiar phonal form of the root in the primitive syllabary of the world may have originated. It then came to mean "side," from the fact that the two portions of impinging matter remained side by side. Then the act of bringing them together and of holding them together, or of their coming together of themselves, were named with the same vowel and consonants. This gave rise to the words belonging to this family meaning "tie," "fasten," "fix." When evenness, physical or moral, had to be spoken of, the same root was used.

SURDS DERIVED FROM SONANTS. 81

But how do we find them spelled in Old Chinese? Chiefly with *b*. Yet in part also with *p*. "Evenness," "impinging," "side," "bringing side by side," are all *bang*. To "assist," "squareness," a "territorial square," to "tie," a "wing," to "imitate," are all *pang*. The reason of this is evident. Language instinctively seeks to enlarge her bounds when they become cramped by an increase of words and of ideas. She aims to remove ambiguity by introducing differences in pronunciation between like sounding words.

In the example given the words initiated by *b* are the older. Those in *p* are the newer. The obvious conclusion is that *p* derives its origin from *b*, and that *b* is an older letter than *p*. The primeval syllabary did not need so many letters as are now in use. It started with *b*, and added *p*, *p'*, and *f* afterwards as they were needed. In the Mongol syllabary there is no *p*, *p'*, or *f*. There is a fully developed *p* in the Indo-European and Semitic families. Hence the *p* may have sprung up contemporaneously in the Chinese and Indo-European families after their separation. In both cases it was by a natural putting forth of creative strength on the part of language to increase its alphabet and its syllabary. It is thus that the preponderance of *b* over *p* in the Sanscrit and Hebrew vocabularies may be best accounted for. That Latin and Greek dictionaries devote so much larger a space to words in *p* and *f* than to words in *b* is an indication of recent origin in the vocabularies.

What is true of *b* in the old Chinese syllabary is true also of the other letters in the sonant and surd series. The sonants *g, d, b, z,* are the old letters; the surds *k, t, p, s,* are more recent; *f* and *h* seem to be the newest of all. In the Japanese transcription all Chinese words in *h* are written with *k,* while those which in modern Chinese commence with *f* are written with either *b* or *h.* But as *h* is the regular Japanese equivalent of the Chinese *p,* the weight of evidence is in favour of the statement that *p* and *b* were the old equivalents in all cases of the modern Chinese *f.* If we carry back the inquiry another stage, *p* and *b* coalesce in the primeval and world-wide *b.* The Japanese, indeed, have an initial *f*; but as it is used to write Chinese words in *p* as well as in *f,* it is probably a new letter.

We should expect to find the name *Buddha* transcribed in old Chinese with something like exactness. We learn on investigation that the character 佛 *Fo,* was anciently called *But,* as is shown by the syllabic spelling, in the Amoy pronunciation *Put,* and in the Japanese transcription *Budzu.*

A few more examples are here appended. Among the sonants, 分 *bun,* "divisions," "duties," 臐 *dan,* "revolve in a circle," 復 *bok,* "return," 學 *gak,* "learn," 硬 *ngang,* "hard," 從 *zung,* "follow," 別 *bit,* "other," 羣 *gun,* "herd," 遇 *ngu,* "meet," 謄 *deng,* "go up," have the following correlates in the surd series, viz.: 分 *pun*, "to divide" (Hebrew *bin*, Latin *findo*), 轉 *tun*, "revolve," "turn," English *turn*, 北 *pok*, "north," "back," 教 *kak*, "teach," 岡 *kong*, "hard," "steel," 縱 *tsung*, "let it be that," 別 *pit*, "difference," 軍 *kun*, "a body of troops," 遘 *ku*, "meet with," 登 *teng*, "go up."

But it was not enough for language to add the surd letters to its acquisitions. The syllabary was still too contracted. Words and ideas continued to multiply, and there was a scarcity of syllables to express them. The age of suffixes and prefixes had not yet arrived. It was too soon to think of dissyllables or polysyllables, of a prefixed *s* or an inserted *r*. Language in this time of need seized for the required service those flitting musical intonations of human speech which the orator uses to express decision, sarcasm, doubt, and interrogation. At this time there were in the Chinese vocabulary two great groups of words. Those ending with *ng, n, m,* and the vowels, formed one group, which we will call long in quantity. Those terminating in *g, d, b,* or *k, t, p,* formed another, in which the sound is shortened by the action of the final letters. They check the breath and bring the utterance to an abrupt conclusion. Hence these words become, for the purposes of tonic pronunciation, short in quantity.

But final letters will drop off, through laziness in enunciation, through imitation of the defects of others, and from the circumstance that, when stress is laid by the speaker on some one element of sound, the other elements will suffer. What did language do? She did not resist change? This she never does. She allowed new laws to enter, so that the inevitable changes might be kept under control. A third group of words was formed out of contributions from the other two. By the ancient poetry we learn that 3,000 years ago the words that could rhyme with each other formed three groups, which did not encroach on each other's limits. The new group was mainly composed of what is now called the Shang sheng tone class or second tone. The third, or K'ü sheng, was subsequently formed. The numerals were then pronounced *yit, ni, sam, sat, ngo, lok, sit, pat, ku, zhip*. Of these, *sam*, "three," was in the long tone, now become the first tone; *ngo*, "five," and *ku*, "nine," in the new, or second tone; *ni*, "two," doubtful; and the rest in the short tone. Of the five elements, *kim*, "metal," was first, *mok*, "wood," last, and *shi*, "water," *ka*, "fire," *t'o*, "earth," all in the newly-formed tone class.

Fifteen hundred years passed away, and the Hindoo Buddhists were in China teaching the religion and sciences of India. The Chinese had never thought about the distinction between tones and letters, and when Bengal and Panjáb pandits told them that sound was capable of analysis, and that tones must be distinguished from vowels and consonants, they listened incredulously. But the claims of the alphabetical analysis were gradually allowed, and emperors appointed commissions to settle the sounds and construct dictionaries. Imperial pride condescended to learn the tone distinctions in a flattering sentence constructed by a courtier, which exemplified them in their order. 天子聖哲 *T'in tsi shing chit*, "Heaven's son is holy and wise."

The passage of 1,500 years had seen a new tone formed, the K'ü sheng. It consists of contributions from the second and fourth. Poetry at this time was made according to new laws. Not only the rhyming words were brought into subjection to the tones in groups of four; but all the words of each line were made to conform to a complex harmonic scale, in the construction of which the tones formed the chief element.

Another 1,500 years has passed away, and we now find that still greater changes have taken place than in the preceding period. The first tone class has been split in two. The old sonant initials have been expelled, and their place supplied by surds and aspirates. The words of the fourth tone class, after losing all their final letters, have been distributed among the other classes, and the Chinese modern language has become more changed from the old type than any member of the monosyllabic family.[1]

[1] For a detailed account of these changes, see Mandarin Grammar, Part I. The principal step I have made in advance in the Chinese part

There have been three great periods of 1,500 years each. The first saw the earliest formation of the surd and aspirate series, with that of a triple tone system. The second witnessed an extensive dropping of the final letters *k, t, p,* and *ng,* and the growth of the tone system ending in the quadruple formation of the dictionaries. The third period, perhaps the most revolutionary of all, saw the sonant initials, and the finals *k, t, p, m,* for ever dismissed, one of the primeval tone groups completely broken up, and the syllabic spelling of the Hindoo Buddhists thrown into chaotic confusion.

All this may be taken as proof of the primitive character of the Chinese language. Had it inherited from the Turanian, Indo-European, or Semitic families, any of their peculiar tendencies to polysyllabic formation, it would have had, historically, a very different development. But being itself of the first descent from the primeval mother of human speech, we can trace in it no later elements. Not the Egyptian nor the Hebrew nor the Sanscrit can compare with the Chinese in antiquity of type. They all have a more complex syllabary, and introduce appendages to the roots, which constitute an evidence of the comparative recency of their formation.

of the investigation since the publication of that work, has been in the detection of the law by which the surd series has been regularly formed from the sonants, as illustrated above.

If with these views alone before me, I should be inclined greatly to lengthen Chinese chronology; but the comparison of the ancient civilizations of China and Western Asia compels me to reduce the epoch of the commencement of Chinese isolation to very nearly that of accepted history. The similarity between old Chinese life and that depicted in the Book of Genesis is so striking and so multiform, that it seems impossible to date the eastern migration of the Chinese earlier than a few centuries, at the most ten, before the time of Abraham.

The laws of position in Chinese sentences are the same with those already given as belonging to the natural and primeval speech of man. The actor is mentioned before the action, and the verb before its object. The adjective precedes the substantive, and the specific noun the genus to which it belongs. The adverb precedes the verb, and the attribute the substance to which it is attached. The subject is first mentioned, then the copula, and lastly the predicate. The only peculiarity to be here mentioned as not of natural and primeval growth is, that locative auxiliaries are made suffixes and not prefixes. "In a city," is more natural than "city in." The Chinese, however, prefer in their ancient and modern language to say the latter. Our phrase, "the world," is with them 天下 "heaven under." These locative postpositions are best explained as substantives. *Hia* is "that which is below." The original force of such words was verbal. "To go down," is also *hia.* As in the Turanian languages, so in Chinese, the verb became strongly substantival. Act became action. It is indeed the same in English. "Act," is a verb and a noun, and the mind learns to abstract the act from the actor, and look at it by itself. It is then spoken of as any other noun. Thus, *c'heng nei* is translated "the city's interior" or "in the city." The word *nei* is *nip,* to "enter," the *p* being dropped. The modern form is *ju.* That which is entered is the interior. The language forming faculty performs the necessary transformation, and applies the name of the act *enter* to the inside of a city or house. It then becomes a locative suffix.

All Chinese suffixes of this sort were originally verbs. So the other locatives *shang,* "above," *hia,* "below," *t'sien,* "before," *heu,* "behind," etc., were all verbs originally. As such their places would, before they assumed the locative character, be before their nouns.

The germ of the Turanian and Indo-European system of declension appears here for the first time. What the Chinese did for the locative, the ancient communities, who founded those types of language, proceeded to do for the instrumental, ablative, and dative cases. All the case suffixes, whether locative, instrumental, or dative, were simply verbs robbed of

ORIGIN OF THE POSSESSIVE CASE. 89

their activity and placed after nouns as signs of locality, direction, instrumentality, and so on, in order to facilitate the more speedy and convenient allocation of the objects of thought in the categories of space and time.

The Chinese has also a sort of possessive case, the history of which is simple. In the earliest Chinese the possessive case was included in the law by which species precedes genus, subject precedes attribute, and the particular notion goes before the general notion. "Man's body" was *jen shen*. Soon one of the demonstratives, *ti*, was used as a connective—人之耳目 *Nin ti ngi mok*, "men's ears and eyes." There was originally no possessive force in this connective, anciently 之 *ti*, now 的 *ti*. The possessive force was conveyed in the order of the words, in accordance with what may be regarded as a law in the primeval language from which the Chinese was derived. A hiatus is felt in the modern language if *Wo c'hai shï*, "my duties," is said for *Wo ti c'hai shï*. The Tibetan would perceive a similar hiatus. The remedy is found in the introduction of the particle *ti*. In the Shanghai dialect the particle used to fill the hiatus is *ko*. In Tibetan *ki* is employed. In Fu kien province, as in the Amoy dialect, *e* is the word. In all these cases the possessive force would be acquired subsequently. The origin of the possessive was simply a want felt, to make the sentence square, a rhythmical feeling which is not contented until the laws of proportion are obeyed in language. It is the same feeling which prompts us to say "a long and happy reign," rather than "a happy and long reign," and which lies at the foundation of prosody.

The order of verbs, when they represent two or more consecutive actions, is in Chinese that of time. This principle would be adopted from the primeval type. Thus, primeval man would say without any inversion, "Sit down eat food," in the language of command or of narration. The word *dòwn* would be a verb, and thus three verbs would stand in juxtaposition before the solitary substantive *food*. The modern Chinese says *Tso hia c'hï fan*, "sit down eat rice." The Semites were the first to introduce a conjunction *and*, as in Gen. xviii. 2, "And he lifted up eyes his, and saw, and behold three men standing by him, and [he] saw and ran to meet them." The words *lifted, saw, behold, ran,* are all introduced by *and*. The prepositions "by," עַל *ngal*, and לְ *le*, "to," are originally verbs, the one meaning "to ascend," and the other "motion towards." The whole sentence thus consists of nouns, pronouns, and verbs, and the order in which the verbs stand is that of the time in which the actions symbolized by them took place. Not one of them is put out of its natural position.

The order of time is the basis of the position of

verbs in all languages. But it was subject to frequent inversion in the Hebrew, as in Gen. xx. 6, "And said, Sarah, laugh made to me God," for "Sarah said, God has made me laugh." The dative participle *le* before *me* is redundant. The verb *laugh* is placed before the verb *make*, and both stand before their nominatives.

Such inversions do not appear in the Chinese language, which is unimaginative. The popular instinct is satisfied when it describes events in the order in which they took place, and could take no pleasure in those bold transpositions which delighted the Semite race.

CHAPTER VI.

THE SEMITIC SYSTEM OLDER THAN THE TURANIAN; YOUNGER THAN THE CHINESE.—TRILITERAL ROOTS.—INSERTIONS.—SUFFIXES.—PREFIXES.—GROWTH OF INFLEXIONS.—SEX.—PERSONIFICATIONS.—SYNTAX.—THE VERB PLACED FIRST.—POST-POSITION OF ADJECTIVE AND OF GENITIVE.—POST-POSITION OF GENITIVE BORROWED BY EUROPEAN LANGUAGES.—SEMITIC RELATIVE AND EUROPEAN RELATIVE COMPARED WITH THE CHINESE AND TURANIAN EQUIVALENT.

THERE is no good reason to doubt the correctness of those views by which Gesenius and other Semitic philologists were led to seek affinities between the Indo-European system and that which formed the more peculiar object of their researches. The number of common roots found in these two systems is indeed very great. Thus, among the numerals, *Hhad*, "one," in Chaldee seems to agree with the Greek *heis*, *eĩs*, "one," the Latin *solus*, and with the third among the common Chinese roots *tan*, *yid*, *kit*, all meaning "alone," or "one." The Chaldee *shetē*, "two," becomes in the ordinal for *thinyana*, "second." The original dental initial *t* resumes its place instead of the favourite Hebrew sibilant *sh*, and points to an old connexion with *duo*. The very law which frequently changed *t*

THE SEMITIC FAMILY OLDER THAN THE TURANIAN. 93

and d to sh or z or ts in Hebrew, prevailed in the Greek when tu, "thou," became συ, and still operates in German when $tide$ becomes $zeit$. Where there are roots in common, there will also be found laws of change in common. But this is anticipating. Our task of comparison must for the present be rather limited to the linguistic systems of Eastern Asia.

The Semitic family has older features than the Turanian, for in the progress towards a polysyllabic formation it has not gone far beyond the dissyllabic root. In the Turanian languages, words of four or five syllables are not uncommon. Another mark of superior antiquity in the Semitic system is the absence of case suffixes in the nouns and of temporal and model suffixes in the verbs. The earliest Semites bent their energy, unconsciously but surely, to the formation of a system of speech in which as much as possible should be done by prefixes, while the Turanians directed their language-forming power to the development of suffixes. Now, since the Semites never prefixed more than one syllable, while the Turanian instinct, by the creation of the polysyllabic suffix, has caused the upgrowth of immense lingual variety in the speech of more than half the area of Europe and Asia, the Semitic type must be regarded as less developed, and therefore more primitive, than the Turanian.

When it is remembered that Mongol, Greek, and Sanscrit case suffixes are metamorphosed pronouns and verbs put after instead of before their nouns, it must be admitted that the language-systems to which they belong are of recent origin. But where, as in Semitic speech it happens, the verb, which is required to do the duty of a case particle, becomes a preposition, and stands before its noun, we feel ourselves to be in the midst of speakers who retain closely the tradition of the earth's primeval language. No one will object to the statement that the Arabs have more primeval characteristics than the Greeks. Their life, their customs, and their modes of thinking, bear the stamp of immense antiquity; and as is their life so is their language. Every language carries on it the impress of the genius of the people that formed it. If the Chinese type is the most conservative among families of languages, the Semitic comes next to it. It never went far beyond the primitive model transmitted by "the earth's gray fathers."

The date of the formation of the Semitic type being thus shown to be older than that of the Aryan and Turanian families, it must now be proved that it is more recent than the Chinese, and that its origination constitutes the second great step in the progress of language.

The most obvious point of contrast is in the triliteral roots. The ancient Chinese said for "happiness," *pok*, a root which has the connected meanings, "rich" and "vast." In Sanscrit we find *bhaga*, "good fortune," in Latin *fortuna*, in Greek πλοῦτος, "rich," in Persian *bakht*, "rich," in Mongol *boyin*, "happiness," in Russian *bogatie*, "rich." The confusion between riches and happiness is easily accounted for. Among what people is it not common to make wealth the measure of happiness? In Hebrew the root occurs in *barach*, "to bless." Here we have a triliteral root *brk*. The vowels were not written by the early Phœnicians and Hebrews. We have, therefore, only the consonants to consider. An *r* has been inserted. There is in this nothing uncommon. The difference of an inserted *r* in the English word *world* as compared with the German *Welt*, does not render doubtful the identification of these words.

There is a root very widely spread in most languages. It is our English verb to *cut*. It is in Chinese *kat* 割, Latin *cædo*, Mongol *hadomoi*, Japanese *katana*, "a sword," Tamul *katti*, "a knife." Gesenius says[1] that the syllable *gad* has in Hebrew the notion of cutting in common with *gaz*, as in *gazaz*, from which it is derived by the loss of the sibilant; but on the other hand it may be traced still farther to the harder syllables *Kats*, *Kash*, *Kas*, *Hhats*, *Hhaz*, and, the sibilant disappearing, *Kat*, *Kad*, *Hhat*, *Hhad*. All these syllables have the sense of cutting. They appear as roots in the forms *Gazaz*, *Katsats*, *Hhatsats*, *Kadad*, *Hhadad*. To these may be added *Gadah* and *Gadang*

[1] Lexicon Manuale, under Gadad.

When this great philologist proceeded to compare with the large family of words here cited the Latin *cædo* and *scindo*, the Greek σχίζω, the Persian *chidan* and *khudan*, and the English *cut*, it is evident that he regarded the triliteral form as the formal root, and the biliteral as the real. He was manifestly right in this, as the examples now given from the eastern Asiatic languages sufficiently show. But there can be but little doubt that he was wrong in assuming the priority of the *s* final to the *t*, and of the *k* initial to the *g*.[1] The Chinese syllabary shows that a sibilant final to a root syllable is an innovation, and the history of the changes of letters in that language renders it probable that the whole surd series is derived from the sonant. Hence we learn that the root *gad* changed its initial to the strong aspirate *Hh* or to the pure surd letter *k*. The final *d* became *t* or *s* or *sh* or *ts*. We need not be surprised if we often meet with an interchange between the dental *t* and the sibilant *s*. This may be illustrated by the second personal pronoun in *t*. This form for the second person does not occur in any families but the Semitic, the Indo-European, and the Tartar branch of the Turanian. It is firmly fixed in all these. The Mongols take the *s* form, *ch'i* or *t'si*, as do the Manchus when they say *si*, and the Turks when they say *sen*. The Greek συ has followed them. The Sanscrit *tuam*,

---

[1] Under the word שְׁנַיִם *shenayim*, "two," Gesenius states that the primary form seems to be תְּנִי, thus admitting the priority of the *t* sound.

Persian *tu* and *to*, Latin *tu*, German *du*, English *thou*, agree with the Hebrew *atta*, Arabic *ant*, and Egyptian *entok* in preferring *t*.

We also learn that the first speakers of the Semitic languages, in forcing the roots to assume a triliteral form, added as a third letter the consonants *ng* and *h*, or doubled the final letter when it happened to be *d*, *ts*, or *s*. There were similar laws of change attendant on the other letters of the Semitic alphabet where they occur. The second *k*, for instance, was added in *mathaq*, "was sweet," connected with the Sanscrit *madhu*, "honey."

I now give examples to show that the phenomenon of a sibilant prefix, so common in the Sanscrit, and in the European languages, is also a favourite way of modifying the sound of a root among the Semites. The word *saphak*, "strike," is used[1] in the causative form in the sense of "strike a covenant," which is in Latin *pepigit fœdus*, or in the completed form *pactum*. In Chinese *p'ak* is "to strike," and *bang*, in the modern form *p'ing*, is a "proof," "evidence." In the verb *saphak*, "to strike," "to punish," there is a variation in the sibilant initial, *samech* being used for *sin*. The Hebrews also said for to "cleave," to "open," *bakang*, *bakar*, which meanings are expressed in Chinese by *p'ik*. May it not be regarded as probable that *s* was prefixed to the biliteral root in *p*, *k*, just as we say

[1] Gesenius, Lex. Man. in voc. Saphek.

smelt, and the Germans *schmelzen*, for *to melt*? If so, then *tsakhaq*, "laugh," may be derived from *kak*, the root syllable of cachination, the German *Kichern*, and the Greek καχάζω. So *shakab*, "recline," from *kub*, the root of *cubo*, and κύπτω, Mongol *hebt'emoi*, "lie down." So again, *sagab*, "to be high," from *gab* in *gibeah*, "a hill," and *gabahh*, "to be high." The word *sabar*, "to hope," derived from *bar*, a root meaning "to pierce," "scrutinize," as in the preposition *per*, and the verbs *pierce*, *bore*, may be compared with the Latin *spero*, "to hope." *Tsadik*, "just," will then be the same with the Greek δίκαιος and the Latin *rectus*, and agrees still more nearly with our own *straight*.

By these and similar processes the primitive biliteral roots have become triliteral, and it was thus that the Semites pointed out the path of change to the more youthful Indo-Europeans. Finding among the two families similar laws of change, we assign to the Semitic system, on account of its more simple syllabary, a higher antiquity than to the Indo-European; and so, when we compare the Semitic system with the Chinese, we must call the Chinese the older, because its roots are in a more rudimentary and primitive form.

The Chinese *chï*, "straight," is in the oldest ascertainable pronunciation *dik*. The Tamul-speaking people say *takuti*, and the Mongols *t'egshi*. The Greeks used the root *dik*. The Latins changed it to *rek*. The English and Arabs prefixed *s*, and the Hebrews *ts*.

That the Hamitic and Semitic languages were closely connected is now generally admitted. Egyptian words show signs of a more modern form than corresponding Chinese words. I select a few examples[1] from "Egypt's Place in Universal History."

| CHINESE. | | MEANING. | EGYPTIAN. |
OLD.	NEW.		
mo	ma	hemp	hma
mo	wu	is not	m or am
pui	fei	fly	pai, pui
ban	p'an	to sin, offend	ban
put	pu	not	bu
bak	pe	white	ubeχ
kit	hi	rejoice	haa
pak	pei	carry	fa, fai

The tendency to assume a dissyllabic form is manifest in these words. The language of Ancient Egypt belongs to a newer formation than the Chinese.

When the structure of the Hebrew conjugations, the syllabic suffixes to express the dual and plural, and the pronominal suffixes to nouns, are examined, the advance of the Semitic system from the primeval monosyllabism towards the polysyllabic form becomes still more clear. For example, *n* is prefixed to make a passive and *hith* to form a middle voice. The prefix *h* makes the verb causative, as does the insertion of

---

[1] These examples have been kindly corrected for me by a distinguished Egyptologist.

go and *gol* in Mongol. The root of the verb *to cause* is in Chinese *ko* or *kok*, and this, as *h* grows out of *k*, may be the parent of both these forms. The root thus becomes lengthened into four or five letters and two or three syllables.

The extensive use of *l*, *r*, *s*, and *ts*, as finals to the monosyllabic or biliteral root is another mark of more recent formation. These peculiar finals, entirely unknown in the ancient Chinese vocabulary, occur abundantly in the Hebrew, Turanian, and Indo-European syllabaries. The Chinese has *l*, but not *r*, in its alphabet, and the Japanese *r*, but not *l*. In modern Chinese *r* is struggling for recognition. In Mongol and Tamil *l* and *r* are fully developed, as in the Semitic and European systems.[1] They occur either as initials or as finals. The same is true of the sibilants *s*, *ts*, and *sh*. To the Semitic stock, therefore, should be assigned the honour of developing the syllabary of human speech in this direction. It was this system that first distinguished between *l* and *r* as initials, and added them, with *s*, *sh*, *z*, *ts*, to the list of final consonants. From them the Turanians took them during their ancient residence in South-western Asia, but subsequently to the time when they sent away the Japanese offshoot, and left it to pursue an independent existence in the far east of Asia; for the inhabitants of that island-empire are very deficient in this part of

[1] Not as initials in Tamil.

their syllabary, and their language seems to be the oldest of the three Turanian systems.

The vowels being represented by three letters in the earliest Semitic (that is, the Phœnician) alphabet, it is probable that when the ancestors of the Semites left the primeval stem of language, the vowels *a*, *i*, *u*, were sufficient for the needs of human speech at that time.

Thus much for the Semitic syllabary. Another mark of advance to be now noted is the growth of the Semitic inflexions. Imagination was always powerful among the men of this race. It gave to the Old Testament in its poetical portions their metaphorical imagery, brilliant description, and rapid movement. This same gift was their inheritance long before the days of the prophets, at an earlier time during the formation of their languages. We see its effects in the attribution of sex to the lifeless objects of nature. *Cedar, gem, bunch of grapes, death, enemy, book,* were masculine. *Pillar, egg, castle, intellect, year, sleep,* were feminine. Some words, such as *earth, fire,* were masculine or feminine. The Chinese and Turanian languages know nothing of these distinctions, and hence we infer that this characteristic of the Sanscrit, Greek, and Latin tongues has been derived from the influence of the earlier Semitic type. The feminine was marked frequently by a special suffix, as by *h*, or *th* in Hebrew, and by *a* in Greek and Latin.

Among the personal pronouns, *ani*, the first, was the common property of the Hebrew man and woman, but in the second person a distinction commenced, and was also maintained in the third. In the verb also, when woman or any feminine objects were spoken to or spoken of, a special suffix was used. But in this the Indo-European system did not follow the Semitic example, preferring to express the distinctions of person by the pronominal suffixes, without giving attention to sex. The Semitic languages gain little by this laborious system of conjugating according to gender, and it has, therefore, nearly lost its place in language. The predisposition of the human mind for poetical and rhythmical expression leads to the introduction into language of many laws, which, on account of their burdensome nature, must ultimately be given up, and cannot be expected to continue their existence in newly formed linguistic families. To such laws the Semitic conjugation by gender must be referred. The distinction of gender in pronouns has lived for a longer period, having lasted from the commencement of the Semitic age down to the modern English, the newest and freest form of Indo-European speech, which, while rejecting the distinction of gender in inanimate objects, has retained it in the personal pronouns *he, she, it.*

One of the most striking phenomena in Semitic speech, the result, like the genders of nouns, of boldness in imagination, is the inversion noticeable in the order of words. In the first verse of Genesis we read *Breshith bara Elohim eth hashshamayim ve eth ha-aretz.* " In the beginning created God the heavens and the earth." Why is the verb placed before its nominative ? It is in consequence of a law of inversion which it pleased the imaginative faculty to introduce. It was rendered possible by the previous formation of an objective case. The prefix *eth* being used to mark the object of the verb's action, there can be no confusion between the nominative and accusative, and it is, therefore, at the option of the speaker to place the actor before or after the verb, as he pleases. Guided by a poetic instinct, the Semite usually preferred to mention the verb before the actor. In so doing he departed from the old primeval law of human speech, still remaining in the Chinese and Turanian systems, and allowed the imagination to triumph over the logical faculty, according to which the nominative, as the first in nature and time, precedes its verb.

Another instance of the effect of inversion is seen in examples where the verb stands first, the nominative comes last, and the object is between them. *Ki Yebiaka Yehova*, "For shall bring thee Jehovah," instead of, "For Jehovah shall bring thee." This order is rendered possible by the object *ka*, "thee," the pronominal suffix to the verb, being always accusative, so that there can be no confusion between actor and object.

The laws by which the adjective follows the substantive, and the demonstrative pronoun its noun, are also caused by this tendency to inversion. The article came into existence opportunely to allow of this being conveniently done. The sentence, "This good land," is in Hebrew, *Ha-aretz hattobah hazzoth*. *Ha*, the definite article, is used three times. *Tobah*, "good," follows *aretz*, "the earth," and *zoth*, "this," comes last. This law also meets us in the Malay and Polynesian languages, where, however, the article is wanting.

A more important inversion perhaps than the preceding is what may be called the post-position of the genitive, as in the Arabic *zill Allah*, "the shadow of Allah." The natural order is "Allah's shadow," as in all the languages east of Persia (including the Sanscrit), excepting the East Himalaic, Malay, and Polynesian systems. Our primeval ancestors, there can be little doubt, spoke of the possessor first, and then what he possessed. The Semitic imagination first seized the name of the object possessed and then that of the possessor. This caused what is called the "construct state." The first word had its vowel shortened, and the plural termination appeared in a clipped form. Thus, דְּבָרִים *devarim*, became דִּבְרֵי *divre*, in the phrase *divre hangam* דִּבְרֵי הָעָם "words of the people."

When in Greek we find the post-position of the genitive well established, as in ἄναξ ἀνδρῶν, "king of men," and also remember the contiguity of the Greek and Semitic areas and the ancient intermixing of the Phœnicians with the Hellenic race, it seems quite a natural supposition that the Greeks derived it from the Semites. The near neighbourhood of the Assyrian empire and civilization would aid powerfully in the introduction into the Greek language of this and other Semite idioms. The same strong and long-continued Semite influence caused its entrance into the Persian as in *Mushk-i Khoten*, "musk of Khoten."

In English the two modes of arrangement are both in use, and this, as in other European tongues, adds much to the freedom, fluency, and variety which characterize modern speech. Thus the Shorter Catechism commences, "What is the chief end of man?" and says in the answer, "Man's chief end is to glorify God, and enjoy him for ever." If there had been any difference in intelligibility or propriety of use between "man's chief end," and the "chief end of man," a preference would have been shown here for one of these modes of speaking, to the exclusion of the other. In the English of the nineteenth century there are still no certain signs indicating that the Semitic mode of speech is coming near the end of its reign; and yet it is possible that the post-position of the genitive may pass into an archaism after no very long time. The Greeks said υἱὸς Θεοῦ, for "Son of God." The Latins rather preferred to say *Dei filius*. The Sanscrit-speaking Arians could not transpose their genitive, thus showing that they were under strong Turanian influence, and showed very little sign of Semite connexion.

Of the remarkable inversion of order, which in the Turanian and Indo-European families led to the system of case suffixes, there is scarcely any trace in the Hebrew, except in the suffix *ah*, expressing motion towards a place. But we do not know what this *ah* was. In the case suffixes of the Sanscrit and Greek we find, or think we ought to find, metamorphosed demonstratives placed after their nouns. Perhaps we should rather say verbs metamorphosed. Looking for an old verbal equivalent to this suffix, we find the Chinese *hiang* 向 *hung, kung*, "towards."

One of the greatest improvements in language due to the influence of the Semitic mind is the introduction of the relative pronoun. This pronoun is originally formed from the interrogative or demonstrative. In English the demonstrative *that* has acquired a relative force, and so it may be said of the interrogative *who*.

In Hebrew, the relative pronoun אֲשֶׁר *asher*, is not so easily accounted for. We find in Chinese an interrogative *zhok*, "who?" which appears in the modern form as *shui*, after dropping its final and changing its *zh* to *sh*. We also have *si*, "this," and *zhi*, "this," both old words; *shat*, "what?" a dialect word; and *shen*, "what," or, in an older form, *zhim*, a Mandarin word. Gesenius prefers to derive *asher* from the primitive demonstrative in *s*, in Sanscrit *sa, sas*, English *so, she*, German *sie*, and finds the final *r* in our words *there, der, er*, etc. The old word 斯 *si*, "this," and its equivalent 此 *t'si*, "this," show that the ancient Chinese had the same sibilant demonstrative. But the Hebrew *sh* has in some words the value *t* in cognate dialects. Thus, שָׁם *sham*, "there," was *tam* in Chaldee, Latin *tum*. Our word *asher* may therefore be a disguised form of the demonstrative in *d*, used in so many languages and dialects, Indo-European and Chinese. Thus we have in old Chinese *di*, "this," and the same in Tibetan, equivalent to the German *der, die, das*, and the English *this* and *that*. In Chaldee we find *da min da*, "this from that," reminding us of the Tibetan *di*, "this," and Malay *dia*, "he." We also meet with *di* in Chaldee for "who," "which," "that," and as a sign to connect a genitive with its prefixed nominative.

The relative is a device for continuing a description without coming to a full stop, and it allows the speaker to proceed without being compelled to commence again with a repetition of the noun. Hence the demonstrative pronoun is taken for this service as the representative of the noun, and as most suited to undergo the change in meaning which is required by its new position. The Hebrews often omitted the relative, an indication that in the early stage their language was without it. כָּל־יֶשׁ לוֹ *kol yesh lo*, "all was his," that is, "all that was his." They afterwards introduced *asher* to fill the gap, and make the sentence entirely coherent. The device was successful. They used for this object an obsolete demonstrative, *asher*, not needed for any other purpose.

When the Semites introduced the relative, it was in accordance with the genius of their language, which seizes on the central idea and then describes it in detail. The second verse of the second chapter of Genesis reads, if translated according to the Hebrew order, "And finished God on day the seventh work his which he did, and he rested on day the seventh from all work his which he did." The emphatic verbs *finish* and *rest* stand first. *Day* precedes its adjective, *seventh*. *Work* precedes the relative clause describing it. The action if a verb and the nominative if a noun must in all cases stand out in their clear individuality first. Then the particulars follow, whether expressed by adjectives, by pronouns, or by the relative clause. Such was the mode of constructing sentences which was most agreeable to the Semitic imagination. The eastern Asiatic languages have been content to be guided by the logical faculty.

The old Chinese would say, "Seventh day, God's work being completed, then he rested."[1] Here the

---

[1] 七 日 上 帝 工 竣 乃 憩 息 *Tsit nit zhiung te kong tsiun nai k'i sik*, "Seventh day Supreme Ruler work completed then

time is put first, because it is (viewed grammatically) a subordinate circumstance. The nominative stands first because the actor in the order of nature exists before the act. The verbs *completed* and *rested* take the order of time, and one nominative, *God*, serves for both. The order of nature allows of brief description. If this order is broken in upon, the penalty must be paid in tautologies and circumlocution.

The contents of every relative clause are capable of being inserted as a subordinate clause in the principal sentence under the control of the nominative to that sentence. This insertion is what the Chinese make use of instead of a relative clause.

The Mongol reads " God," *uberon uileduksen uilesi,* " self-done work," *jirgogan edure t'egusgeged*, " sixth day being finished," *dolodogar edure*, " on the seventh day," *uberon uileduksen uiles eche*, " self-done work from," *amorabai*, "rested."[1] Here the principal verb, *rested*, stands last, according to the invariable law of the Turanian languages. The nominative, *God*, stands first, ruling the subordinate and the principal clause. This is the fixed order of clauses in Chinese and in the Turanian system. What in Hebrew would be a relative clause is here constructed in immediate connexion with

stopped rested." From Translation of the Scriptures by Medhurst and others into Chinese.

[1] From the Translation of the Scriptures into Mongolian, by Messrs. Swan and Stallybrass.

the nominative by means of the possessive suffix attached to the reflexive pronoun *self*.

The influence of Semite speech appears to have been less on Sanscrit than on the other Indo-European tongues. The post-position of the genitive is entirely foreign to Indian grammar, and it seems to make but sparing use of the relative. The Hindoos did not commonly by its means construct a new subordinate clause after the principal sentence. They placed it as a Chinese or Mongol would do in a clause by itself before the chief sentence. They were fond of antithesis, and introduced a demonstrative *he* to correspond with the relative. In Williams' Sanscrit Grammar, the following example is given. "What you have promised, that abide by." *Yat pratijnátam tat pálaya*.

The Chinese would say in their modern language, *tsen mo shwo, tsen mo hing*, "how speak," "how do," meaning, "as you have spoken so do." Here, *tsen mo* is an interrogative, "how?" The Sanscrit *yad, yah,* is simply an old disused interrogative "who?" "what?" employed to perform the simpler duties of the relative according to the limited Hindoo conception of them. It is to the European languages that we must look for the examples of the full development of the relative, as a main help to the attainment of that fluency in narrative and accuracy in description for which they are distinguished.

CHAPTER VII.

THE HIMALAIC LANGUAGES YOUNGER THAN THE CHINESE; OLDER THAN THE TURANIAN.—EASTERN HIMALAIC BRANCH.—SIAMESE PHONAL SYSTEM.—COCHIN-CHINESE TONES.—CHINESE NATURAL TONES.—VOCABULARY.—SYNTAX.—WESTERN HIMALAIC BRANCH.—TIBETAN PHONAL SYSTEM.—TIBETAN AND HEBREW COMMON WORDS.—TIBETAN TONES.—POST-POSITION OF CASE PARTICLES.—DERIVATIVES.—TIBETAN VERB.—ANTIQUITY OF THE TIBETAN TYPE.

ON approaching the Himalaic languages on the western side, we find ourselves in contact with a system of case suffixes for the first time. For these we look in vain in the Semitic family, and in Chinese they are limited to the locative case. The Tibetan race connects itself by monosyllabic structure and tones, as well as by a large number of identical words, with the Chinese. But by its system of case particles it is seen to approach to the Tartar and Indian languages. The Tibetan belongs to a system younger than the Chinese, because it places the substantive before the adjective, and the verb at the end of the sentence. In the same way it may be shown to be older than the Turanian family, because, though it strongly resembles that system in placing the case particles after their nouns, and the verbs at the end of the sentence, yet its monosyllabic character and system of tonic pronunciation cause it to approximate to the Chinese.

The existence of the case suffixes in the Tibetan language, and the circumstance that the verb is there uniformly found at the end of the sentence, are sufficient to justify us in ascribing to the Himalaic family to which it belongs a later origin than to the Semitic. The third great step in the development of human language was made, therefore, in the formation of this family.

At the same time it must be kept in view that the Eastern and Western Himalaic languages are diverse in several important respects. The Cochin-Chinese and Siamese languages have an order like and yet not like the Chinese in the combination of the prepositions with the nouns. All the case auxiliaries are prefixed, whether locative, instrumental, dative, or ablative. In the Chinese the locative auxiliaries follow, and the rest precede their nouns. In the Tibetan they are all suffixes. The Eastern and Western branches of the Himalaic family thus appear to differ in character very materially, and a division is rendered inevitable. Yet their common tonic pronunciation, and their advance beyond the Chinese in the extended capacity of their syllabaries, may still be regarded as furnishing sufficient ground for retaining them in connexion as branches of one family.

In the Cochin-Chinese and Siamese languages, which are the chief members of the Eastern Himalaic branch, an alphabetic series and syllabary exist, much resembling the Chinese. The words are monosyllabic. The finals are in Cochin-Chinese, besides the vowels, *k, t, p, ng, nh, n, m,* and *ch*. Of these *nh* is a variation from *ng* and *ch* from *k*. An effort has been made to throw off some of these finals. We find *nhot*, "day," the Chinese *nyit*, also spelled *ngai*, where the *t* is lost. There is a limited use of *r* and *l* after the initials *b* and *t*. Thus, *tron, blon, trot, blot,* all mean "perfect," "whole," and are the same with the Chinese 全 *t'siuen*, formerly pronounced *zien* and *dzien*. In exchange for *dz, dj, ch, ts*, the Cochin-Chinese introduced gradually the initials *tr* and *bl*. They also developed the modern letters *r* and *l* out of the old *l*. The Siamese have done the same, and have also added *f*, as the modern Chinese have done, to the old alphabetic elements. No other member of the Himalaic family has the letter *f*. The area of this letter is also limited among the Turanian languages to Japan, Manchuria, and Turkestan. The Siamese have no *sh*, but they have, like all the members of the Himalaic family, an abundant supply of aspirated surds. Thus, *k, t,* and *p*, with an aspirate, are extremely common. These aspirated mutes exist in certain localities in Europe, and constitute a main peculiarity in the colloquial Irish pronunciation of the English language, but it is only in the speech of Eastern Asia that they have been made to take the part of distinct letters. From Jones's "Grammatical Notices of the Siamese Language," it would appear that there has been no change in the finals: *k, d, b, ng, n, m*, rule undisturbed as the favourite consonants for terminating all closed syllables. Perhaps *d* and *b*, which come in place of *t* and *p*, are of even greater antiquity than these last. They may be the vestiges of an era when the surds *k, t, p*, were still unknown as initials or finals, and when in the primeval alphabet, as now in the Tartar languages, the aspirates and sonants were the only representatives of the triple series known as gutturals, dentals, and labials.

The tones are in the Siamese phonal system closely intertwined with the syllabary. The letters are divided into three series, high, middle, and low. The aspirates *k', t', p', s, f, h, c'h*, are pronounced in the upper and lower series, that is, for example, in a high and low *do*. The surds and sonants *k, ch, t, p, d, b*, are in the middle series, *e.g.*, in the key of *sol*. The remainder, *ng, n, m, l, r, w, y*, are in the lower *do*.

The words being arranged on a scale with a triple pitch, of which the two intervals, taken together, vary from, perhaps, a half to an entire octave, the inflexions and even-tones, five in number, still remain to be applied to them. These consist of a slow even-tone, a circumflex, which is a curve of the voice, first down and then up, a slow falling, a quick rising, and a slow rising inflexion.[1] The English and French interrogative tone is the same as what is here called the quick

[1] See Grammatica Linguæ Tai, by Bishop Pallegoix.

rising inflexion. In the sentence, "What! not obey me?" the tone of *what* is the quick rising inflexion, and that of *obey* is not unfrequently the slow falling circumflex.

The Cochin-Chinese tones are also arranged on a triple pitch, which we may again think of as upper *do*, *sol*, and lower *do*, remembering, however, that the breadth of the intervals and the general pitch of the voice depend on the habit of the individual and the state of his feelings. The tones in this language are like the Chinese, and are not distributed among aspirates and non-aspirates, as are the Siamese and Tibetan, but are themselves set in *sol*, and the lower and upper *do*.

COCHIN-CHINESE TONES.[1]

NATURAL CHARACTER.	MUSICAL NOTATION.	ENGLISH EQUIVALENT.
1. quick even	upper *do*	monotone
2. quick rising	*sol, si*	interrogative
3. falling and rising { circumflex	*sol, fa, la*	satirical circumflex
4. slow even	*sol*	monotone
5. quick falling	*fa, mi*	interrogative
6. slow falling	lower *do*	{ tone of remonstrance { tone of decision

This system differs from the Chinese only in having a triple pitch, while the tones of Chinese dialects are,

[1] Prof. des Michels, "Sur les Intonations chez les Annamites." 1869.

perhaps, usually content with a double key. The Chinese, also, often use the other circumflex, namely, that which is bent first upward and then downward.

The Chinese, as having a greater variety of dialects, have, of course, a fuller development of tones than the sister races can be expected to possess.

They have the quick and slow even-tone, the quick and slow rising inflexion, the quick and slow falling inflexion, and the circumflex of two kinds, first rising and then falling, or first falling and then rising, and each of these in slow or quick time. They may be represented by straight and curved lines, thus :—

CHINESE NATURAL TONES.

Even stroke	— — —	quick and slow monotone
Down stroke, straight or curved	⟍ ⟍	quick and slow falling slide
Up stroke, straight or curved	⟋ ⟋	quick and slow rising slide
Curve down and up	⌣ ⌣	quick and slow falling circumflex
Curve up and down	⌢ ⌢	quick and slow rising circumflex

Each of these may be placed in a higher or lower pitch, and perhaps there may be an intermediate or triple pitch in some cases.[1]

Each dialect selects from this set of tones as many as it requires. The least number of tones that any dialect

---

[1] The intervals may be *do, mi, sol,* or *mi, la, do,* and for the double pitch *do, sol,* or *la, do,* which last is the interval in Peking for ordinary voices.

in China is known to use is four, as the Pekinese; and the greatest nine, as in the Hok lo *patois*, in Canton province.

The waves of the voice in these inflexions are better represented by *curved lines* than by the musical scale of modern Europe, because the sound of the inflexion is continuous and not broken up into quavers and crotchets. But to convey a correct idea of the variation in *pitch* noticeable in tonic elocution, reference to the musical scale is highly useful.

The vocabulary of the eastern Himalaic languages is in many respects like the Chinese.

ENGLISH	fish	honey	earth	clothing	mother	breath
CHINESE	ngud	mid	da	wei	mo	k'ui
COCHIN-CHINESE	ka	mot	dat	ao	me	k'oi
GREEK, LATIN	ἰχθύς	μέλι	terra	vestis	μήτηρ	halitus

ENGLISH	two	three	four	five	six	fire	fowl	head
CHINESE	shong	sam	si	ngu	lok	hwa	koi	du
SIAMESE	song	sam	si	ha	hok	fai	kai	how

In Siamese *h* takes the place of the Chinese *l* and *d*. The Siamese *l* corresponds to the Chinese *h*, as in Chinese *hit*, "blood," Siamese *luit;* Chinese *hwang*, "yellow," Siamese *leuang;* Chinese *hung*, "rainbow," Siamese *lung*. The modern Chinese *h* corresponds to an older *k*, and will bear comparison with our western *cruor, crudelis, gore, clot.*[1] So *hwang,* "yellow," may be compared with our *crocus.* The word for "rainbow," *hung,* is doubtless a variant of *kong,* " a bow." The *ng* final of Chinese words sometimes corresponds to our western *m.* So here the Persian *kemán* and Greek κάμπτω, " to bend," are derived from the same root.

The Siamese pronouns *ku,* "I," *meung,* " thou," and *k'ea,* "he," may be compared with the Chinese *nga,* "I," the Hainan, Kwangsi, and Kweicheu aboriginal word *mu,* "thou," and the Chinese *gi,* " he." The extension of the second personal pronoun *mu* over the area occupied by the Blue and White Miau of South China, the Hainan islanders and the Shan tribes of Burmah and Siam,[2] helps materially to connect these scattered dialects, stretching from the Gulf of Siam, N. latitude 14°, to Kweicheu in China, N. latitude 26°, into one system.

The Western Himalaic languages, including the speech of the Lo lo in the Chinese province of Kweicheu, the Burmese and the Tibetians, do not appear to have this pronoun. They use instead of it for our *thou,* in the Lo lo dialect, *kai,* and in Tibetan, *k'yed.*

---

[1] These words all branch from the primeval root *kit,* "coagulate," "join together." Hence our *kith, catena,* and the Chinese *kit,* "tie," and *gin,* "near."

[2] See Bishop Bigandet's comparative vocabulary of Shan dialects in Logan's Journal of the Indian Archipelago.

The Siamese, the T'ung tribe in Kwangsi, the White Miau in Kweicheu, the Li tribe of Hainan, and the Shans, all say for "I" and "my," *ku, hau,* or *k'au.* These are all merely variations from the widely spread root *nga* common to the Chinese and Tibetians, and occurring as *aham, ego, ich,* in Indo-European languages.

The third personal pronoun *k'ia,* in Chinese *gi,* has nearly as wide an area. The White Miau of China say *kwa* for "he," the Tibetians *ko.* The Japanese say *kono* for "this." The Latin is *hic,* and the English *he.* As an interrogative, the same root takes the form of "quis?" "quid?" "who?" and "what?" It is also extensively used in the Turanian and Semitic languages, as in the Mongol *k'en,* "who?" and the Hebrew *hu,* "he."

The laws of position in the Eastern branch of the Himalaic family are very peculiar. In all the dialects, whether those of the Miau aborigines in South-western China,[1] or the Li in Hainan, the Cochin-Chinese or the Siamese, the adjective follows the substantive. It is the same in the Western branch. The Chinese, Mongols, Turks, and Hindoos, encircling these languages on all sides, place the adjective before the substantive. The Malays only form an exception. The Himalayan races have not then, in the adoption of this inversion,

---

[1] My authorities for Miau dialects are the Chinese works Hing i fu chï, Kwangsi t'ung chï, and for Hainan a manuscript vocabulary by Robert Swinhoe, Esq.

imitated any of their neighbours. Shall we trace this law to Semite influence, or attribute it to their own independent efforts to effect changes in the primeval type? Perhaps the latter view may be most favourably received. But an early connexion with the Semites is not unlikely, certainly not impossible.

On the other hand, the Eastern branch of this family is, in regard to the position of the locative case particles, older than the oldest of its neighbours. The verbs which mark the cases of nouns are all found before their nouns, and very curiously we see the same principle in operation in the Semitic languages. The Tibetians and Tartars belong to more modern migrations, and at the very commencement of their independent linguistic existence they performed with decision and the most thorough success the feat of transferring the verb to the close of the sentence. This process included necessarily the post-position of all case particles. There can be no doubt that this Turanian idiom is new, and the Ultra-Indian idiom old. The geographical situation renders this conclusion inevitable. If also it be remembered that the tribes called in the oldest of the Chinese classics, the San Miau,[3] were the first known occupants of the Chinese area, it seems difficult to resist the conclusion that the Eastern Himalayan

---

[1] The reign of Shun, B.C. 2255, in the Shu king, included the pacification of the San Miau, or three aboriginal tribes, among its chief historical events.

races are older than the Chinese. For how can it be accounted for that the Chinese should have taken the first step in the post-position of the case particles, and that their southern neighbours should show no trace of a similar phenomenon, except on the supposition that in the early migrations from the west, the Ultra-Indians came first and the Chinese next? Yet they continued uncivilized till Buddhist teachers visited them from India and covered the peninsula with monastic institutions and Hindoo practices and beliefs. This was nearly 2,000 years ago. At about the same time, the light of Chinese ancient culture penetrated also among them, especially in the reign of Han Wu ti, B.C. 100. They never originated, like the Hindoos, a mighty *kosmos* of the imagination, nor, like the Chinese, a complete practical system of the arts of life. The vast Cambodian temples, with their long colonnades, now hidden in the glades of unfrequented forests, the shining kiosks of modern Bankok, the books of prayers written on the palm leaf, the invocations to Gautama, and the ascetic and convent life, are all Hindoo. The agriculture, the usages of commerce, the mode of government, are all Chinese.

Hence their languages have probably changed more than the Chinese. Speech owes its persistence to civilization. Ancient words are crystallized in literature, even if they are dropped from their place in the familiar intercourse of men. Barbarous idioms alter rapidly. Laws of grammar, words, sounds, meanings, accents, are in perpetual transition. Hence the novel aspect of much of the vocabulary of these races. Living as separate tribes, the language of each has undergone rapid changes. But through all the principles of grammatical structure and the outline of the phonal system appear to have retained their ancient features. The marks of primeval formation are most remarkable, and their consanguinity to the Chinese type is as undeniable as is their likeness in lineaments to the common mother from which all languages sprang.

We do not meet with any full representative of the Western branch of the Himalayan race till we arrive at Tibet and Burmah, and perhaps the Chinese Lo lo. The Karens are in a half-way position between the two branches. They place the adjective and the demonstrative pronoun after the substantive, and the case particles before the object, whose relations they define. The possessor precedes the object possessed, as in all the Eastern Asiatic languages. They have six tones and a strong attachment for vowel finals. All the consonant finals have been thrown off, except *ng*. Although in vocabulary they have borrowed much from the Burmese and Tibetan languages,[1] they cannot with these laws of position be rightly classed anywhere but in the Eastern branch.

What strikes the eye most remarkably in the Tibetan

[1] Logan's Journal.

syllabary is the prefixed letters. The early speakers of this form of human speech, not having before them the idea of terminations, that happy device made use of by the founders of the polysyllabic languages, bent their strength unconsciously to add letters at the beginnings of the roots. In so doing they remind us of the Semite system, which, in the conjugation of the verb, prefixes *n* to make a passive, *m* to make a participle and an agent, and *h* to render the verb causative. The favourite prefixes of the Tibetans are *g, d, b, h, m, r, l, s*. Csoma de Körös says, they are in modern speech seldom heard. Hence this effort to extend the monosyllabic root at its beginning must be regarded as a failure. The letters thus ineffectually placed at the commencement of the words are *k, g, d, b, m, r, l, s*, and *h*. They help to distinguish words having the same sound, and thus in the written Tibetan they serve a useful purpose. Two letters are also added occasionally at the end of the root, namely, *s* and *h*. Csoma de Körös says, *mi-rnams* is pronounced as it is written, but when the *r* is not preceded by a word in close combination it is silent. When these prefixes and suffixes are cleared away from the word, it is reduced to the radical form. *Mi* is the substantive root *man*, and *nam* is the plural suffix.

The six consonant finals of the Chinese language occur again in the Tibetan, but with a slight variation. The mute surds *k, t, p*, all occur in the sonant form *g, d, b*. The Tibetian cannot shape his vocal organs so as to pronounce *k, t, p,* at the end of a syllable. This peculiarity is more fixed in the Tibetan than in the Siamese, where *k, d,* and *b* occur as finals. In this respect, therefore, the Tibetan has the palm of antiquity; for, as before remarked, there is a strong probability that *k, t,* and *p* are newer letters than *g, d,* and *b,* and have been derived from them.

The capacity of the Tibetan syllabary is much enlarged by the addition of the finals *r, l, s*. By the separation of *r* and *l,* the Tibetan phonal system is shown to be more modern than the Chinese, which has only *l,* and to stand on the same footing with the Eastern Himalaic and Semitic systems. *R* is very abundant in Hebrew as a radical and a suffixed letter, and its extensive use in Tibetan warrants a suspicion of ancient intercommunication between the two families. The Bod race left Western Asia later than the families lying more to the east, and would naturally remain in contact with a Semite population for a much longer period. In Genesis it is said that the sons of Ham were Cush and Mizraim, and Phut and Canaan. As Cush had eastern and western branches, so may Phut have had also, and he may be the race-father both of the Libyans and of the modern Tibetians, now spread over the whole of Tibet and Bootan in the Himalayas. That section of the armies of Gog and Magog mentioned in Ezekiel as belonging to the

Phuttian race may have been contributed by the Eastern branch.

However this may be, the Bod race and the Semites are, at any rate, alike in their fondness for prefixing various letters to their words, and in adding r and l as suffixes. The Hebrews said *gilgal, galgal,* for a "wheel," and *gulgoleth,* for a "skull," from which comes *Golgotha,* the Aramaic original of the Latin Calvary in the Gospels. The Tibetians say *kor,* "a circle," *khor,* "a wheel." The Chinese have *gu,* "a ball," and *ku,* "a garland," "a hoop." To this root the Tibetians added r, the Semites l, and then farther west it took the forms *circulus,* κύκλος, κυλίνδω. The Sanscrit *chakra,* "wheel," and *chakrawat,* "circular," are from the same root, by the common change from k to *ch*. The Hebrew, עָגוּר *ngagur,* "revolving," עָגַל "revolve," עָגֹל "round," may be also included, because the primitive value of *ayin,* the initial consonant, is *ng* or *g.*

Among the letters the surd mutes k, t, p, are very weak. They scarcely fill a page each in the dictionary. The first k is the most important. The aspirated forms *kh, th, ph, k', t', p',* abound, as do the sonants g, d, b. Much the same law appears to exist in the Hebrew vocabulary. The two k's together cover fifty-one pages, while the aspirate *heth* covers seventy, and g and *ng* together ninety-seven pages. The surd t, the aspirate *th,* and the sonant d, occupy respectively, five, forty, and twenty-three pages. The labial series includes, p and f together, eighteen, and b seventy pages.

Compare these results with the Sanscrit vocabulary, and it will be found that the tables are turned, k and its cognate ch occupy 108 pages, their aspirates eleven, and the sonants g and j fifty-seven. The dental series, t, d, and dh, has the numbers thirty-one, forty, twelve. The labial series p, b, and p', b', has ninety-six, eleven, twenty-one. Here the surds have a clear superiority, and the influence of the aspirates has greatly diminished.

These facts reveal the existence of a great general law, according to which the aspirates and surds grew out of the sonants. The older vocabularies, as the old Chinese, the Turanian, the Tibetan, and the Semitic, have a preponderance of sonate initials and finals, b, c, d. Then the limits of language were extended to satisfy the ever-increasing wants of the historical races and the advance of civilization, and the aspirates appeared, k', t', p', h', h, θ, ϕ, f, with the surds k, t, p, h. These would spring up in some countries contemporaneously. In others, as in the Tibetan and Tartar languages, the aspirates grew into use alone, and the surds slowly followed. This law embraces the celebrated Grimm's law as one of its particulars. The reason why *dip*, *deep*, *door*, are in German *taufen*, *tief*, and *Thür*, is that the English vocabulary is in this respect older than the German, and that the German has advanced one stage farther than the English in the development of the surd initials. *K, t, p,* have grown out of *g, d,* and *b,* just as we have seen *r* and *l,* in the Semitic and Himalaic systems, grow out of an original *l* in the old Chinese. Our English *f* and *th* have grown out of a more ancient *b* and *d*. *Father* is in Hebrew *ab,* in old Chinese *be,* in Turkish *baba,* in Tibetan *yab,* in Latin *pater,* in German *Vater*. In the older syllabaries it was *ba* and *ab,* and here we see another lurking similarity existing between the Tibetan and the Semitic families meeting as they do in the use of *ab, yab,* " father." It is found with *p* in some southern Chinese dialects, and in Sanscrit, Greek, and Latin. Modern Chinese agrees with English and German in giving the *f* sound. New vocabularies have a preponderance of surds, as old vocabularies delight in sonants. Grimm's law is not so much a circular law, as one of perpetual advancement.

TABLE OF TIBETAN AND HEBREW COMMON WORDS.

TIBETAN.	HEBREW.	ENGLISH.	MISCELLANEOUS.
yum	em	mother	
lang	lakahh	receive	GREEK λαγχάνω.
lug	rahhel (*ewe*)	sheep	
log, *side*	tselang	rib, side	CHINESE lok, *rib*.
rum	rahham	womb	
rab, *exalted*	rab	great	
ring	rahhoq	long, far	CHINESE dung.
la	l'	to	
lha, *gods*	eloah	God, angels	
langs, *vapour, ghost*	ruahh	spirit, wind	
rogs, *friend*	ré-ang	friend	

In this list of words common to the Tibetan and Semitic vocabularies, the circumstance that *r* agrees usually with *r*, and *l* with *l*, is itself evidence that the two families grew up together in their early youth.

The Tibetan, like the Mongol, Cochin-Chinese, and the Indian languages, has not to this day admitted *f* into its alphabet; but *sh*, which is not used in Mongolia or Japan, has here, as in the Semitic and Chinese languages, a full development.

The tones of the Tibetan language are mentioned by Georgi, but no allusion is made to them by De Körös or by Schmidt. They are attached, like the Siamese tones, to the letters of the alphabet in sets, and are, I believe, arranged in a scale of two elevations, as is usually the case in Chinese.

Dr. Jaeschke, a missionary long resident in Ladak, and who has extended his researches into the various provincial dialects, informs me that the tones are limited to the central provinces. To compensate for the loss in colloquial pronunciation of letters recognized in the written language, the Lhasa dialect has introduced (1), an aspiration which may be symbolized by the forms *dh, gh, bh, jh;* (2), a deep tone. The word *chang,* "beer," sounds high, short, and sharp. The deep tone is a lower slow rising inflexion. By comparing Dr. Jaeschke's remarks with my own notes on the Lhasa pronunciation, as taken from the lips of a native visiting Peking, I believe it is correct to state that surds are pronounced with the upper quick falling intonation, and sonants with the lower slow rising. Among the sonants, however, there has been a loss of *g*, *j*, *d*, *b*. These are by the Lhasa people pronounced *kh*, *c'h*, *t'h*, *ph*. The loss thus sustained is compensated for by the lower or deep tone. This change resembles that which takes place in China in passing from the old middle dialect to Mandarin or to the Hakka, when *du*, "map," becomes *t'u* with the aspirate. In both countries the sonant is the older, and the aspirate with its special tone the newer form.

What caused the tones? I believe Dr. Jaeschke to be right in his view, that it was the loss of letters. When certain initial and final letters, faithfully preserved in the book language and in the dialects of the western provinces of Tibet, became mute in the neighbourhood of Lhasa, the tones were affixed by an unconscious effort of language to maintain distinctions between words that would be otherwise confounded. This hypothesis of the origin of tones agrees with that advocated long since in my "Grammar of the Chinese Colloquial Language."

After the researches of Dr. Jaeschke, which show that the mute letters of the Lhasa dialect and of the written language, are all heard distinctly in the pronunciation of some of the frontiers, philologists must regard the written form of the Tibetan, with its troublesome compound letters, as faithfully representing the old state of the language.

A Semitic principle here appears working itself out in a somewhat exaggerated manner. The language made too great an effort to expand itself by prefixes and suffixes, and is now throwing them off, and gradually assuming the primeval monosyllabic form.

The tonic element seems destined to extend itself in Tibetan, as it has done in Chinese. It is now in the Lhasa dialect doing the work which was formerly done by the difference between surd and sonant initials. The syllables *kha* and *ga* have assumed tones, and *ga* has changed to *kha*, so that they are now separated only by intonation. A native of Lhasa reads *kha* for *ga*, and intones the syllable.

A subject of great interest in Tibetan is the post-position of the case particles. Excepting the locative case suffixes of the old and new Chinese, there was no earlier family from which the Bod race could borrow this idea. It manifestly originated in the post-position of the verb. For it is more likely that the case particles should take their place after their nouns, as an instance of a general law which drew all the verbs into that position, than that they should first go there themselves, and then draw the other verbs after them. There is little difficulty in conceiving the way in which the locative case particles came, in the old Chinese, to occupy a position after their nouns. They are in fact, as explained in a previous chapter, treated as substantives following other substantives in the relation of the part to the whole. In the phrase *t'ien hia*, "the world," literally "heaven under," the word "under" is viewed as a noun, "that which is under." The possessive particle *chï* might be inserted, *t'ien chï hia*, showing that we are quite right in regarding the Chinese post-position of the locative as only an instance of the juxtaposition of substantives.

The Chinese language cannot, therefore, explain the great inversion of the Tibetan and Turanian languages, according to which the verb with the case particles comes after the noun. Perhaps the best explanation is found in a general tendency of these races to collect the energy of linguistic expression at the end both of sentences and words. The boldness of the Semite imagination was caused by religious culture, the habit of meditating on the objects of the spiritual sphere, and the possession of the primeval revelation made in the antediluvian period, and handed down from age to age. Hence poetic laws control the language and literature of the Semites. They attribute life to inanimate things, and action to objects that are at rest. They filled the world around them, as they did their grammatical paradigms, with the distinctions of gender. The Tibetians and Tartars are at the opposite pole. They are almost destitute of imagination. The sun and moon, the river, the stone, the mountain, are to them simply what their names imply—

> "A yellow primrose was to him
> A yellow primrose, and no more."

They take the world quietly. Things are to them before action. Personification is to them an absurdity. The effort required to look on the universe as animated with living forces is to them almost impossible. Their books are translated, their alphabets are borrowed, and they have learned the arts of life from their neighbours. They let go with facility the old Turanian religion, and took in the place of it the Buddhistic faith, a creation of the dreaming Hindoo. This pleases them because it teaches inactivity. The thought of Nirvana imparts to them consolation, because it consists of unbroken rest. The Tibetians have two substantive verbs, *nyug* and *dod*, which mean either "to sit," or "to be." Sitting is being. Races of active intellect do not form substantive verbs thus.

In conformity with this predisposition to inactivity, they postpone the place of the verb in a sentence to the end. All the details are carefully completed before action commences. A nation with very little poetry will have an unpoetical language, for the child is father of the man. A language, the work of a race in its childhood, will be found to resemble the literature which that race achieves in its maturity. So the Mongol and the Tibetian, in introducing the principle of the post-position of the verb, have only done what we might expect from the dullness of their literary development.

The case particles in Tibetan are few. There is a possessive, *kyi, gi, gyi, hi,* and *yi*. In Chinese dialects occur as possessives, *ku* at Shanghai, *ge* and *é* at Amoy. They are probably identical with the Tibetan and with the demonstrative roots *ki, gi, i*.

An *s* appended to the possessive particles makes them instrumental, and the sense, "by means of," "by the use of," is thus conveyed.

Among the dative case suffixes the commonest, *la*, may be the Semitic *le*, used as a dative prefix. The Tibetians may have borrowed it at some ancient period of contact, before the Persian race separated them from the Semite area, and before they migrated to their present locality. The case suffixes, expressive of motion towards, *tu* and *du*, as in *lag-tu*, "into the hand," *Bod-du*, "into Tibet," are probably the Chinese *to*, in Mandarin *tau*, "towards," "to." The Mongol corresponding case suffix is *de*. After a vowel *ru* is used by the Tibetians for *tu* and *du*. This I incline to think is changed from *du*. Thus, *ring*, "long," is in Old Chinese *dung*, in Mandarin *c'hang*.

The locative suffix *in* is *na* or *la*, and the ablative *nas* or *las*.

Such is the beginning of the declension of nouns, which expanded itself somewhat in the Turanian languages, and grew to its fullest dimensions in the Sanscrit.

We have also in Tibetan the rudiments of the system of derivatives. The following forms are in use :

Monosyllabic Suffixes: pa, ba, ma, po, bo, mo, ka, k'a, ga, nga, ge, nge, ni, p'o, mo, bu, hu, gu, ngu, nu.
Dissyllabic Suffixes: papa, pama, papo, pamo, bapa, bapo, bama, bamo.
Closed-syllable Suffixes: chig, zhig, chag, dag, nams.

The various significations of these suffixes are as follows :

Plural Suffixes: chag, dag, nam.
Diminutives: gu, ngu, nu, bu, hu.
Masculine: po, bo, pa, papa, papo.
Feminine: ma, mo, pama, pamo.
Agents or Verbal Substantives: po, ba (*masc. or fem.*).

It is the tonic pronunciation which prevents derived words from becoming dissyllables and polysyllables. The inflexions attached to the root and the suffixes have a tendency to check the consolidation of the syllables into a unity. Yet this is in time overcome. In the Peking pronunciation of Chinese a suffix very frequently loses its tone and becomes *de facto* a part of the word which precedes it.[1]

The verb forms its infinitive by appending *r* to *pa*

[1] Mandarin Grammar.

or *ba*, as *byed par* (pronounced *ched par*), "to do." *Byed pa* is either a present participle or a verbal noun, "doing." *Byed* alone is an indicative present, "he does."

In many cases verbs are placed in the indicative present by adding *byed*, "do," as an auxiliary, as in *za par byed*, "he eats," *gro par byed* (pronounced *tʻo par ched*), "he walks." Other auxiliaries, *zhin pa*, *hdug*, *snang*, are used with the same force.

Verbs are made preterite by affixing *s*. An auxiliary verb, *hdug pa*, "was," placed after a verb, changes it to the imperfect tense, as *hong hdug pa*, "he was coming." The future adds *hgyur*.

In the form for the imperative we meet curiously with a Semitic peculiarity. The vowel *a* or *e* is changed to *o*. *Za*, "he eats," becomes *zo*, "eat." *Sel*, "he cures," becomes *sol*, "cure." In the Hebrew paradigm, *katal*, "he killed," becomes in the imperative *ktol*; and *sabab*, "he surrounded," becomes *sob*. To a change like this there is no parallel in Chinese or Mongol, and it is difficult to conceive any explanation but that of ancient Semitic connexion.

A precative is formed by the suffix *chig*, *zhig*, or *shig*. This may be the Chinese root *sik*, "give," or *shung*, "reward." The Mongols in their imperative add a verb "to give" just in this way,—*Tʻa naded helji ug*, "you me for speak give," that is, "be kind enough to speak for me."

The conditional suffix *na* is undoubtedly derived from the root *nak*, which now appears in Chinese as *jo* and *ju*, "if." Thus, *byed na*, "if you do."

The changes in the prefixes of the Tibetan verb are due to a principle which was also at work, as before noticed, in the formation of the verb. To "call" is *hgugs*, in the indicative present, *bkug* in the preterite, *dgug* in the future, and *k'ug* in the imperative. The Chinese root is *kok*, "call," in Greek καλέω, in English *call*. The prefix *h* frequently marks the present, *b* the preterite or future, and *d* or *g* the future.

Another principle, to which attention should be drawn, is the change, with the moods and tenses, from sonant to surd and from aspirate to sonant, *e.g.* from *g* to *k* and from *k'* to *g*.

TIBETAN.				CHINESE.		INDO-EUROPEAN.	SENSE.
Present.	*Pret.*	*Future.*	*Imper.*	*New.*	*Old.*		
ht'ags	btags	btag	t'og	chï	tek	texo	*weave*
htogs	btags	gdags	t'ogs			Saxon tig, *a tie*	*tie*
hbigs	p'ig	dbig	p'ig	p'iau	p'ok	prick	*pierce*
hbyed	p'ye	dbye	p'ye			πράττω, πρᾶγμα	*do*
ht'sog	btsogs	btsog	tsog	siau	sok	seco, section	*cut*
hdzem	bzem	gzem	zem			schamen, shame	*shame*
hgegs	bkag	dgag		kie	kak	check	*hinder*
hgebs[1]	bkab	dgab	k'ob	kai	kap	κύπτω, *Heb.* kafar	*cover*

[1] This is a widely-extended root. The Chinese *kap* means "head," "covering," "coat of mail," and "to cover." The Tibetan has *k'ob*, "a covering," and *mgo*, "head." The Western languages have *caput*, *Haupt*, *head*, κεφαλή, *crab*, *cope*, etc.

But these principles, the first of prefixed augments and the second of the interchange of allied letters, have not been carried through the language, and they have failed to acquire the authority of irresistible law. This may have been owing to the want of strong will in the race speaking the language. Although characterized by this weakness, the principles here alluded to are deeply interesting as examples of very early efforts of the human race to conjugate their verbs in a way neither Semitic nor Indo-European. The geographical position occupied by the Tibetians indicates that their language may be expected to be a stepping-stone between the oldest and the newest types. The Chinese are on one side and the Persians on the other. But no early literature crystallized the language in its ancient form. How far it may have lost features which once belonged to it, it is now impossible with accuracy to determine.

The antiquity of the Tibetan type, as compared with the Turanian and Indo-European, cannot be questioned, when its monosyllabic character and stunted derivative system are properly considered. The only modern-looking feature is, indeed, the post-position of the verb and of the case particles, as already alluded to. The personal pronouns show that the long neighbourhood of Mongols, Turks, Hindoos, and Persians, has failed to have any effect on the Tibetan towards introducing into it their favourite words, *thou* and *me*, *be* and *become*. The first personal pronoun in *b* or *m*, the second in *t* or *s*, and the substantive verb in *b*, are used over the whole vast extent of the Indo-European and Tartar area, but into no Tibetan or Chinese dialect have they ever forced their way. The long continuance of linguistic differences between races that have been living side by side for thousands of years is at least as remarkable as the mutual influence they exert on each other's vocabulary and grammar. In the Tibetan pronouns and substantive verbs we see a Chinese impress. *Nga* for "I," *k'hyed* for "thou," *k'o* for "he," with *yin*, *yod*, for "to be," "to have," reveal a cousinship with the countrymen of Confucius. They are apparently no other than the old Chinese words *nga*, "I," *ni*,[1] "you," *gi*, "he," *wei*, "be," *u*, "have."

[1] The common Western equivalent for the Chinese *ni* is *k*, *g*, or *k'*.

CHAPTER VIII.

The Triple-Branched Turanian Family: Japanese, Dravidian, and Tartar. — First, the Japanese. — Japanese Syllabic Alphabet.—Common Roots in Japanese.—Formation of Compounds.—Case Particles.

We now pass the boundary between the monosyllabic and polysyllabic languages. The dividing line is a sharp one, which the traveller crosses from the region of tone systems and carefully-pronounced inflexions of the voice to the freedom of polysyllabic speech. He suddenly finds that he is where tonic laws have been thrown away, and all accented and inflected elocution has been transferred from the region of the syllabary and the vocabulary to that of the passions and the will. It is but a short distance from the Chinese city to the Mongol encampment, but the change of scenery is great. An agricultural plain, studded with villages and clumps of trees, with all the signs of industry, is left at the foot of the chain of mountains, along which the Great Wall is built. These mountains must be ascended, and at the height of 2,000 feet commences the tableland, which has received the name of "the land of grass." Field labour suddenly comes to a termination, and everywhere are seen the marks of pastoral occupations. It is the land of the roaming deer, the patient camel, the vigorous ox, of tents and fleecy flocks, and droves of ponies; of vast plains without trees, and a limitless horizon, only varied by the undulations which this immense prairie has retained from the far distant time when it formed part of the bottom of the primeval ocean. Such is nature's own well-defined line of separation between the monosyllabic and polysyllabic languages.

But it is necessary to begin with an older stock than the Tartar. The Mongol and the Turk are much nearer to the Western type of language than are the far-off Japanese, nor apparently can the Indian Tamul compete successfully with the Japanese and the Corean for the prize of superior antiquity.

In looking at the Japanese alphabet, with its forty-seven syllables, generally terminating with a vowel, we remark at once several limitations. The letters *r* and *l* are not separated. The Japanese use *r*, and the Chinese *l*, and these letters are employed only to commence a syllable. In Mongol both are used at the commencement and close of syllables. The Dravidian languages have a very full development of *r* and *l*. As a child whose mother-tongue is English learns to distinguish the other letters first, and *r* and *l* last, so it is in the comparative chronology of languages. The distinction between *r* and *l* is a sign of late formation. Judged by this test, the Japanese and Chinese are older than their Western neighbours.

The word *mid*, "honey," has final *d* in old Chinese, and in the Sanscrit it is *madhu*. In Hebrew we find *mathak*, "was sweet," doubtless the same word, and here the final *k* is a Semitic addition. The Greeks had a wine called μέθυ, "mead." The Turks and Mongols use *l* final, and change the initial *m* to *b*, saying *bal*. The Japanese have *mits*, and the Tamul *madu*. The Greeks and Latins appear to have followed the Turanians in the use of the final *l*, as in *mel*, μέλι, "honey," μέλισσα, "bee." Here the Greek is more under Turanian influence than either the Sanscrit or Germanic branches of the Indo-European family. Also, the Tamul and Japanese both appear to be older than the Tartar subdivision of the Turanian family. Take another example. The Mongol *gol*, "river," is in Japanese *kawa*, in modern Chinese *ho*, and in old Chinese *ga*. The addition of *l* seems to have been made after the separation of the Tartar and Japanese races. The word for *crow*, κόραξ, in Latin *corvus*, is in Sanscrit *káka* or *karada*. The Mongol is *k'eriye*, and the Japanese *karasï*. The Chinese have *kwa*, in the modern compound *laukwa*, "crow," where *lau* means "old." The Chinese and Sanscrit forms indicate that *r* is an addition to the primeval root. The Hebrew form is עֹרֵב, where *ayin*, as very frequently happens, represents *k* or *g*, and the word may read *goreb*. The *r* medial connects the Hebrew, second Sanscrit, Mongol, and Japanese forms in one group. The last addition, *b* in Hebrew, *v* in Latin, *ks* in Greek, *h* in German (*Krähe*), *d* in Sanscrit, *ye* in Mongol, *sï* in Japanese, must, from its variety, have been made after the separation of the races. Thus, the Japanese, although to the east of China, are connected more closely with the Western than with the Chinese system. It may also be inferred that the Japanese brought *r* with them in their migration eastward, and the question then arises, whether the initial *r* of Western languages is older or younger than the Chinese *l*, to which it corresponds? The Old Chinese *lut*, "musical tubes in definite lengths, used for regulating weights and measures," agrees in idea with the Greek $\rho\nu\theta\mu\acute{o}\varsigma$; and the Latin *ritus* of the same group corresponds to the Chinese *li* or *lit*, "ceremony." As *l* is easier for young children to utter than *r* (mothers tell me that they can say *l* a year and a half sooner than *r*), the palm of priority in the history of language should be accorded to *l* in this case; and thus the bulk of Western roots commencing with an initial *r* may with probability be supposed to have taken it in exchange for a more ancient *l*.

Another peculiarity in the Japanese syllabary is, that the aspirates are wanting. If words cross the sea to Japan, whether Chinese or Mongol, the aspirated letters, *k'*, *t'*, *p'*, become simple surds, namely, *k*, *t*, and *h*, or *f*. Insulation seems to be the cause of this change.

The absence of *sh*, *ch*, *zh*, and *j* from the syllabary, gives it a very defective appearance, but this is one of the characteristics of some of the most important Turanian languages, and helps to establish the near kinship existing between them and the Japanese. Perhaps it should rather be said that these letters are used to a small extent. In Hepburn's very valuable Japanese Dictionary the syllables *si*, *tsi*, *dzi*, are written *shi*, *chi*, *ji;* but this mode of writing, though doubtless convenient in some respects, is probably not so accurately descriptive of the real sound as the Dutch spelling. In explanation of the want of *sh* and its cognate letters, it may be mentioned that in the Mongol and Tamul languages they are not found. The Mongol has indeed occasionally an *sh*, but it is only, like the same letter in Japanese, a modification of *si*. So the Mongol *ch'* is in fact a modified *ts'*, and *j* is a disguised *d*, as will be shown.

The surds and sonants are by the Japanese considered as so closely allied, that a short double stroke on the right hand is used to change *k*, *t*, and *s'*, into *g*, *d*, and *z*. The letters *f*, *b*, *p*, are considered as one sound under three modifications. The double stroke denotes *b*, and a small circle *p*. Thus *kami*, " god," "spirit," becomes *gami*, in the combination *ŏnna gami*, "a goddess." Here it is on account of a word preceding it that *k* becomes *g*. That *k* and *g* were originally one letter seems likely also because the sounds of the Chinese language are by the Japanese written with extreme irregularity. Thus *k* and *g* and other pairs of cognate letters, carefully kept separate in Chinese dictionaries, are in the Japanese transcription much intermixed. The Chinese *sin*, "heart," is spelt *sin* or *zin*; and *zhin*, "spirit," "divinity," "the genii," "marvellous," is in Japanese spelt *sin* or *zin*, as in *zin riki*, "marvellous strength" (in the native language, "kami no chikara"); while Japan is called *sin koku*, "kingdom of the genii" (in the native language, "kami no kuni").

This tendency to an interchange of surds and sonants is probably due to the recent appearance of either the surds or the sonants. In the syllabary, it is the surd series that holds the place of honour, and it is therefore likely to be the older. When the Japanese, nearly 2,000 years ago, invented their alphabet, or rather borrowed it from China, they made no provision for *g*, *d*, *b*, or *z*. This was a later addition, dating from the time when Corean, Chinese, and Hindoo Buddhists propagated their religion in Japan. As an auxiliary proof, it may be mentioned that the Mongol *egude*, "door," appears in Japanese as *kado*; *yek'e*, "great," as *ikai*; *maihan*, "a tent," as *makuya*, though this word may be directly derived from the Chinese (*mu,* in the old form) *mok,* "a tent," in Japanese *maku,* a "curtain."¹ Why should *k* always occur? It is very likely that there was at that time no *g,* as there was no aspirated *k.*

But it is necessary to carry this inquiry further. The Mongols have *g, d, b,* and the aspirates, but no hard surd series. I suppose, therefore, that this was also the primitive condition of the Japanese phonal system. As the two races are alike in grammatical structure, and have many identical words, they may long ago have had the same sort of alphabet. The *g* may have become *k* after the progenitors of the Japanese passed to their island home, and subsequently *g* may have been again developed as a sub-division under *k,* or *vice versâ.*

The softness and simplicity of the Japanese syllabary, admitting no final consonant but *n,* and terminating all its forty-seven syllables by the five vowels *a, i, e, o, u,* seem due to the mild and damp climate induced by its insular situation. Its syllables are predominantly Polynesian in form, but certainly not because of near connexion in race. The Polynesian islanders place their verbs before the objects on which their action is exerted, and their adjectives prefer to follow the nouns

---

¹ Compare also Japanese *katai, kataku,* "hard," Mongol *k'at'ago,* and in the eastern dialect, *hat'o.*

they qualify.[1] In Japanese the verb follows its accusative, and the adjective precedes its noun. It may be concluded then that, as Hoffmann pointed out in his notes to Donker Curtius' Japanese Grammar,[2] the family connexion of the Japanese language is with Manchu and Mongol. This being admitted, that difference in the syllabaries which consists in separating final consonants from the first syllable, and causing them to form new syllables, should be attributed to the relaxing effect of sea air on the vocal organs. The Mongols can say *gos, gol, gang, gar, yab, ed, beg*. The Japanese will make dissyllables of all these, thus increasing the influence of the vowels at the expense of the consonants. The Chinese *dok*, "poison," becomes for instance *doku*.

In the present state of the Japanese syllabary, *ng* has taken the place of *n* final, but this has not affected the orthography. *N* is still written. The sibilants *s*, *ts*, and *dz*, also sometimes drop their vowel, and in actual pronunciation take their place as final letters.[3]

The language of the Japanese had already become

[1] Notes by T. Gulich, M.D., on the language of Ponape, one of the Caroline Islands.

[2] Professor Max Müller, writing in 1861, has invested Prof. Boller, of Vienna, with the honour of discovering that the Japanese language ought to be called Turanian. But the resemblance had several years before (1857) been perceived by the penetrating sagacity of the Dutch Professor, to whom we owe so many ingenious remarks on the Japanese language.

[3] Hepburn notices some other final consonants, as *m* and *p* in certain positions.

polysyllabic when transferred from Corea to their islands, for a few Mongol words of three syllables occur in the vocabulary, *e.g. kataku,* "hard," Mongol *k'at'ago.* The root is the same with that of our word *hard,* and the German *hart.* In Sanscrit we meet with *kat'ara,* "hard," *kát'ina, kát'inya,* "hardness," *kaṭ'a,* "rock," Mongol *k'ada,* "rock."

The first two syllables of a native Japanese word usually represent the monosyllabic root. Thus *kit,* in Chinese "to harden," "coagulate," "tie a knot," *kin,* "hard," "firm," occur in Japanese with long suffixes. *Katamari* is "to become hardened," *katame,* "harden," and as above adduced *kataku, katai,* "hard." So also the root *zhut,* in Chinese, *sheu,* "to give," "to receive," formerly distinguished by tone, the one taking the rising (*shang*), and the other the falling (*k'ü*) inflexion, but now amalgamated in the falling tone class, is found in the Japanese vocabulary, with the forms, *sadzukaru,* "to receive," and *sadzukeru,* "to bestow," or *sadzkatta* and *sadzketa.* The Chinese have *chï,* "to stop," in Japanese *todomari,* "to be stopped," *todokori,* "to impede," "stop," *todome,* "to stop," as in *uma wo todomeru,* "stop a horse," *todomerare,* "to be stopped." The Chinese has lost a final *t,* which appears in *dat,* "to stand," "to tread upon," "rest the foot." The Chinese initial *ch* in all cases comes from *t* or *d.* Hence the root assumes the form *dot,* "to stop," and *dat,* "to stand." This is really the root of our "stand," the

Latin *sto*, the Sanscrit *st'ala*, "stand," *st'ána*, "a place." The Tamul has *taṇḍu*, "a stand," the Japanese also say *tatsi* and *tatta*, "to stand." The initial *s* was prefixed by the forefathers of the Indo-Europeans before the separation of their western and eastern branches, for they all have it. The primeval root was probably *dad* and *dan*. It may have originated from the noise of the foot striking the ground. Families of words closely allied are not wanting. Among them may be mentioned the Chinese *ti* or *dad*, "earth." Sanscrit *dhárá*, Latin *terra*, Cochin-Chinese *dat*. The earth on which we stand receives its name from the verb "stand," and is a verbal noun, just as "inkstand," and "the grand stand" at a race course, receive their names for a similar reason.

We are now in a position to compare the Japanese roots with Chinese, Semitic, and Himalaic roots, and with those of the cognate Turanian languages. In doing so the Chinese initial *h* must be read *k* or *g*, *ch* must be read *t* or *d*, and *f* must be read *p* or *b*. Thus *ho*, "fire," is *gal* in Mongol and *calor* in Latin, where the inserted *l* shows that a Turanian influence has been at work in the formation of the Indo-European polysyllable. The Greek καίω, "burn," and German *heiss*, English *hot*, are connected, as also the Sanscrit *kárshanava*, "hot," and the root *kásh*, "shine." The Chinese word *ho*, "fire," was in the time of the creation of the syllabic spelling, A.D. 500, pronounced *ha*. More anciently it was *ka*, and more anciently still *ga*, which is as far as the analogies of the connected languages will carry us. The Japanese have *koge*, "burn," "scorch," in Chinese *k'au*, "scorch." Our word *scorch*, if the prefix *s* be removed and the *ch* changed for its ancient equivalent, *k*, appears to be the same word. The letter *s*, when prefixed to a consonant, never belongs to the root.

The Japanese say for "fire" *hi*. This must for etymological use be changed to *bi*, or *pi*, as in the case of all words beginning in Japanese with *h* or *f*. It may then be compared with the verb *aburi*, "roast," Tamul *pori*, with the Chinese *bun*, "burn," the Greek πῦρ, Latin *comburo*, and the English *burn* and *fire*.

For "warm" the Japanese word is *atatakai*, and for "hot" *atszku*. The root is *at*, for the sibilant form of *t* in the latter example is accidental. We may compare it with the Persian *atesh* and the Hebrew אש *ésh*. The etymological equivalent of the Hebrew *sh* is *t*, as in *shor*, "bull," *taurus*; *sham*, "there," Chaldee *tam*. The Persian final *sh* is thus seen to be a reduplication of the final *t*. Compare the Greek αἴθω and Latin *æstus*, which Gesenius believed to be connected. This author proceeds to say that אור *ur*, "light," belongs to the same family relationship. This is an extremely interesting identification, because the letter *r* occupies a frequent place among the

Semitic initials. For convenience of comparison with Chinese roots it should have the value *d*. For example, רֹאשׁ *rosh*, "head," may be advantageously compared with the Chinese *t'eu*, "head," old form *dut*. The equivalent of *sh* being also *t*, the resemblance is complete.

A fourth Japanese root for "fire" is *yake*, "to be on fire," "bake." The Chinese say *yik*, "flame," "fire," "light." The Sanscrit *agni*, "fire," and Latin *ignis*, are the same word.

An example of a word common to the three branches of the Turanian family will help to show the connexion in which they stand to each other. *Mune* is in Japanese "the breast," and it is found compounded with many words; for example, *muna gawara*, "roof tiles," where the ridge of the roof is called *mune* from its resemblance to the chest. The Mongol has *emun*, "before," "front," "south," and the Chinese *mien*, "face." The Tamul people say *mun* for "before," "front." In Japanese *omote* is "before," "front," "the face," "outside." In Cochin-China the face is *mat*. A door is the front of a house, and in Chinese "door" is *men*, and with this seems to be connected the German *Mund* and the English *mouth*. The interchange of *n* and *t* is easily accounted for; they being allied letters. The final consonant *k* is found in the root of a family of words closely related to this one. The Japanese *mukai*, "to face," "stand with the face towards," *muki*, "frontage," "exposure," is like the Tamul *mukam*, "mouth," "face," and the Sanscrit *mukha*, "mouth," "face," "commencement," "first."

In the preceding examples occur several prefixed vowels. They are very common in Mongol and Japanese. Thus "horse," which is *ma* in Chinese, is *mori* in Mongol, and *uma* in Japanese. The Manchus say *morin*. The prefixed vowel agrees in nature with the vowel of the root, as in *omote*, "before," *ishi*, "stone," Chinese *zhak*. If a vowel be appended to the final consonant of the root, when already thus augmented, our primeval monosyllable is already extended to a trissyllable, and this without the addition of new words to make compounds. Thus "honé," to be read "boné," the German *Bein*, and English *bone*. We have the same suffixed *e* in *kake*, "to hang up," "hook on," in Chinese *kwa* or *kak*, and in English hook.

The next step in additions to the root we may suppose to have been the appending of consonants. Thus from *ma*, "grind," in modern Chinese *mo*, in Latin *mola*, in English *mill*, is derived the Japanese *maru*, "circle." From *kak*, "black," came *k'ara* in Mongol, and *kuroi* in Japanese, the final *k* being lost in both cases. The *r* and *l* do not mean anything. They are not abbreviated words. They are merely phonetic additions. The Mongols are content to add an *r* or *l* to their roots, without supplementing it by a vowel, as *gar*, "hand," *i.e.*, the "holder." The

Japanese prefer to add a vowel. Hence arose several syllabic suffixes in ordinary use for forming derivatives, and they gradually, as they grew in length, assumed distinctive characteristics as nominal, qualitative, or verbal terminations. Thus *e* in *hate*, "an end," "to end," from a root *bat*, "to end," in Chinese, our word *butt*, and the French *bout*, does not distinguish between parts of speech. So *eshi* and *ashi* in *hateshi*, "the end," and *hatashi*, "to end," are appended to the same root without any mark of difference between verb and noun. But in Mongol the suffix *si* or *t'si* marks nouns distinctly. The following derivatives occur to the roots *maru*, "circle," and *kuroi*, "black":—

marui, "circular."   *kurai*, "dark."
marume, "make round."   *kurami*, "grow dark."
marushi, "round."   *kure*, "darken."
maruku, "round."   *kuroku*, "black."
marusa, "roundness."   *kurasa*, "degree of darkness."
maroi, "round."   *kuroshi*, "black."
mari, "a ball."   *kurosa*, "blackness."

Of the suffixes here used only *me, mi*, have a decided verbal sense, and they are probably connected with the verb suffix *meri, meru, mere*, which is translated "becoming."

Of the substantive suffixes, *sa* is the only one that seems to be exclusively used of nouns.

The word *siro*, "white," takes the derivative forms *shiroi, shiroku, shiroshi*, "white," *shiromi*, "whiten," *shirosa*, "whiteness." The root is *sit* in Chinese, meaning "snow." In Mongol the *t* is lost and the suffix *gan* appended, the sibilant initial taking as a prefix *t* aspirated. The Manchu form is *shayan*. *Shiromi*, "to become white," is also used as a noun in the sense "white of an egg," and "whiteness," as in *shiromiga aru*, "it has whiteness," where *ga* marks the objective case, and *aru* is the substantive verb used possessively.

Generally speaking, the final *mi* marks a verb; *oi, ui, ku, si,* mark an adjective; and *sa, ru,* a noun. But these distinctions are not strictly adhered to. Language is in the Japanese only approaching to accuracy of conception. It was in fact first in the Sanscrit that the parts of speech arrived at their full form, with accuracy of outline and suitable variety of expression. The Mongol conjugates the adverb as he does the verb, because language, in its ever-advancing development, has not yet reached the epoch of accurate grammatical distinctions. So it is in the Japanese derivatives. The terminations are wanting in sharpness of definition. This was for the first time attained in the Indo-European system, and even there the separate independence of the parts of speech is far from being complete.

The next step in the progress of development is the formation of compounds. *Ki*, "a tree," becomes *kiburi*, "shape of a tree," from *furi* or *buri*, "shape," "manner."

Species precedes genus. This law of position is invariable. *Kado bi*, "door-fire," is the name of the fire in front of a dead person's house to light his way to the next world. In Mongol compounds are not used without the intervention of the possessive suffix. In Tamul, however, they abound, as also in the Himalaic and Chinese languages. In Mongol, inflexions have more power, and hence the genitive or accusative mark cannot be omitted, except where the case is one of simple apposition. Take the following example: English *cowherd, cowkeeper*, Japanese *usikai*. Here *kai* is "keeper," and as a verb means "to keep." Mongol *uk'erc'hi*, from *ukher*, "cow," with the suffix *c'hi*, which is equivalent to our *er* in *shipper, mouser, chandler*. They also say *uk'eri sahikc'hi*, "cowkeeper," where the verb *sahihu*, "to keep," governs the accusative in *i*, and takes itself the suffix of agency, giving it the form of a present participle. The Tamul has *kôpâlar*, "cowherds," and the Sanscrit *gopa*, where *pa* means "ruler," and may be compared with the Semitic *Baal*, "lord." The Greek βούτης and Latin *bubulcus* are formed like the Mongol from words meaning "cow," with a suffix of agency. In *pecoris custos* the Latin order is strictly Turanian. The Mongol would say *uk'erun ejen*, literally "cow's lord." Take the common Latin word for "cow," *wakka* (i.e., *vacca*), and the resemblance is still more striking. The etymological value of the Latin *v* is always *w* or *u*, as in *volo*, "to will." And it may also be asked, What is the Greek suffix of agency της, as in ἱππότης, but the Turanian *ch'i*, of which the etymological value is *si*? The letters *s* and *t* are convertible in Greek and Latin. Apposition of substantives preceded in the Turanian languages the formation of the suffix of agency. The formation of compounds by apposition, as in Japanese, is an older principle than that by which in Mongol a derivative of agency is formed by a syllabic suffix. It has also been destined to achieve a longer lifetime. The derivative suffixes of agency in European languages have not the prevalence now that they had 2,000 years ago, and especially in the Germanic stock they show signs of approach to extinction. *Cavalier* will become in English an obsolete word before *horseman*. The Manchus and Turks agree with the Mongols in the use of *c'hi* as the suffix of agency, but the Turks have also the form *dji*. Its origin may be in *sak*, "to make," in Chinese *tsok* and *tso*, as in *mutso*, "carpenter," from *mu*, "wood."

In proceeding to the case particles, it may be observed that they originated in the great Tibetan and Turanian inversion, found also in the Sanscrit, by which the verb and the demonstrative pronouns were transferred from their primeval position, before the noun, to the end of the sentence. Prepositions are verbs. The case suffixes of the Turanian and Indo-European languages are modified prepositions, and originally verbs or pronouns. The post-position of the transitive verb took place first, and subsequently the verb roots of the case suffixes became changed and shortened in form, and now appear to the investigator as suffixes, more or less closely combined with the substantives to which they belong.

The Japanese genitive *no*—as in *ki no ha*, "leaf of a tree," where *ha*, i.e., *ba*, "leaf," suggests a connexion with the Siamese *bai*, "leaf," and with *folium* and *blatt* —is in Manchu *ni*, and in Mongol sometimes *nu, nai*.

We have beside this possessive, four others in China and its neighbour countries. They are, *ti* in Chinese, *gi* or *go* in Tibetan and the old middle dialect of China, *i, e,* or *u* in Mongol and the South Fukien dialect, and *in* or *un* in Mongol and Turkish. The Eastern Himalaic languages have adopted the Semitic inversion, and place the nominative before the genitive, as in Cochin-Chinese *luai dau*, "edge of knife," where *dau* is "knife."

Our five possessive suffixes are all, let it be observed, in form demonstrative pronouns. *No* is the Chinese *na*, "that." *Ti* is *di*, "this." *Gi* is *gi*, "he." *E, i,* or *u*, is *i*, "he." *In* and *un* are other forms of the third personal pronoun. Here we may see, therefore, a confirmation of Bopp's view, that the Sanscrit genitive suffix *sya* is an old demonstrative pronoun and is equivalent to *tyam* and *tyat*, "that." He adds[1]

[1] Vergleichende Grammatik, von Bopp. § 194.

that, "in *sya* and *tya* are contained the two stems *sa* and *ta*, 'he,' with the relative stem *ya*, 'which.'" The Chinese *ti*, usually read *chï*, is in the ancient books used not only as a possessive particle, but in the sense of *it* or *that* after verbs, and also as a verb with the meaning of *go to*.

The Greek and Latin genitives in *i* and *u* we may perhaps derive from the Mongol possessive *u*, affixed as a genitive ending to nouns closing with *n*. But I do not lay stress on this resemblance, for it is possible that *u* is here in fact *nu*, the Japanese genitive. The modern last Mongol dialect allows the possessive *ne* to be used with more nouns than the grammar of the book language would admit.

The case of direction "towards" is in Japanese expressed by the suffix *he* or *be* and *ye*. The Tibetan has *la*, the Mongol *de* and *dor*, the Turkish *ga* and *yeh*, the Tamul *ku*. The Chinese has the verbs *to*, *ti*, or *tau*, the same as our "to," and *gip* or *ki*, "arrive at." In Greek πέδονδε, "to the ground," agrees in form with the Mongol. Examples abound in Homer, as δόμονδε, "to the house." The Greeks afterwards preferred to prefix εἰς, "to," with an accusative. That is, as it appears to me, they were under Turanian influence while they used the suffix δε in the sense, "to a place," and emancipated themselves from it in this instance when they changed the suffix for the preposition. This took place soon after the time of

Homer. In confirmation, it may be remarked that there is an aspirated form of the Mongol, namely, *t'or*, which corresponds to the Greek θι, an old dative.

Other Chinese verbs, which may be referred to in explanation of some of the forms now given, are *wang*, "go towards," *hiang*, "towards." *W* and *y* are interchangeable initials, and the final *ng* is frequently dropped, as in the Chinese *ta*, "beat," anciently *tang*. The ancient equivalent of initial *h* is *k*. Hence these two verbs become *ye* and *ka*.

The Japanese *be*, "to," suggests a connexion with the Greek πρὸς, "to," and παρὰ, "beside," "towards," etc. The word *proximus*, "nearest," is of the same family, and the Chinese *bing*, "unite," *bang*, "beside," *bang*, "to strike against," are probably related. Hoffmann says *be* is the side or direction of a thing. The verbs *heru* and *furu*, mean "to pass from one place to another." This is undoubtedly the same word. The Chinese words for "unite," "union," "side," "neighbourhood," "collision," all tend to meet in an ultimate root *bang*, "strike against," derived probably from the noise of collision, and preserved in the familiar English expression, "bang the door." In the Japanese and Mongol languages, the final *ng* of Chinese roots is usually lost. Thus in *kwang*, "light" (at an older period *keng*), the *ng* is dropped, and the word reappears in Japanese as *karui* and *akari*, and in Mongol as *gerel*. It was then by the Turanians that the *ng* was dropped and an *r* substituted. In this state the root was introduced into the Indo-European vocabulary, as in the German *hell*, "clear," and the Latin *gloria* and *clarus*, where *l* is inserted.

Motion "from" or "by" a place or route, is expressed in Japanese by *kara* and *yori*. With the Mongols *ec'he* is the word. But this is etymologically *ese*. They also have *yiar* as in *eguden yer*, "by the gate." The corresponding case suffix in Turkish is *den* or *dan*, and in Manchu *deri*. The Chinese has the verbs *yeu*, "take origin from," "let a man do as he thinks best," and *dzung*, "to follow," "obey." As prepositions these words appear with the sense "from." *Yeu* (Japanese *yori*, Mongol *yer*) has lost a final *k*, for the character 由 *yeu*, is frequently used as a phonetic in words which to the present day retain final *k*, in Southern Chinese dialects, as *dik*, "flute." The old value then is *ok*, the *ex* of Greek and Latin. The other word, *dzung*, early lost *ng*, and appears commonly in Chinese in the form *dzi*, the modern 自 *tsï*. All the words having *ts* as their initial had anciently *s* or *z*. The old form of this verb is therefore *zung* or *zu*. The Mongol, having no *z*, adopted it in the form of *se*, and prefixed to it the vowel *e*.

Another old Chinese verb, taking the sense of *from* as a preposition, is *tang*, "to strike," in modern pronunciation *ta*. This may be the source from which the Manchu and Turkish forms are derived. The Turkish *den, dan,* is found in the Greek θεν, the old epic suffix for " from," as in οὐρανόθεν, " from heaven."

The Japanese *kara,* "from," is compared by Hoffmann to the High German *her,* "from that place to this." It may be derived from the Chinese verb *k'ai* or *k'i,* "to open," "to begin," and hence in colloquial usage "to start from." The Japanese use *ake, akeru,* for "to open," and *aki, aku,* for "to be open," as in *to wo ake,* "open the door," where *to,* "door," is the same word, perhaps, as the Manchu *duk'a,* "city gate," and the Greek θυρος. The vowel *a* is a prefix, not radical.

The locative particles used by the Japanese are *ni, te, de,* and *nite.* The Turkish has *der,* the Mongol *de* and *dor,* the Manchu *de,* the Tamul *il* and *idattil.* The Chinese have the prepositions *yü,* "at," "in," *dzai* or *zai,* "to be in " or " at." As local suffixes they use *li* or *lai, nei* or *nip,* "within," *chung* or *tung,* "in the midst of," or "within." Of these, *nei* is from *nip,* "to enter," in Modern Chinese *ju*; and *chung* is either "the middle," or "to strike the middle." The *p* and *ng* being dropped, most of the locative forms now given may be derived from these two locative auxiliaries.

The Greek epic dative in θι may, from its correspondence in form and sense with the Japanese and Mongol locative, be regarded as of Turanian origin. Thus, οἴκοθι, "at home," ἄλλοθι, "elsewhere," may be compared with the Mongol *ger t'or* or *ger t'e*, "in the house," where the usual *de* or *dor* becomes *t'e* or *t'or*, on account of *r* preceding; and *ober oron dor*, or more colloquially, *ore oron de*, "at another place." To illustrate the Greek dative suffix θι, Bopp also cites ἔνθα, ἐνταῦθα, "here," as compared with the ablatives ἔνθεν, "hence," ἐμέθεν, "from the place where I am," forms which resemble the Turkish ablative, as above stated. He also refers[1] to the Sanscrit suffix *dhas* in *adhas*, "under," as connected with the Greek forms, and derives all of them from the demonstrative stem in *t*. I ask, will it not be more satisfactory to trace the forms in δε and θι through the Mongol, as a modern type of the old Turanian language, to the Chinese 到 *tau*, "to," used as a dative suffix, and the other word already mentioned, *tung*, "in the midst of," used as a locative? The English *to* and the German *zu* have the dative force, as well as that of motion "towards" and "arriving at"; and the extension of the meaning of the word *tau*, to embrace a dative force, is no more than what we should expect when it became a postposition and was employed in case formation.

This word *tau*, "to," has in Chinese and English the surd form. In Sanscrit and Mongol it appears with the sonant *d*, as also in the Latin *ad*, where *a* is perhaps a prefix for sound's sake. In Mongol and Greek it has the aspirated form, and in German it

[1] Bopp. Zweite Ausgabe, § 223.

occurs as a sibilant, through the fondness of that language for the initial *ts*.

The Turkish *dah*, "in," "at," "within the limit of space or possession of,"[1] with *n* before it in *kandah*, "where," *bundah*, "here," much resembles the Japanese locatives *te* and *nite*. May not this be pointed to as the possible origin of the Sanscrit ablative in *d*? The Turks say *buradah*, "here," where the *r* is a mere phonal extension of *bu*, "this." The final *h*, now silent, may possibly represent an old *k* or *g*, which would render the transition easy from the Chinese *tang*, "from." The Sanscrit *kutas*, "whence," is not far from the Turkish *kandan*, "whence," especially when compared, as by Bopp, with the Greek πόθεν, where *n* final replaces *s*.

The Turkish *kani*, "where," contains the Japanese *ni* as its locative suffix. Compare it with the Sanscrit *kadâ*, "where." The other Japanese locative is here used, *d* being the representative of the Mongol *d* in *dor*, *da*, and the Japanese *t* in *te*. Who doubts that the Japanese proceeded from the same part of the world from which the Hindoos proceeded? If there be any one, the occurrence of resemblances such as this should cause him to pause. The Turkish for "when" is *kachan*, and the Mongol *heje*; but the Mongol *j* represents *d*, and *h* is *k'*, so that the Sanscrit and Mongol forms agree, except in the circumstance

[1] Redhouse's English and Turkish Dictionary, p. 700.

that the Mongol *k* is aspirated. Can we doubt that the period during which the Indo-Europeans lived beside the Turanians in Bactria, Persia, and Armenia, was fruitful in linguistic results? Take another form. The Sanscrit *kati*, "how many," is in Mongol *hedui*, *k'edui*, or, in the modern colloquial, simply *hedi*. The Latin is *quot*. The Chinese original of these words, *ki*, "how many," is unaspirated, and has probably lost a final *t*.

The instrumental case in Japanese is formed by the suffixes *ni*, *nite*, *de*, *te*, *motte*, the last of which is derived from the verb *motsi*, "to employ." The Mongol has *ber*, *yar*, *loga*. In the Dravidian languages are found *ál* (Tamil), *án* (Sen-Tamil), *im* (Kannaḍa),[1] in newer forms *inda*. The Chinese *na*, "to take," *tan* or *twan*, "to carry," *pa*, "to take in the hand" (in Mongol *barihu*, "to take in the hand"), and *i*, "take," 以, are the roots of these forms. The Japanese *ni* as a locative is derived from the Chinese *nei*, "within," and as an instrumental from *na*, originally *nap*. The Russians have the word *nosish*, "to carry." The second word is *tan*, "to take up" or "carry." We also find *tai*, to "carry," or "lead," old form *tak*, the English *take*. We also have *tam*, "carry on the shoulders," and *tang*, "to undertake." Since *se*, "the back," seems to be derived by dropping *n* final from

[1] Reise der Novara um die Erde. Linguistischer Theil, von Dr. Friedrich Müller. 1867.

senaka, "back," I suppose that the first of the four words is the root here sought for, and that the Japanese instrumental *de* and verb *tori,* "take," are the Chinese *tan.* The third Chinese instrumental verb is *pa,* Mongol *barihu,* "seize," Russian *brat,* "to seize." This originated the Mongol *ber,* when the verb was placed after its noun by the Turanian inversion. Here too we find a probable origin for the Sanscrit instrumental suffixes *bhyâm, bhih,* and the Latin *bus.* The Sanscrit suffix *nâ* I suppose to be the Chinese *na,* "carry." This seems to be a more natural way of accounting for it than to refer it to the pronominal root *a,* as Bopp does, a supposition which requires the insertion of *n* for euphony. The last Chinese verb to be considered is *i,* "take," "regard as," "use." It was much used in the style of the Chinese classics. Now it has given way to *pa, tsiang, na,* and *tan.* It affords a probable origin to the Mongol instrumental *yer* or *yar,* and the Sanscrit suffixes *ya, a,* used in an instrumental sense. The Tungus suffix *dji* is probably the same with the Japanese *de,* by change of *d* to *j.* The Zend instrumental is *a,* agreeing with the prevailing Sanscrit form.

The Lithuanian instrumental suffix *mi* should be compared with the German *mit* and the Greek μέτα. The Japanese instrumental *motta* and *motsu* are no other than this. *Motsi,* is "to hold," *motsiyi ru,* is "to use," "employ." Bopp's derivation from the Sanscrit *bis* seems forced, but he had so firm a conviction that the Indo-European case suffixes are all to be derived from pronominal roots, that he neglected nearer and more probable analogies. It is, however, a remarkable fact that the Chinese instrumental verbs bear a close resemblance to the primeval pronouns. The old instrumental *i* is like the old pronoun *i*, "he," and the modern *na*, "take," is like the modern pronoun *na*, "that," and in sound they are distinguished only by tones.

The Japanese accusative suffix *wo* is like the Turkish *yi* and Mongol *i*, and is probably derived from the old pronoun *i* for the third person. The Chinese *i* usually comes from an older *ui* or *wei*, and the transition from *wei* to *wo* is not great. In Manchu the accusative *ba* reminds us of the Chinese *pa*, which is used to introduce the accusative, when in the colloquial language the speaker desires to place it before the verb which ordinarily governs it, as in *pa t'a sha liau*, "he killed him," literally, "take him kill finished." Another accusative ending in Mongol is *gi*. This may be the Chinese third personal pronoun *gi*. Thus Bopp's view that the Indo-European accusative is of pronominal origin may receive confirmation from the formation of the Turanian accusative. The Tamil accusative in *ei*, the Telugu in *ni*, and the Tibetan in *gi*, appear to be all constructed in a similar manner.

The Japanese case suffix *to* has the sense "for the sake of," and "in conjunction with." In the former sense it agrees with the Mongol *to'la*, and with the Chinese *t'i*, "instead of." In the latter sense it agrees with the Mongol *t'ai* and *t'o*, as in *hamt'o*, "together," and the Chinese *dung*, "together." The Chinese have also *dai* and *wei*, meaning "for the sake of," and "on account of." I suppose therefore the Japanese *to* to be a mixture of two words, which are in Chinese *t'i* or *dai*, "for," "instead of," and *dung*, "with."

The Japanese nominative *ba* is used like the Mongol *inu*, and as the nominative termination in Greek, Latin, and Sanscrit, was probably first used. Without doubt it is a metamorphosed third personal pronoun. In the Turanian languages this suffix is not part of the word, but is a pronominal repetition of the nominative. Such too was the origin of the termination *s* in the Greek οἶκος, in Chinese *ok*, "house," in the demonstrative ὅς in Greek, and *is* in Latin, in Chinese *gi* and *i*. But the final has in these languages been taken into the word, and forms a part of it. The Turanian is the older, and the Indo-European the newer mode of doing the same thing. Let it not be said that the Turanian languages as now known are altogether too modern for the philologist to regard them as constituting a stepping-stone between the Indo-European system, and the venerable mother from whom all languages, eastern and western, have sprung. The Japanese writing, being 2,000 years old, secures to that language a claim to a very respectable antiquity, and when the Dravidian languages are taken into account, that antiquity is greatly increased. As the three races, Tartar, Dravidian, and Mongol, have not been neighbours since 4,000 years ago, the approximate time of the Arian invasion of India, all common features existing in the three branches must have belonged to the old Turanian stock from which all of them proceeded. For example, the postposition of the verb, and the formation of cases had then already taken place. Among the case particles which resemble each other most closely are those which mark the accusative and conjunctive relations, viz., *ei* in Tamil and Mongol, and *wo* in Japanese for the accusative, and *ôḍu* in Tamil, *to* in Japanese, and *t'ei* or *loga* in Mongol for the conjunctive, or, as De Castren calls it, the comitative case. For example, in Tamil *pilḷeiyôḍu wandân*, "he came with the child."[1] It also appears from this instance, that at that early time the final *ng* of the Chinese word *dung*, "together," was already thrown off in cognate languages, a phenomenon which occurs in the history of many Chinese words, such as *wu*, "not," formerly *mo*, and still earlier *mong*, as known from the fact that the character 口 *mong*, was frequently used for it in the ancient Chinese books.

[1] Pope's Tamil Handbook.

CHAPTER IX.

SECOND DIVISION OF THE TURANIAN SYSTEM. — THE DRAVIDIAN LANGUAGES.—PROOF THAT THIS FAMILY IS TRULY TURANIAN.— COMMON WORDS. — COMMON LAWS OF SOUND. — SURDS AND SONANTS. — DEFICIENCY IN SIBILANTS. — ABUNDANCE OF LIQUIDS. —SYLLABLES USUALLY OPEN.—DERIVATION.—COMPARATIVE LIST OF WORDS. — THE VERB. — THE PASSIVE NEGATION. — TENSE FORMATION.—DRAVIDIAN SYNTAX.

PROFESSOR FRIEDRICH MÜLLER has expressed doubts respecting the Turanian character of the Dravidian languages. The proofs of this rest on a multitude of common roots, resemblances in alphabet and syllabary, identity of syntactical construction, and the similarity observable in their system of suffixes.

First, the roots are the same. Thus, we find resemblances like the following:

COMMON TURANIAN ROOTS.

TAMIL.	MONGOL.	JAPANESE.	CHINESE.	INDO-EUROPEAN.
kâl, *foot*	k'ul		kak	to kick.
talei, *head*	tologai	atama	du, dud	
silei, *stone*	c'hilagon	isi	zhag	saxum.
karam, *hand*	gar			SANS. kara.
nây, *dog*	nohai	inu		
marei, *rain*	boron	ame	mo, *mist*	PERS. baran.
kiragam, *house*	ger		ke	casa.
tammulu, { *younger brother* }	degu	ototo	de	'ἀδελφός.
irâ, *night*		yoru	ya	
adigam, *much*		dake		

TURANIAN ORIGIN OF THE DRAVIDIAN FAMILY. 169

TAMIL.	MONGOL.	JAPANESE.	CHINESE.	INDO-EUROPEAN.
wegu, *much*	yek'e	okini		
teyilam, *oil*	t'ossa			
ter, *chariot*	t'ereg		t'e	dray, drag.
paṭṭini, *hunger*		hidaru		
maram, *wood*	modo		mok	
agam, *sin*	Ma ek'e	aku	ak	wicked.
kâr, *blackness*	k'ara	kuroi	kek	caligo.
aṇḍam, *egg*	undug			ὠόν.

There is a law in all true Turanian languages, according to which the vowel of the root repeats itself in the prefixes and suffixes. If it does not repeat itself exactly, it takes the form of an allied vowel. In Mongol *a* and *o* are allied; *e* and *u* are also allied. The vowel *i* is doubtful. Hence the syllabic alphabets of Turanian languages. The vowels are regarded as inherent in the consonants. The consonants are essential, and the vowels are secondary. The vowels only attained their full and individual importance in the Indo-European languages.

The sounds of the Tamil and other languages of the Dravidian family are such as to confirm the fact of their Turanian origin. There is noticeable a deficiency in the development of the letters *sh*, *ch*, and the surd series generally. Thus *k*, *t*, *p*, become *g*, *d*, *b*, when they occur in the middle of a word. Analogy, Japanese, and Mongol, shows that the original sounds were *g*, *d*, *b*, which become surd at the beginning of words or when doubled. In the Japanese language, words in *h* or *f*, for instance, take *b* for *h* or *f*, when they follow another word. *Hito*, "man," becomes *bito* in certain cases. Thus *hito bito* means "men." Hoffmann has shown how the Japanese *h* of this century was, last century and previously, *f*, and that it really belonged anciently to the labial series. But it is necessary to go further than this, and to reduce the *h* in all cases to *b*, as its ancient form, as *hatashi*, "to complete," Chinese *ba*, *bad*, Mongol *barahu*. So in the plural *kuni guni*, "kingdoms," corresponding to the Manchu *gurun*, "kingdom," it is better to avoid being misled by the Japanese orthography, which make *g* a modification of *k*, and to regard *k* as being rather a modern modification of *g*. Here I use the word *modern* with a wide acceptation. The history of the Japanese alphabet shows that *k* and *g* have been divided in Japan for 1,500 years. The fact is that the Turanian ear formerly recognized no such distinction. Nor does the Mongol of the present day. When naming his little tent images to his foreign visitor, he will call this one *Kalin ejin* or *Galin ejin*, "lord of fire," that one *Shiggamuni Borhan* (that is, *Shakyamuni Buddha*), and another *Gesser Han* or *Kesser Han*, the hero who in Tartary takes the place of the seven champions of Christendom. It is nothing to him whether he attenuates his initials into *k*, *t*, and *p*, or thickens them into *g*, *d*, *b*. His language has not yet arrived at this stage. The Japanese have gone forward most successfully in the division of the surds from the sonants. The Tamil-speaking people are in a midway position. The Mongol has still to arrive at the consciousness of the distinction. But he makes use of aspirated surds as a substitute for the pure surds. He has a fully developed k' and t' in his alphabet. It may be concluded by analogy that the Tamil k, t, p, have come out of g, d, b, and that the true ancient sound is heard when it occurs in the middle and end of words, *e.g.*, *ug*, "to desire," Chinese *yug* or *yuk*, Sanscrit *vaç*, Greek εὔχομαι, English *wish*. Here the final g becomes k in modern Chinese, and *sh* in Sanscrit and English, while in Greek it prefers the aspirated form. The importance of the Tamil is shown by this example, for with the intermediate form *ug* as a guide, there can be no just ground of hesitation in identifying the Chinese root having the initial y with the Indo-European root having the initial v, or, which is the same thing, w.

The Tamil sibilants are very defective. When s is doubled or follows $\d$ or r, it is pronounced *ch* as in Charles. The analogy of the Mongol and Japanese languages shows that s is the true old sound. The Mongol has s and $t's$, the latter of which is called $c'h$, but its value in comparative philology is simple s, as in *c'hi*, "thou," Manchu *si*, Greek σύ. The Mongol has no true j, the j in use being a modern corruption of d, as *jirohe*, "heart," the same as the Persian *dil*.

So *jigahu*, to "teach," to "point to," is the same as the Latin *doceo, digitus,* the English "teach," and "betoken," the German *zeichnen,* etc., and the Chinese *chi* or *ti,* "to point," *chï* or *dik,* "straight." So the Tamil *tagu,* "to be just," and *tagudi,* "justice," have the same etymology. Nor has the Mongol an *sh* proper, the initial having this orthography being modified from *si*. The same occurs in Japanese, where *si* is pronounced like *shi,* and *tsi* like *chi*. Thus in Mongol *c'hagan,* "white," seems to be connected with *c'hasa,* "snow," but *c'hasa* is evidently connected with the Chinese *sit,* "snow," and snow is a substance which in all countries where the winter is cold, originates adjectives indicating whiteness. The Manchu *shanggien,* "white," is apparently formed from the Mongol by dropping the initial *t*. After the letter *sh* had been thus introduced many Chinese words were perhaps borrowed, such as *shu'min* and *shum,* "deep," Chinese *shim*. I suppose, therefore, that the Tamil *s,* though sometimes pronounced *ch,* is really the *s* of Tartary and Japan.

The three *r*'s, two *l*'s, and three *n*'s of Tamil reveal the existence of a principle that has been at work among all the Indian populations since the intrusion of the dominant Arian element. The Sanscrit language has among the vowels a long and short *r* and *l,* and an *r* and *l* at the bottom of the cerebral and dental *t* series, respectively. The sister language,

Zend, has one *r* and no *l*; and hence it may be concluded that this rich development of *r* and *l* took place in Sanscrit after the migration to India. It was, therefore, probably the effect of climate, for it characterizes the Dravidian languages as it does those of Sanscrit origin. Hot and moist climates induce luxury and softness of manners. The vowels and liquids then become extensively subdivided, while letters which in their enunciation require decision and physical energy suffer in proportion. The remarkable completeness of the Sanscrit alphabet, wanting only *f* among the consonants, and *eu* and *ü* among the vowels, was due to the Arian race having first been located in a temperate region and afterwards migrating to a hot and moist one.

That the Tamil and other Dravidian languages have, when compared with the Sanscrit, so poor an alphabet, is partly due to the fact, that the Turanian stock from which they sprang was itself poor. To this should be added, that deterioration had followed on their separation from it. A softening process deprived Dravidian speech of much of the pith and force which belonged to it at an earlier stage, when it was one with the Mongol and Japanese. Proof of this will now be given by adducing the deficiencies of the Tamil syllable.

The syllable admits in modern Chinese of a prefixed *t* before the initials *s* and *sh*. This liberty is also used in Mongol, and *t* becomes *ts* before *i* and *u* in Japanese. In Tamil, *s* becomes occasionally *ch*. In old Chinese the six final consonants by which a syllable could be closed were *g, d, b; ng, n,* and *m*. In Mongol the same rule prevails. The Japanese language restricts this law, and takes pleasure in changing the old monosyllable into a dissyllable. The Mongol went farther and added *s, l, r,* to the number of finals by which their syllables might be closed. The Tamil people are more like the Japanese than the Mongols in this respect, and give their syllables no consonantal letters with which to close them, except *n, m, l,* and *r*. The Telugu and Kannaḍa languages know no finals to their syllables but the vowels, and they thus assume in regard to this feature a completely Polynesian aspect.

The following examples of derivation in the Tamil language will at the same time show that the roots are found alike in the Chinese and in the European vocabulary. They have been chosen within the space of a very few pages in Dr. Winslow's Tamil Dictionary, and in a part where the identity of words is very easily detected, because the features of family resemblance have not been much defaced by the processes of secular corruption. In Chinese words three sounds are sometimes given, the first modern, the second that of the dictionaries A.D. 500, the third that of the era (according to tradition) of the formation of the phonetic

DERIVATION IN TAMIL. 175

characters, B.C. 2000. The Japanese *h* is replaced by its ancient equivalent *b*.

Paḍi, "step of a ladder," *padam*, "foot," "road," "metrical foot." Chinese *pu*, "step," *bo, bod*. Indo-European *pada, foot, pes, passus, pace*. The Tamil here uses as suffixes of derivation *i, am*.

Para, "spread," "be diffused," *paravu*, "lay open," "spread," *parambu*, "to spread," "become diffused," "multiply." Japanese *fure, bure*, "publish," "promulgate," *haru, baru*, "spread over," "extend," "display." Chinese *pei, bi, bid*, "coverlid," "to spread over," "extend to." Indo-European *bed, spread, pando, pateo, broad, breit*. Tamil derivative syllables *a, avu, ambu*.

Paḍar, "widen," "ramify," "extend," "pass," *padam*, "path," i.e., "that by which we pass" or "proceed," *padavi*, "road." Mongol *badarahu*, "to extend," *badaral*, "extension." Chinese *fa, bat*, "to expand," "go forth." Indo-European *forth, path*. Russian *razbrasivat, razbrosat*, to "dissipate," "extend." Tamil derivative syllables *ar, am, avi*.

Paru, "to be increased," *parambu*, "to multiply," *paṭṭu*, "fold." Betel nut in folds for guests. Hurdles in folds for folding cattle. Cloth either as spread or as folded. A "plait" or "doubling" of cloth. Japanese *hida, bida*, "fold," "plait," *futa, buta*, "two." Chinese *pei, bi, bit*, "double," "add as much again." Indo-European *both*, German *beide, fold, plait, to boot*, *i.e.*, "add," *freebooter, i.e.,* "one who wanders freely." (Here the sense of spreading is approached.)

Pari, "to part," "separate," *piri,* "to part from," "separate," *pâdi,* "part," "proportion," *pâdiḍa,* "distribute," *pâdu,* "sharing," *pâtti,* "division." Mongol *buda,* "group." Japanese *hedate, bedate,* "to separate from." Chinese, *pie, bit,* "to separate," "other," *fen, pun,* "divide," *pu, bu, bud,* "division," "class," *fen, bun,* "a division." Indo-European *pars, separo,* Sanscrit *bheda,* "dividing," *bhedita,* "divided," *bhinna,* "separated."

Paḍu, "to suffer," "to be acted on," "to perish," "die in battle." This word forms a passive when joined to the infinitive of active verbs. Japanese *hate, bate,* "end, to end," *batashi,* "finish." Mongol *barahu,* "finish." Chinese *pa, ba, bat,* "to end," *pei, bi, bit,* "to be acted on"; used as a sign of the passive, as in *pei sha,* "was killed," *pai,* "destroy," "be destroyed," *ba, bad*; *fa,* "strike," "cut down," "make to fall," *bat.* Indo-European *bout, butt, patior, passus, beat, batuo.*

Pari, "burden," "load," "speed," *pâri,* "to be heavy," "to feel heavy," "to be thick." Mongol *bidugun,* "thick," *bidu gulig,* "thickness." Chinese *fu, bu, bud,* "burden," "to bear." Indo-European *bear, fero,* φέρω, *porto, bahren,* βαρύς, βάρος, *berden, speed,* σπεύδω.

Padam, "boiled rice," "eating," *pâdeyam,* "pro-

EXAMPLES OF DERIVATIVES IN TAMIL. 177

visions for a journey." Mongol *bada*, "food." Manchu *but'a*, "cooked rice." Chinese *fan, ban,* "cooked rice," "food." Indo-European *food, feed, fodder, petayu* (Russian "nourish"), *bwyd* (Welsh "food").

Padivu, "stooping," "lying near the ground," *padukkam*, "servility." Manchu *budun*, "vile." Mongol *begen* or *bogen*, "low" (*g* is apparently part of the suffix, and *d* is probably dropped). Japanese *hikui, bikui*, "low." Chinese *pei, pi, pid*, "low." Indo-European *bottom, base,* βάθος.

Pal, "many," *palam*, "force," "strength," "fruit," "result," "profit," *palan*, "profit," "fruit." Japanese *batashta*, "to result," *hodoshi, bodosi*, "to give," "bestow." Mongol *butogehu*, "fulfil." Chinese *pei, pi, pid*, "add to," "give," "annex to," "benefit," "assist." Indo-European *fructus, fruit, fortis, abundo.*

Paṛeiya, "old," "decayed," *paṛeimei*, "oldness," "decay." Japanese *furui, burui*, "old." Chinese *pai, ba, bad*, "to decay," "destroy," "decayed," *fa, bad*, "wearied," "worn out." Indo-European *fatigatus, fetid,* παλαιός, *beaten* (in the sense of "weary").

Para, "fly," "move quickly," "be dispersed." Japanese *hashiri, basiri*, "flee," "move fast." Chinese *fei, pi, pid*, "fly," *po, pad*, "scatter," "winnow." Indo-European σπείρω, πετάννυμι, *bird, fly, Flügel,* πετεινά, *flee, fast.*

Padi, "resemblance," *pôlu*, "to be like," *pôli*, "likeness." Mongol *budut'u*, "likeness." Chinese *pi, pe,*

12

ped, "compare." Russian *podobie*, "resemblance," *upodoblenie*, "comparison."

These, and many other words like them in form, appear to have sprung from a very few roots, such as *bad, bid, bud*, which may easily have originated in the imitation of natural sounds. These sounds would be, for example: the noise of the foot in stepping, of a bird beginning to fly, of striking with a hatchet, or of a heavy object falling to the ground. The many sharp sounds heard in nature favour the opinion that closed syllables were common in the primeval syllabary. It is not likely that our first forefathers ended their words with vowels exclusively.

The preceding examples show that a close comparison of the vocabularies of the Turanian languages with the Chinese old vocabulary is likely to be most fruitful in results. Philology, indeed, has at hand no vocabulary of roots so complete and so ancient in form as that found in the Chinese dictionary.

Among the additions to the root in Tamil are *m* and *l*, marking substantives, as *kâdam*, "killing," *kâdal*, "act of killing." The *m* reminds us of the Semitic *m*, which is a demonstrative root, and is used to form participial substantives from verbs and also to mark the participle. The suffix *l* is the same with the Mongol suffix for verbal nouns. For instance, the Mongols say *c'hidal*, "strength," "ability," derived from *c'hidahu*, "to be able," by adding *l*. Chinese *t'sai*, "power," "riches," *ze*, *zat*. The root is also found in the Sanscrit *sattva*, "vigour," "power," and *sattra*, "wealth," "sacrifice" (Chinese *tsi*, *tse*, *sat*, "sacrifice").

The vowels *i* and *u*, added to the root, are sounds, and nothing more. Thus, *parru* is "a grasp" and "to grasp." The same is true in Japanese. They are therefore used merely to make a second syllable, by giving a vowel to the final consonant of the root. They show that language has an inherent tendency to become polysyllabic.

The Tamil, like the Japanese, but more freely, makes compounds by annexing words to each other. Thus, from *tarisi*, "to see," are formed *tarisanam*, "vision," and *sandarisanam*, "the capacity to see all things in common," where the first syllable is the root *sam*, "all," "even," "common," Latin *simul*, English *same*, Greek ἅμα, Chinese *t'sam*, "equal," Tamul *samam*, "evenness," "sameness." From *palam*, "strength," is formed *samabalam*, "equal power." It is only in the Indo-European languages that we find a parallel development of compounds. But the prepositions παρά, *pro*, *super*, etc., which make so prominent a figure as prefixes to words in Greek and Latin dictionaries, are not able to take the same position in any Turanian language, because their nature as verbs requires them to be placed last. This exception being made, there can be no doubt that the transition from the Turanian languages to the Indo-European system is, in regard to the formation of compounds, most easily made from the Dravidian branch. The Turkish and Mongol in regard to this feature afford no foothold for comparison, for in those languages the loose compounds which exist cannot be regarded as single words. The intervention of possessive and other particles prevents the fusion of the two words into one.

A glance at the verb will enable us to judge of the relation held by the three branches of the Turanian family to each other.

The essential identity of the verb and noun is plainly taught by the Chinese and Turanian systems of languages. This identity is not in idea, but in sound. The framers of language did not confound action and thing, but they gave them the same name. Thus, *dong* in many languages expresses the sound of a bell. So anything that gives a ringing even sound, as also the sound itself, and any action that causes it, would be called *dong*. The Chinese say *ta*, old form *tang*, "to strike," *chung*, old form *tang*, "bell," *dung*, "copper." Of the Dravidian roots, Caldwell says, as quoted by F. Müller,[1] "When case-signs are attached to a root, or when without the addition of case-signs, it is used as the nominative to a verb, it is regarded as a noun: the same root becomes a verb without any internal change or formative addition, when the

[1] Reise der Novara. Linguistischer Theil, p. 95.

signs of tense and the pronouns, or their terminal fragments, are suffixed to it."

Thus, in Tamil occurs *kúttu*, a word which means either "union" or "to join." Changing the vowel, we meet with *kattu*, "a tie" and "to tie," "a fabrication" and "to fabricate," "a bundle" and "to bind." The Chinese *kit* means, in the same twofold manner, "a tie" or "to tie," "to coagulate," "to solidify." But if we observe the same root in Mongol and in the Indo-European languages, a difference is perceptible. The Mongols say *hada* for "a rock," *hat'ago*, for the adjective "hard," *hat'aho*, for the neuter verb "to harden," and *hadaho*, "to make fast" (by hammering), *hat'agaho*, "to dry," "to harden," in a causative or transitive sense. The Japanese, like the Mongol, has advanced beyond the stage when the verb and noun were one. Thus, we find in the Japanese vocabulary *katai*, "hard," *katameru*, "congeal," "harden," *katasa*, "hardness," *kataku*, "hard" (the same with the Mongol), *katamaru*, "become hardened," *kata*, "a mould," "shape," *katatsi*, "figure." Among the suffixes here observable, *i* and *ku* serve for the adjective, *sa* and *a* for the noun, *maru* for the verb in a passive or increscent sense, *meru* for the verb in a neuter or transitive sense. The naked root does not appear, nor do the verb and noun meet in any one form.

Hence it may be concluded that the Tamil and

Chinese types of language are both in this respect older than the Japanese and Mongol, while the English combination of the noun and verb in one form as "a tie," and "to tie," is a return to primeval usage after the language had been temporarily subject to the laws of derivation which reigned in the Sanscrit, Greek, and Latin.

The Sanscrit vocabulary contains the forms *kaṭhora*, "hard," *kaṭhoratâ*, "hardness," *kaṭhina*, "hard," *kaṭhinatâ*, "hardness," *kâṭha*, "rock," *kâṭhina*, "hardness," *kâdambara*, "the skim of coagulated milk," *kiṭaka*, "harsh," *kil*, to "bind," "fasten," or "nail" (*l* for *d*), *kila*, "a nail," "pin" (Mongol *hadagaso*, "a nail"), *kuta*, "a hammer." To these correspond the English *hard, hardness, harden*, where an *r* has crept in before the final letter.

It was this system of terminations, beginning in the Turanian languages and culminating in the Sanscrit, Greek, and Latin, that obscured the original identity of the verb, noun, and adjective, separated with precision the parts of speech, and thus gave origin to Indo-European grammar in its broadest aspect. This vast superstructure of derivatives raised on the original basis of the monosyllabic roots is now, and has been for two thousand years, gradually crumbling away. The contrast between the Anglo-Saxon and the English in regard to the extent of the principle of derivative suffixes is a measure of the change steadily advancing in the whole Indo-European world. If the human race should last long enough, we might expect, supposing that the present law of decay continues, to find the whole superimposed system of derivative forms swept away from language, leaving behind only the primeval vocabulary of monosyllabic roots. But the working of other laws, and the insatiable craving of civilization for new words, will prevent this.

The verb in Tamil appears as transitive, neuter, causative, passive, and negative. A neuter becomes transitive by doubling the final consonant of the root. Thus *pogu*, "to go away," becomes *pokku*, "to drive away." Professor F. Müller has noticed that this is a Semitic peculiarity. I would add that it should be traced to the influence of the Semitic form of speech on the Turanian at an ancient period, when they were geographically contiguous, or mixed in one older system. In Hebrew the doubling of a consonant is intensitive or causative. The syllables *pi*, *bi*, and *vi* are appended in Tamil to make causal verbs out of transitives. Thus *sey*, "do," the Chinese *tso*, in the old form *sak*, "do," or "make," when pronounced *seyvi*, means "cause to do." From *kal*, "to learn," and *kân*, "to see," are formed *karpi*, "to teach," and *kâṇbi*, "to show," *i.e.*, "cause to see." The Mongol inserts the syllables *ga* and *gol*, to impart to verbs a transitive or causative sense. This may be the Chinese causative verb *kiau*, old form *ko*. The Japanese causative suffix is *se*. Thus from *miru*, "see," and *naru*, "be," are formed *miseru*, "cause to see," *nasi*, "make to be." This syllabic addition reminds us of the Chinese causative verb *shi*. In passing from Chinese to the Turanian languages, as before remarked, *sh* becomes *s*. The causative syllable in the Telugu and Kannaḍa divisions of the Dravidian branch is *su*, which may be referred to the same origin as the Japanese. The Turks insert *al* or *ar*, to give the sense of "coming into the state of," and add *d* or *t* to add the causative signification, as *kararmak*, "to become black," *karartmak*, "to cause to become black." Here *mak* is the sign of the infinitive. The Sanscrit causal *p*, inserted before the causal suffix *aya*, as in the example given by Bopp, *sthâpayâmi*, "I make to stand," may be referred to the Tamil causative *p* for a probable origin.[1] The great philologist just mentioned derives the *c* of *doceo*, "to teach," from the Sanscrit causal *p*, and finds the root in *disco*, ἐδάην and διδάσκω. In Chinese we have the roots *ti*, "to know," in Mandarin *chï*, and *dik*, "to lead," *tok*, "to superintend," *to*, "lord." These words will furnish a natural and probable etymology for *doceo*, *dux*, διδάσκω, the Persian *dânem*, "I know," and other connected words. Bopp derives the *p* in *rapio*, "to snatch," from the same Sanscrit causal *p*,

[1] The Manchu, also a Turanian language, has *bu* for a causative syllable, *cholimbi*, "carve," *choʻlibumbi*, "cause to carve."

"in case *rapio* corresponds to the Sanscrit *râpáyâmi*, 'I make to give,' of which the root is *râ*, 'give,' formed from *dâ*, 'give,' by a weakening of the *d*." When we have the word *rob*, "to plunder," in English and German, it seems to be useless to seek for any other origin for the Latin *rapio* than the root *rab* or *lab*, "to take with the hand," "to take violently," "to receive," etc.; in Chinese *nip*, "take with the fingers," *nap*, "to take," "bring," in Mandarin *niĕ* and *na*.[1]

In the eastern Asiatic languages the passive is a derivative verb. Thus, in Tamil the suffix *paḍu* gives to verbs a passive sense. This is the same word with the Latin *patior*, "to suffer," and the Chinese *bad*, in Mandarin *pei*, which from the original meaning "to cover," "to spread," "reach to," etc., has taken the sense of "being acted upon," and so come to be used as a passive auxiliary. As such it is quite common in the modern speech of the country. In some dialects, as at Shanghai, its tone (4 or 8) indicates that a final *d* has been lost.[2] The Japanese changes final *i* to *e* to form a passive. Thus, *umi*, "to produce," becomes *ume*, "to be produced," "to be born"; *yomi*, "to read" (Chinese *niem*), becomes *yome*, "to be read." The

[1] The original root for the causative *p*, Manchu *bu*, I think is the Chinese *bad* or *pet*, "to give," for in the Shanghai dialect *peh* for *pet* is used in a causative sense. Edkins's Shanghai Grammar, p. 140, *Peh la ngu k'iuk kwen sz*, "he caused me to suffer a lawsuit."

[2] The lost letter might be *d* or *b*, but the phonetic shows it to have been *d*.

Tungusian adds *wum* to the active form. Here *m* is a personal ending, and *wu* is the addition, which may be the verb *ui*, in Mongol meaning "to do," and in Chinese "to do" and "to be." The Mongol passive is formed by inserting *da* or *de*. The Turks insert *il*. Thus, in Tungusian *silkim*, "wash," *silkiwum*, "to be washed"; in Mongol *abho*, "take," *abdaho*, "be taken"; in Turkish *deugurum*, "strike," *deugilurum*, "be struck"; in Tamil *adikkappadu*, "to be struck"; in Mongol *t'ugsedehu*, "to be struck."[1]

The Turanian verbs are negatived by the insertion or addition of the negative roots *al, ne, ak, ma*, common in Semitic and European languages. The Tamil inserts *a*, as do the other Dravidian dialects. Its full form, says Caldwell, as quoted by F. Müller, is *al*. The Telugu simply changes *u* to *a*, as in *pampu*, "to send," *pampa*, "not to send." The Tamil allows the usual terminations to follow. *Seygindadu*, "it makes," *seyyâdu*, "it does not make." This negative may be identified with the Hebrew אל *al*, "not." The Japanese negative element, says Hoffmann, is the sound *n*. From *siri*, "to know," is formed *siranai*, "I do not know." From *ake*, "to open," is formed *akenu*, "not to open." From *yuki*, "to go," are formed *yuku na* or *na yuki so*, "do not go." This negative may

[1] The root *dig, dug*, "strike," occurring in three Turanian languages, is in Chinese *tang*; in English, with prefix *s* and insertion of *r, strike*; in Hebrew הקמ "he struck," דקק "beat small"; Arabic *dak*, "strike a bell."

be identified with the Latin *non, ne*. The Manchu negative is *ak'o*, "not," as in *ak'o oho*, "I have it not," *ak'uc'hi*, "if it is not," *ak'ungge ak'o*, "nothing is wanting," *ak'ungge*, "it is not." The Mongol *ugei* is the same word with the aspirate omitted. In the eastern Mongol *w* is inserted in this word, as in *bada idesen ugwei*, "I have not eaten food." Here *bada* is the English *food*,[1] *ide* the English *eat*,[2] and *ugwei* the Greek οὐκ and οὐ. It is marvellous that the roving inhabitants of the Tartar plains should be daily using words so familiar to the inhabitants of European countries, but it is not the less true. These three negative roots, *a, ne, οὐκ*, have absolutely no representative in Chinese. Hence they must be regarded as of Semitic and Turanian origin, and the introduction of the last two into the Indo-European languages must be attributed to the influence of ancient union, or mutual influence and juxtaposition of the races.

It is otherwise with the remainder of the negatives in the Turanian languages. They are chiefly words identical with Chinese negatives. Thus, the Chinese *wu* or *mut*, "do not," is in Mongol *bu*, as in *bu bic'hi*, "do not write," *bu oro*, "do not enter." The Turkish uses *ma*, as in *olmah*, "do not be," *olmaz*, "he is not."

---

[1] Compare the Russian *pitat*, "to feed," German *füttern*; Russian *pishc'ha*, "food," German *futter*, English *fodder*.

[2] Compare the Sanscrit *anna*, "food," *ad*, "eat," Latin *edo*, Greek ἐσθίω, German *essen*, Russian *yest*, Greek ἔδω.

The Tibetan has *ma, mi,* "not." The Chinese denial of existence is expressed by *mo, mong,* in Mandarin *wu* and *mei yeu.* The Greek μή, in μὴ γένοιτο, "let it not be," is evidently connected with the same root. The two Chinese words are probably one in origin. In prohibitions they preferred the final *t* or *d*. In the denial of existence they chose the final *ng*.[1]

Another Chinese root is *pi, put,* in Mandarin *fei, pu,* used to express contradiction, as in *pu hau,* "it is not good," *pu lai,* "he does not come." The Mongols say, *boso,* "it is not so," in the eastern dialect, *bishi.* In Europe this root appears in the Latin *pereo* and *perdo, perfidus* and *perjuria,* in all which the prefix *per* has the sense of destruction or badness. It is also our own word *bad.* As a transitive verb it is in Chinese "to destroy" *(fei)* ; as a neuter, it is the substantive verb negatived; as an adjective, it denotes moral badness *(fei lui,* "bad people"); as an adverb, it is *pu,* "not."

The formation of the tenses preceded that of the personal endings. Thus, in the Tamil the form *sey-gind-en,* "I do," has for the mark of present time (*gir*) *gind,* and for the first person singular *en.* The first person singular in the aorist tense is *sey-v-en,* "I did." The perfect is *sey-d-en,* "I have done." In the older Turanian types, represented by dialects bordering on China, the personal endings do not occur. Thus, in

---

[1] *Mong,* in Mandarin *wang,* is used for "to die" or "be destroyed." It is the Latin *morior,* Sanscrit *mara,* Persian *mardan.*

the eastern Mongol, "I kill," "thou killest," "he kills," are expressed by *bi alana, c'hi alana, t'ere alana*, while in Buriat-Mongol, spoken on the shores of the Baikal Sea, *alanap, alanas, alana* are used, where *p* is *bi*, "I," and *s* is *c'hi*, "thou."

The distinction of masculine, feminine, and neuter is found in the personal endings of all the Dravidian dialects. Thus, in Tamil the third person singular of the perfect indicative is, masculine *sey-d-ân*, feminine *sey-d-âḷ*, neuter *sey-d-adu*. This peculiarity, being unknown in the languages of Tartary and Siberia, is best referred for its origin to ancient juxtaposition with Semite or Indo-European races. If traces of Semite influence occur in Dravidian speech, it may have been from the neighbourhood of some early people of that descent in Persia. The Cushite settlements stretched eastward along the sea-coast from Arabia to the mouths of the Indus,[1] and the language of the Cushites differed but little from that of the Semites. In Coptic and other Hamitic languages the distinction of masculine and feminine is still found in the personal endings of verbs.[2] When it is also remembered what striking indications of Semite in-

[1] Compare the geographical names, Cutch, in the Gulf of Kutch, near Bombay; Gujerat; Katsh, the name of a Tibetan province; the Vale of "Cashmere," etc.

[2] Reise der Novara. Linguistischer Theil. In old Egyptian, *t* marked the feminine. A neuter gender was unknown to Semitic or Hamitic grammar. The Arians probably introduced this distinction into language.

fluence are observable in the Tibetan language, it seems fair to conclude that the races which occupied the Persian area immediately before the Arian, being partly Semite and partly Cushite, imparted Semite elements to the Dravidian languages.

The Dravidian tense marks are, present *gindu, giṛu*, in Tamil; *ta, te*, in Kannaḍa; *chu, tu*, in Telugu. Perfect *t, d*, and *i*. Future *t*. Aorist *b, v, pp*.

On the origin of the marks for the present no light is thrown by reference to the Turkish *ar* or *ur*, as in *korkarum, korkarsen, korkar*, "I fear," "thou fearest," "he fears," where *um* and *sen* denote the first and second persons and *kork* is the root; nor to the Mongol *moi, na, namas*, in *bi abomoi*, "I take," *t'a abomoi*, "you take," *t'ere abomoi*, "he takes," in the eastern colloquial Mongol *abana*, and in old books *abonam*.

The forms for past time are, on the other hand, remarkably similar to those found in the connected languages. The Turkish preterite inserts *d*, as in *korkdum*, "I have feared," where *m* is the first pronoun—our own *me*. The Mongol gerunds have among them a form in *d*, which may easily have originated the indicative preterite in *d*. For example, in the eastern Mongol, *noyin moran onad jidan beriji iheu hashigaran oroba*, "the chief, mounted on his horse, and holding his spear, entered his great court-yard." *Noyin* is "any chief." *Moran* is the second accusative of *mori*, "horse," and as such bears a possessive signification.

Onihu is "to ride." Its gerunds are *onad, onaman, onaji*, which may be used in succession in a sentence composed of several clauses like the preceding. *Jidan* is the second accusative of *jid*, "spear." *Berihu* is "to grasp with the hand,"—the Chinese *pa*. *Iheu*, "great," is the Japanese *okii*, "great." *Hashigar* is "a palisaded enclosure." *Oroba* is the past indicative of *orohu*, "to enter." The form in *d* resembles our English participial form in *ed*, which agrees with the past tense indicative, as in, "he was mounted on his own horse," or, "he mounted his own horse." The Latin *equitatus*, or *equo vectus*, "mounted on a horse," are also equivalent. So is the Sanscrit participle in *ta*, as *patita*, "fallen," from *pat*, "fall."

The third Mongol gerund in *ji* appears to be the same wide-spread form disguised by phonetic change, for the Mongol *j* has *d* for its etymological equivalent.

The Japanese gerund in *te* nearly agrees in form and use with the Mongol. I take an example from Hoffmann: *Te wo aghete fito wo manekiyubu*, "elevating his hand, he calls the people by signs." *Te* is "hand." *Wo* is the accusative case suffix. *Aghete* is the gerund of *aghe*, "lift up," the Chinese *gu* or *kü*, and Greek ἐγείρω. The Turanian prefixed vowel has, if this identification be correct, been retained by the Greeks from that time in hoar antiquity when the forefathers of the Japanese were next-door neighbours to the world-famous Hellenes. *Fito wo* is "man" or "men," in the accusative, and *manekiyubu* is a compound verb, consisting of *maneki*, "to beckon," and *yubu*, "he calls." Hoffmann remarks that the suffix *te* means "at the time of," or "by means of," and is locative, modal, or instrumental.[1] The Japanese past tense takes the suffix *ta*, as in *watakusiga mita*, "I have seen," where *watakusiga* means "I," and has the honour perhaps of being the longest word in the world in use for that pronoun. *Mita* is the past of *mi*, "see," connected with the Chinese *mok*, "eye." I suppose that, as in English, the past tense is of later formation than the gerund form and founded upon it. So in Greek, the participle λείπων preceded the imperfect or aorist ἔλιπον, and both are later than the Mongol infinitive or participle in *n*, with which they are connected by a distant relationship. So also ἐβούλευσα, "I counselled," and ἐβουλεύθην, "I was advised," may be viewed as more recent forms, founded on the older βουλεύσας and βουλευθείς. The Indo-European past tense in *s*, *d*, and *n*, is based on the participle, and this again upon the Turanian gerund. The Turanian intellect nominalizes the verb. Every verb is looked at as a substantive, and hence those parts of the conjugation which were first formed approach in their nature to the substantive. The Turanian in describing a succession of events gave to his verbs the forms of gerunds, and added to them, when needed, the case

[1] Grammaire Japonaise, p. 177.

suffixes. Thus, each clause was a substantive. Yet, by the nature of the case, they retained a verbal energy. Time was an inherent element which was inseparable. The union of verb and noun in one word thus originated the participle of both the Turanian and Indo-European families. Then from this were derived certain indicative forms denoting past time.

The origin of the past tense and past participle in d may be looked for, perhaps, in the ancient Chinese pronoun *ti*, "him," Mandarin *chi*. This word is used as a preposition, "to a place," and as a possessive particle. I take an example from M. Julien's Syntaxe Nouvelle de la Langue Chinoise: *Kwo chi kiun*, "the kingdom's prince." The Mongol use of the suffix *de* in the sense of "towards a place" is parallel. In the dialects of China the same word is used in the same way as the Mongol gerund. *Tsu tsï ping, tang tsang k'i tse*,[1] "he has become a soldier and gone to fight." *Tsu* is to "do," "be," "act as," old form *sak*, in Tamil *sey*, "do." *Tsï* is the common sign of the possessive, here used as a mark of the gerund. *Ping* is "soldier." *Tang tsang* is a compound verb, "to fight." *K'i* is "to go," and is put in the past by the last word *tse*, a particle fixing past time. In M. Julien's examples of the use of *chi*[2] may be seen, *Wei shu sheng chi*, "only millet grows," said of the barbarians of Tartary, whose country will not grow rice or wheat.

[1] Shanghai Grammar, § 252.   [2] Syntaxe Nouvelle, p. 75.

At present the northern boundary of wheat cultivation passes at about 200 miles to the north of Peking. The word *chi* is here, says M. Julien, without signification. But may there not be here the commencement of a gerund formation like that seen in compounds formed with the word *cho* in Mandarin? Thus, in *Wo chan cho ti shï heu*, "while I was standing," *wo* is "I." *Chan* is "stand." *Cho* makes it a gerund. *Ti* is the possessive sign to the verb-noun, *chan cho*. *Shï heu* is a compound noun meaning "hour," "time." Looking at the use of *chi* in this way, and keeping in mind the Shanghai usage above adduced, the history of the gerund formation in *d* would become clear. The root *ti* appears in old Chinese literature, (1) with the meanings "this," "him," "towards," "go towards"; (2) with the possessive sense, thus becoming a mere auxiliary particle; (3) with a gerund-like signification, which comes out more distinctly in the dialects.[1]

The other Dravidian perfect in *i* and the aorist in *b* or *v* are interesting from their striking resemblance to the Latin perfect in *ui*, *vi*, and imperfect in *bam*. In Mongol the ordinary past tense ends in *ba* when the root has *a* or *o*, and *beu* when the root has *e* or *i*, e.g., *yababa*, "he went," *helebeu*, "he said." The

---

[1] If this is not the true origin of the Mongol gerund in *d* and *ju*, it may be possible to find it in the Chinese Mandarin gerund *cho*, meaning originally "to hit the mark," "strike," "take fire," etc.

CONDITIONAL TENSE. 195

form in *ba* differs in nothing from the Latin imperfect, except that the Latin has proceeded to affix the mark of the personal pronoun, a stage which the older Mongol dialects have not reached. The Buriat-Mongols, however, have added *b, s, t,* to the three persons, thus making the identification complete. The Turkish and Persian languages, which have always been neighbours, both have *m* for the first person, as in the Persian imperfect *budam, budi, bud,* "I was," "thou wast," "he was," corresponding in Turkish to *boldim, boldung, boldi.* The Manchus also have a past tense in *bi.* In Japanese *ba* is used to serve as a suffix to the verb in a subordinate clause with the sense "when," or "as." This appears to be the same as the Mongol conditional suffix *bel.* Hoffmann gives the example: *yama no ne kumo tsigiretaraba yagate fare,* "should the clouds on the top of the mountain be dispersed, it becomes forthwith clear." Here *no* is the possessive, *yama* is "mountain," *ne* is "the summit," *kumo* is "cloud," *tsigiretara* is "disperse," *yagate* is "forthwith," and *fare* is "becomes clear." *Ba* is "should" or "if."

As to the origin of *ba* and *bel* as conditional suffixes, or as signs of the imperfect indicative, there is perhaps nothing more probable than an ancient connexion with the Chinese *pi,* "to compare," and *pei,* "to give." The lost *d* of the latter of these words is recovered by comparing the Shanghai form *peh* for *pet* with the

Japanese *hodokoshi*, "to give" (N.B. Japanese $h = p$ or b). The Japanese for "compare" is *haiszru*, "to match," "equal." The Chinese, as at Shanghai, use both words in compounds, as in *sung peh la ngu*, "present it to me," literally "present give to me"; *siang pi*, "mutually compare." The Tamil has these words with or without an initial *o*. Thus, *oppanei* is "simile," "parable," *pol*, "like as," *oppâri*, "comparison," *oppi*, "give," *poli* or *oppu*, "likeness," "congruity," *polu* or *oppu*, "to be like," "resemble," *oppumei*, "similitude," *oppuvi*, "to give," "deliver." The Chinese has also the aspirated words *p'i*, "a comparison," *p'ei*, "to match," "correspond to," and *p'i*, "a match," where the root is in all cases *p'it*. In the Indo-European languages, the Russian has *podobie*, "resemblance," and *upodoblenie*, "comparison," where the prefixed *u* is curiously like the *o* in the Tamil forms. The English has *pair*, and the Latin *par*, "equal," and *comparo*, "to compare." The Latin *paro*, "prepare," is the Chinese *bid*, "prepare," in Mandarin *pei*. In Chinese there are also other members of this numerous family, namely, *pi*, "he," and *pit*, "other," already adduced in a previous chapter.

The explanation now proposed of the conditional and past tense suffix in *b* is, that its original meaning was "resemble" and "give," and that it was appended as a verb, in juxtaposition with a preceding verb, as in the modern eastern Mongol *helji og*, "speak for me," where *og* means "give," and *helji* is the gerund of of *helhu,* "to speak." In Japanese and Mongol it became suppositive, and in Dravidian and Mongol preterite. In this state it passed over into the Latin, when the ancestors of the Romans were still in Asia, and in close connexion with the Turanians. What is given is passed over to another. The very word *past* means transferred.

Bopp has derived the Latin imperfect from the substantive verb *fui, fore,* but there is this objection to that view. The same suffix for the past tense exists in Dravidian languages which have not this substantive verb. The substantive verb in *b* first comes into view in the Tartar languages. The older branches of the Turanian family, the Japanese and Dravidian, have it not, nor do they contain any traces of the first personal pronoun in *m*, which is always found in the company of the substantive verb in *b*.

The other Dravidian past in *i*—as in the Kannaḍa aorist *uv* and in the Tamil perfect in *i*—resembles the Latin *ui* and *vi*, in *docui* and *amavi*. Though it does not appear in the verb paradigms of the Mongol and Japanese languages, there is no difficulty in finding it in Chinese. It is the word *i*, "already." By analogy the old form of this word may have been *i* or *wi*. The Latin, Sanscrit, and Tamil *v* is the equivalent of the Chinese *w*. The word *i*, "already," is in Chinese used in the sense "past and gone" (lower second tone), and perhaps originated the final particle *i*, for which it is sometimes used.¹ It differs in nothing from the third personal pronoun *i*, except in tone : a quality which, as has been shown, may be treated as having been non-existent 4,000 years ago. The same word also means "other," "different." Hence the fundamental idea of it is "difference," in space, in person, or in time. Combined with *jen*, "man," it means "a man of another country," "a barbarian" (lower first tone). It is a noun, "difference," in the sentence, *ta t'ung siau i*, "great similarity and small difference." In *i ti*, "a different place," it is an adjective (lower third tone). As an adverb it means "again," and as such it is the word pronounced in Mandarin *yeu*, but in the Shanghai dialect *yi* (lower third tone). As the third personal pronoun (upper first tone), it is still used in the south-eastern dialects.

The Dravidian future in *i* or *e* is evidently identical with the Mongol future in *ya*, and these forms together constitute an old type from which the Latin future in *e* and *ie*, as in *regam, reges*, and *audiam, audies*, may have been formed. Its origin may perhaps be discovered in the Chinese *yau*, which takes the old form *ok*, "wish," "desire." It is a common sign of the future in Mandarin-Chinese. The *k* was early

¹ For an example of the use of *i*, "already," as a final particle in a predicative sentence, *vide* Syntaxe Nouvelle of M. Julien, p. 186.

lost in the colloquial language. The corresponding western word is *volo, wollen, will,* βούλομαι, and perhaps *wish*.[1] That this identification is not unlikely to be correct may be shown by reference to the other Chinese signs of the future. *Tsiang* (old form *siung*) contains in it the *sya*, which is the Sanscrit sign of the future, and the *s* of the Greek and Latin future, as in βουλεύσω, "I will advise," θουλεύσων, "about to give counsel," and *ero*, "I will be" (*r* for *s*). Another sign of the future in Chinese is *pit*, in Mandarin *pi*. It means "certainty," "certainly." "It will certainly be so." The word is the same with the Latin *fides*, the Greek πίστις, and the Hebrew בָּטָה *bata*, "he trusted." This I suppose to be the source of the Latin future in *bo, bis, bit*, where *bi* marks the tense and *o, s, t*, the person, as in *amabo*, "I shall love." This affords a more natural explanation of the future tense formation than to derive it in the manner of Bopp from the substantive verb, *fuisse, futurus*, etc. The Latin future in *r*, as *ero, amavero*, etc., is coincident in a curious way with the Manchu future in *ra, re*, which again strikingly resembles the Mongol supine in *ra, re*. A supine is a sort of infinitive put in future time, and hence in English the supine and the infinitive are not distinguished. The Mongols use

[1] Compare *wash*, in Chinese *og*, Mongol *ogahu*. *Sh* is a western equivalent for the old Chinese final *g* or *k*. In German, the inserted *n* in *wünschen*, "to wish," causes a difficulty in the identification.

for the future both the present tense in *moi* or *ne*, and also the infinitive in *hu*. Thus, in Turanian grammar there is not a little mutual interchange between the present, the future, the supine, and the infinitive. Hence it should be regarded as open for consideration, whether (if *yau*, "wish," is not satisfactory) the Chinese substantive verb *wei*, "to be," "to do," and in the third tone "for," "for the sake of," may not be the source of the Mongol future in *ya*, and so of the Dravidian and Latin forms already adduced. This verb exists in Mongol in *uile*, "an act," and *uiledhu*, "to do"; and is probably the root of our western *am*, *was*, *werden*, *est*, *esse*, Sanscrit *asti*, Tamil *iru*, "to be," Japanese *iru*, *oru*, "to be," "to dwell."

The syntax of the Dravidian languages is similar to that of Tartar and Japanese speech. This will be understood from some examples of Tamil sentences, taken from Pope's Handbook. "Open the door" is *kadavu tira*, where *kadavu* is the Mongol *egude* (or in modern vernacular *ude*) and the Japanese *kado*, "door." The Chinese equivalent is *gud*, in Mandarin *hu*. The verb *tira*, "to open," stands last. So in Mongol *ude nehe*, "open the door," where *nehe* is the Greek ἄνοιγε.

An example of the participial construction is the following: *nán paditta pádam*, "the lesson which I have learned." *Nán* is "I." *Paditta* is the past participle of *padi*, "to learn." *Pádam* is a verbal noun from the same root. Compare in Mongol *bi omsihu ne bichig*, "the book I am reading." Here *omsihu* is the infinitive or present participle "reading." It is in the possessive case, with *ne* to connect it with the following noun, "book." The past participle would be *omsisen*, the other words remaining the same, and the meaning would be, "the books which I have read." The Chinese construction is similar, *wo nien ti shu*, "the book I am reading," or "which I have read." Here *ti* is the possessive (the verb *nien*, "read," being treated as a noun), and corresponds exactly to the Tamil *tâ*.

The gerund construction will be perceived from the following instance: *naḍandu wandân*, "walking he came," Mongol *yabaju irebe*. As *j* takes the place of *d*, the suffix *ju* is the same as the Tamil *du* and the Japanese *te*. The Chinese has the same order, *tseu lai*. The Indo-European languages invert the order, as in ἦλθε, βλέπων, "he came seeing," *rediit videns*. Another example is *kêṭṭu wasittu eɴudinân*, "hearing, reading, he wrote." We should say, "he heard, read, and wrote." The Mongol would use one gerund in *d*, another in *ju*, and then close with the indicative.

There can be little doubt in regard to the probability that the order of verbs in this Turanian construction rests on the older law ruling the order of verbs in Chinese, viz., that of succession in time. Hearing and reading precede writing. Walking precedes coming. After the Turanian period, when an indicative was fully formed, it was possible to transgress this order. The rich Indo-European verb paradigms allowed of verbs being easily distinguished from each other, and language was no longer obliged, in the interest of clearness, to maintain a strict adherence to the order of time in the arrangement of her verbs.

A more complex example from Mongol will illustrate the syntax of an expanded sentence: *t'ere mande helsen ne uge bi mart'asen,* "the words that he said to me I have forgotten." *T'ere* is "he." *Mande* is "to me." *Helsen* is the past participle of *helhu,* "to speak." It has the possessive particle *ne*. *Uge* is words. *Bi mart'asen* is, "I have forgotten," the participle being used as an indicative in the colloquial language. In the book language it would receive after it the substantive verb in the indicative, to complete its expression. The construction, with the participle, is here seen performing the duty afterwards assigned to the relative pronoun. *Helsen ne uge* is a relative clause. This was, in the early state of language, rendered possible by the fact, that the verb was viewed predominantly by the Turanian mind as a substantive; and, as such, the office of finding room in a sentence for the relative clauses of western languages was considered to belong to it in one of its cases, viz., the possessive. But the more lively and energetic attributes of Semite language had in this respect greater influence on the Indo-European mind. The relative pronoun became the hinge on which the clauses of compound sentences could conveniently turn, and the honour of accomplishing this duty was no longer assigned to the verb in the possessive.

CHAPTER X.

THIRD DIVISION OF THE TURANIAN SYSTEM.—MONGOL AS A TYPE OF TARTAR LANGUAGES. — AN OLD TURANIA IN WESTERN ASIA. — THE TARTAR TURANIANS COME NEAREST TO THE INDO-EUROPEANS. —SYSTEM OF SOUND.—*S* AND *J* FOR *SH* AND *D*.—*CH* FOR *S*.— FINAL *NG* DROPPED. — NO *F*.—SEVEN VOWELS. — TONE. — ACCIDENCE. — SUBSTANTIVE VERB AND FIRST PERSONAL PRONOUN. — MONGOL DECLENSION.—PRONOUNS.—THE MONGOL VERB CONJUGATION. — A MONGOL VERB. —ADVERBIAL SUFFIXES. — MONGOL SYNTAX.

THE great antiquity of the Mongolian type of language is manifest from its being found in several of its leading features in the Dravidian area. The historical events which have separated the branches of the great Turanian family furnish to us an approximate chronology for the early stages of Turanian development. They point to a period anterior to the dispersion of the Indo-European families, when there was a primitive Turania in Western Asia, from which the Japanese, Dravidian, and Tartar races proceeded. This time cannot be later than 2,000 years before the Christian era. At that time the Turanian verb had already its gerund, its past participle, and its three indicative tenses, a scale of case suffixes, several polysyllabic derivatives, and a common syntax. The suffixes were attached more loosely to the root than in the Indo-European system. It could not have been otherwise. For the Turanian type stands midway between the monosyllable of China and the richly elaborated polysyllabism of modern Europe. The difference between the agglutinated and inflected languages is simply a question of lower and higher development. Linguistic types come one out of another, like orders in architecture, or ages in geology. The Indo-European system rests on the Semitic and Turanian systems, as they do on the Chinese, and as the Chinese does upon the primitive speech of Western Asia.

The special interest of the Mongolian type consists in the fact that it comes nearest of all the three Turanian branches to the Indo-European. As Iran and Turan stood opposite to each other with hostile front, but in close contiguity, in ancient Persian remembrance, so Arian and Turanian speech, in many respects varying, stand to each other in the closest proximity. Their remarkable resemblance consists mainly in the formation of tenses by suffixes and in the extensive use of the same substantive verbs and personal pronouns. The verb "to be," the first personal pronoun in *m* or *b*, and the second and third in *s* or *t*, are as widely extended in Tartary as they are in Europe, and they form an incontrovertible argument for common origin in language, race, and ideas. The same mental constitution which led the Tartar tribes to develope these roots in a declined and conjugated form, as the convenient expression of their ideas of existence and personality, led the Indo-European races to adopt them for the same use, instead of the more ancient substantive verbs and pronouns found in the Semitic, the Chinese, and the older Turanian languages. That the Fins, Manchus, Mongols, and Turks should have borrowed this striking feature from the Indo-Europeans seems very improbable. It is worked thoroughly into the texture of their languages, and has nothing of the appearance of a foreign element.

The Mongol and other Tartar languages have suffered less from phonetic decay than the Japanese and Dravidian branches of the same family, which have been exposed to the enervating effects of mild or hot climates. Hence there is found here a greater variety of sounds. Thus, the syllabary includes *ng, n, m, g, d, b, l, r, s*, among the finals. Of these, the last three are beyond the capacity of the Chinese vocal system, and they must be regarded as new. Thus, *gol*, "river," is formed by appending *l* to the Chinese root *ga*, in Mandarin *ho*. *T'os*, "opposite," is formed by dropping *d* in the old Chinese *tod*, "opposite," Mandarin *tui*, and adding *s*. The Tamil has *edir*, "to oppose."

The Indo-European languages allow any letter to end a syllable. Thus, in English, in addition to the nine consonants by which the Mongols can close syllables, we have *f, v, k, t, p, ch, dj, z, sh*, and the surd and sonant *th*. This is an unmistakable proof of the advance in freedom which language has now made. In the Mongolic stage it had added three finals to the Chinese and Himalaic phonology. In Sanscrit the finals are *ng, n, m, h, t, d, s, r*; differing very slightly from the Mongol. In Latin, when we have repeated *haud, aut, in, hic, collis, clam, frater, multiplex*, we seem to have exhausted the capacities of the syllabary, and have only eight final consonants, *d, t, n, k, s, m, r, x*, of which the last, *x*, is a compound of two others, *k* and *s*. It is only in the Gothic and Sclavonic speech that language assumed the power of ending syllables with whatever consonants it pleased. Among these two, the Gothic has more freedom than the Sclavonic, and probably there is no language in the world that can compare in this respect with the English. This, however, is a distinction which has been acquired only after long and patient waiting. Language passed from the monosyllabic stage into the Turanian, from this to the early or southern Indo-European type, and from that to the later or northern type of the same family, before venturing on so great a leap. In Semitic phonology, on the other hand, language, with characteristic boldness, claimed the privilege at a most ancient period of using as finals the sibilants and liquids, in addition to the mutes and nasals which were the finals of the primeval monosyllable.

The unaspirated surds *k, t, p,* do not exist in Mongol or Manchu. These letters, as written by De Castren and Schmidt in their Grammars, represent aspirated surds.[1] They appear to have grown out of the sonants. Thus, *t'ologai,* "head," is in Chinese *du,* Mandarin *t'eu.* So also *t'ola,* "for," "on behalf of," is in Chinese *t'ek* and *dak,* in Mandarin *t'i* and *tai,* "instead of."

The aspirated *k* has in the eastern Mongol, which is that spoken in the neighbourhood of Peking, become *h,* but *k'* is retained by the western and northern Mongols.

The want of *sh* in Mongol, or at least its very sparing use, reminds the student of the Greek and Latin languages, which also lack this consonant. The coincidence can scarcely be regarded as accidental when the many remarkable resemblances in words between the Tartar languages and the Greek and Latin are kept in view. In Mongol *k'umun* or *humun,* "man," *ere,* "male," *nehemoi,* "to open," *gar,* "hand," *dalai,* "the sea," *ebur,* "horn," *sara,* "moon," *nom,* "sacred book," may be compared with *homo,* "man," *vir,* ἄρρην, "male," ἀνοίγω, "to open," χείρ, "hand," θάλασσα,

---

[1] What the rule is in Turkish I cannot in Peking learn with certainty. The influence of Arabic and Persian may have led to a change of the aspirates to the pure surds.

"sea," *ebur,* "ivory," σελήνη, "moon," νόμος, "law." It is probable, therefore, that at some distant epoch a strong Turanian influence was exerted specially upon the Greek and Latin sections of the Indo-European family, subsequent to the separation of the Indo-Persian tribes from the common Aryan stock.

The Chinese *d* and *t*, in Mandarin often *ch*, is in Mongol represented by *j*. Thus, *ti,* "to point to," *di,* "to rule," "to cure," *tok,* "candle, "to shine," *ti,* "decree," are in Mongol *jahu,* "to point," *jasahu,* "to rule," "correct," "cure," *jol,* "candle," "lamp," *jerlig,* "decree." In Greek and Latin the corresponding words are δείκνυμι, *indico, rego, luceo, lux, lex.* The law regulating these correspondences is, that words commencing with *d* and *l* in the Latin are found to agree in meaning with words whose initial is in modern Chinese *ch*, in Mongol *j*, and in old Chinese and Mongol *d*. As in the registered old sounds of the Chinese tonic dictionaries, dating from A.D. 400, some of these words are spelt with *t*, it may be reasoned that, as before stated, the old Chinese *t* probably came out of a more ancient *d*, for then it will not be surprising that *l* should be the Latin equivalent. The letters *l* and *d* have a known affinity for each other, and appear to be related, as son to mother. *L* has grown out of *d*, and so also has *r*, and thus has been caused an expansion of the alphabet in Sanscrit, in the Semitic family, and probably in other ancient systems. This will be seen by the following example.

PRIMITIVE IDEA, "TO POINT," *DIK*.

CHINESE.	SIGNIFICATION	MONGOL.	SANSCRIT.	GREEK, LATIN.	GER., ENG.
ti, chï	*point*	jahu		δείκνυμι	zeichnen.
dik, ti	*lead*		daksha	dexter	token.
di, da	*to rule*	jasahu	dakshinât	duco	
di, da	*to cure*	jasahu		dux	
tok, tu	*oversee*	ejelehu		digitus	
tu, chu	*lord*	ejen	rajah	rex	
le, li	*reason*			λόγος, lex	reason.
le, li	*to rule*		raj	rego	Recht.
ti	*decree*	jerlig		decet	law.
ti	*will*			δίκαιος	
dik, chï	*straight*		riju	rectus	straight.

A final *k* or *g* appears to have been lost from all the Chinese words where it is not marked in this list. In the Mongol *ejen*, "lord," *n* final is not part of the root. It disappears in declension, as in the plural *ejid*, and in the verb *ejelehu*, "to rule." In the Sanscrit *daksha*, "right (hand)," *dakshinât*, "southward," the double letter *ksh* has taken the place of *k*. The influence of religious ideas connected with the worship of light is perceptible in the east being regarded as the front and the south as the right. As in common roots the Indo-European *r* corresponds to the Chinese *l*, and the Indo-European *l* and *d* to the Chinese *ch*, the transition from *d* to *l*, observable in the Chinese examples now given, must in all probability have taken place at a time anterior to the separation of the races, and when the forefathers of the Chinese and Indo-Europeans still spoke one language. The primeval root *dig* became doubled by the change of *d* to *l*; and while *dig* and *lig* both remained in Chinese, they originated in the Indo-European languages two sets of derived words, one set with the initials *d* or *l*, and the other with an initial *r*. In the English example *straight*, *s* is prefixed to the root and *r* is inserted after the initial *t*. The same root occurs in the Semitic languages with the sibilant prefixed, as in the Hebrew *tsadik*, "just," Arabic *sadik*.

The Mongol aspirated *ts* or *ch* is found to be the Chinese *s*, *sh*, *ts*, or *tʻs*. Thus, the words *cʻhitgur*, "a demon," *cʻhasa*, "snow," *cʻhohom*, "accurately," "altogether," *cʻhag*, "time," *cʻhilagon*, "stone," are in Chinese *sut*, *suy*, "an evil spirit," "to exercise demoniacal influence," *sit*, "snow," *sik*, "all," "thoroughly," *shi*, "time," "hour," *shig*, "stone." The equivalent in Indo-European is *s* or *sh*, as in *cʻhadaho*, "to be satisfied," *satis*; *cʻhilagon*, "a stone," *saxum*; *chʻi*, "thou," σύ. The change from *cʻh* to *tʻ*, in *cʻhi*, "thou," *tʻa*, "ye," is parallel to the change from the Greek σύ to the Latin *tu*, "thou."

The final *ng* of many Chinese words is dropped in Mongol. Thus, *solaraho*, "to become weak," *lo*, "dragon," *gerel*, "light," are the Chinese *sung*, "loosen," *lung*, "dragon," *keng, kwang*, "light." The same tendency perhaps lurks in the Sanscrit *Râhu*, "the demon of eclipses," and the Latin *gloria*, where an *l* has crept in after the initial. The Japanese and Tamil agree with the Mongol in dropping *ng* final, as in the Japanese *akari*, "light." The word *morning, Morgen*, may be derived from the Chinese *mang*, "bright," in Mandarin *ming*, through the Mongol *maragat'a*, "to-morrow," spelled in books *managar*. Other common forms are *magat'ara, maragasi*. They all mean "to-morrow." There is a verb *manahu*, "to shine," "ascend like the sun."

The want of *f* in Mongol suggests a close connexion in this part of the Turanian sound system with the Sanscrit and Greek. Its place is supplied by *b*.

The vowels are seven. They are called by Schmidt *a, e, i, o, u, ö, ü*. These values answer for the western and northern dialects; but for the eastern Mongol, spoken in the neigbourhood of Peking, and which has not been described by the Russian and German grammarians, the values are rather *a, e, i, ô, o, o* and *u* or *ü*. The fourth is the English *o* in *fond*, the fifth and sixth are divided by tone, and the sound is the English *o* in *bone*. The seventh is sometimes the English *oo* in *tool*, and sometimes the French *u*. The distinction between the fifth and sixth vowels cannot be described in any other way than as a variation in pitch, the fifth being lower than the sixth. The eastern Mongol bears evident marks of being the most ancient of the dialects. It has no traces of the personal endings in the conjugation of verbs which occur in the Buriat dialect. This double tone, therefore, of the east Mongol syllabary must be regarded as a link of connexion with the Chinese and Himalaic systems. In learning the Chinese language the foreign student meets with the tones in the individual words to which they are attached. In the Tibetan, Siamese, and east Mongol, he meets with them in the syllabary. It is the same thing. If the Tibetan and Siamese were written with a separate character, half ideographic and half phonetic, for each word, the tone mark would be attached to the character in some such way as that in use among the Chinese. The difference between the fifth and sixth vowels of the Mongol syllabary would be expressed by saying that all words enunciated with the fifth vowel are in one tone class, and all words enunciated with the sixth vowel are in another.

The existence of this double tone harmonizes with the view that the Mongol language rests on the Chinese as its basis. If a language came between them, it must have had a tone system, which would occupy a midway position between the Chinese system of tones and that of which the last vestiges are now slowly disappearing in the oldest and most easterly of the Mongol dialects.

In the study of the Tartar languages, and the

dialects and languages of the same stock in European and Asiatic Russia, the occurrence of the substantive verb *to be*, and the first personal pronoun in *m* or *b*, is the most striking of all signs of kindred with the Indo-European family. The verb *buhu*, "to be," has a present *boi*, an imperfect *bolai*, a perfect *buloge*, a conditional *bugesu*, a potential *boija* and *bubeja* (?), three gerunds *burun*, *bured* (?), *bugó'te le*, and two infinitives *buhu*, *buhwei*.

The root *a*, found in our auxiliary verb *am*, *are*, *art*, is also mixed with the auxiliary *to be* in a way resembling that to which we are accustomed in English. The parts are, a present *amoi*, an imperfect *abai*, a future *aho* or *ayo*, a conditional *abasu*, a potential *amoija*, a precative *at'ogai*, an imperative plural *akt'on*, two infinitives *aho* and *ahwei*, three gerunds *aju*, *agad*, and *at'ala*, a participle of agency *akc'hi*, and a past participle *ak'san*.

The first of these, *bu*, is the Sanscrit *bhú*, in the infinitive *bhavitum*, "to be," or "become"; the Persian *budan*, "to be"; the English *be*; and in the Turkish *bolmak*, "become." In the Tartar languages the connexion of this root with the ordinary word for *I*, in Mongol *bi*, in Turkish *ben*, in eastern Turkish *men*, in Manchu *bi*, is manifest. The possessive of *bi*, "I," is *manai*, "mine." Thus, then, the English *me* in the accusative is the Mongol *bi* in the nominative, while the English possessive *mine* is the Mongol possessive *manai*, in the book form *minu*. It appears then that the English *me* and *be* are the same word, and that that in which the Mongol differs, namely, the convertibility of *b* and *m*, is derived from some Turanian language, the parent of the present Tartar languages. In the Indo-European family, *m* is appropriated to the pronoun and *b* to the verb. Hence their identification is not at first view obvious. In the Tartar languages, where *b* is used for the verb, and *m* and *b* are both in free use for the pronoun, the identification does not admit of doubt.

The question then arises, what is the origin of the verb *to be* and the personal pronoun *me?* We have in Mongol and Manchu the word *beye*, "body," in Japanese *mi*. This Japanese term signifies both "self" and "body." We have also in Chinese *mut* (Mandarin *wu*) meaning "a thing." The Sanscrit *mâtra*, "matter in the abstract," and Latin *materies*, are by some derived from the word meaning "mother," in Sanscrit *mâtâ*, in Latin *mater*. Further, we have in Mongol *mun*, "it is so," a strong affirmative, and in Hebrew *amin*, "certain." The Mongol and Japanese substantives furnish the ideas of self. The Chinese, Sanscrit, and Latin substantives contribute the notion of substance. The Hebrew and Mongol verbs add the conception of certainty. Why may not these ideas have met in the formation of one pronominal and substantive root, destined to pervade the languages of mankind from

Manchuria to Portugal, and from Calcutta to Finland? That this root is not used in the Semitic, Dravidian, Tibetan, Chinese, or Japanese languages, either as a substantive verb or personal pronoun, affords a strong presumption that it was not originally either the one or the other. If this hypothesis be correct, the combination of ideas, which resulted in the growth of the substantive verb in *b* and the first personal pronoun in *m*, must have taken place in the language which originated the present Tartar dialects. The locality of this language was probably Western Asia, or Persia, or Bucharia, for only in one of these countries could it be in such convenient contiguity to the Aryan race as to allow of the engrafting of this fruitful germ into the mother-speech of that family.

The other auxiliary verb *amoi*, I suppose to be the Chinese *wei*, "to do," "to be." This was, as we learn from the rhymes of the Shï king, anciently called *wa*. In Sanscrit it appears with a suffix *s*, which is retained in our *was* and *were*, in the last of which *s* is represented by *r*.

The present *amoi* seems to be formed from the root *a* by the addition of *boi*, the present tense of the substantive verb in *b*, with *b* altered to *m*.

The imperfect *abai* cannot be derived in the same way, because, as before stated in the foregoing chapter, the Dravidian languages have this tense form, while they are without the substantive verb in *b*. We may refer it rather to a Chinese root, *pet* or *bed*, "to give."

The form in *lai* and that in *loge* may perhaps be derived from the Semitic *le*. The word *le*, or *al*, means "towards," "to," "into," and is used to mark the dative case. The form *el*, with a vowel prefix, gives in a more marked manner the proper and physical sense; and that with a short vowel suffix, *le*, is used for borrowed and metaphysical senses.[1] The Tibetan language has *la* for a dative case suffix. In the Shanghai dialect the same word is used as a dative case prefix, and with the force of a substantive verb in the locative, as in the sentence, *I la a li*, "where is he?" literally, "he at what place." Here the word *la*, translated by "at," has the force of "is at," that is, it is a substantive verb in the locative case. Its Mandarin representative is *tsai*, anciently *ze*. The Mongol imperfect in *lai* and preterite in *loga* may have been formed from the Semitic *le* and Shanghai *la*, by the intervention of a gerund usage, or, in other words, a predominant use of the verb as a substantive. For "he has come back" the Chinese say *hwei lai liau*, literally "return, come, finished." Three verbs are here in juxtaposition. *Hwei*, "return," is a gerund, and is translated into English by the present participle "returning." *Lai*, "come," is indicative, and is made past by the addition of the auxiliary *liau*, "past,"

[1] Gesenius' Lexicon Hebraicum.

"finished," which is a modern particle, formed from a verb, *liau*, "to destroy." The Mongol would say *hairebe*, "he returned," or *haireji irebe*, "returning he came." Put *le* in place of the gerund suffix *ji*, and the sense will be, "in returning he came." Then drop the last verb, "came," and the form in *le* or *loga* becomes a past indicative. So in modern Mongol, as spoken in Peking, sentences such as the following are in constant use.—*T'ere nidenen jil yabaji*, "he left last year," literally, "he last year' left." The gerund form in *ji* is here used as a past indicative tense. It ought to be *yababa*. It is ungrammatical.[1] But language is always busied in making new forms, successfully or unsuccessfully. If the Mongol language needed a past indicative, it might easily be made from the gerund in *ji* or *ju* in this way. So we may suppose the preterite in *loga*, colloquially called *lai*, to have been formed. This is in harmony with the general principle, that tense and mood suffixes in the Turanian and Indo-European languages have been all formed from verbs viewed as nouns and used as gerunds. When gerunds, participles, and infinitives had been formed, they became indicative in past, present, or future time by the simple process of dropping the following verb. This principle of tense and mood formation is at the opposite pole to that which exists in the Semitic languages. Thus, וְחָיוּ עָשׂוּ זֹאת

---

[1] The full form would add *ic'hibe*, "went," after the gerund *yabaji*.

zoth asu vihheyu, "this do ye, and live." Here an imperative is used in both cases. To the Semite mind each verb was instinct with its own energy. He struggled to secure to each verb in a sentence its full activity, and therefore he connected them by the conjunction *and*. This device allowed them each to be indicative. This vital character of the verb has been usually retained in the English version of the Scriptures, as in the same example, "This do, and live; for I fear God." (Gen. xlii. 18.) Luther has altered the Semitic mode of expression. He translates, *Wollt ihr leben, so thut also; denn ich fürchte Gott*, "Would you live, then so do; for I fear God." He has two clauses, of which the conditional contains two verbs, *wollt* and *leben*, the latter with a Turanian suffix; and the affirmative one verb in the imperative. Compare this with the Septuagint rendering, Τοῦτο ποιήσατε καὶ ζησέσθε, τὸν θεὸν γὰρ ἐγὼ φοβοῦμαι, "This do ye, and ye shall live; for I fear God." The imperative and future are here employed. The Greek is only second to the English in its capability of imitating the freedom and energy of the Semitic verb. How different is the Mongol—*T'a ber amit'o baihwain t'ola egoni weiladok't'on hemebesu, bi ber Borhan ec'he aiyomoi*, "Ye, for the sake of life, should do this. I fear God." *Ber* is a particle which marks the nominative *t'a*, "ye." *Amit'o* is "living," *t'o* being equivalent to the English suffix *ing* in *living*. *To'la*, "for," governs the infinitive *baihu*, "to have," "to be," in the genitive. *Egoni* is "it," the final *i* marking the accusative. *Weiladok'tʻon* is the plural imperative of *weiledehu*, "to do." *Hemebesu* is the conditional mood of *hemehu*, "to say," here used as a particle. *Bi, ber,* "I." *Borhan*, "Buddha," is the term used for *God* in the Mongol version of the Scriptures. *Aiyomoi* is the present indicative of *aiyohu*, "to fear," governing the noun *Borhan* by the intervention of *ecʻhe*, "from." The Latin *vereor*, "to fear," which is the same word, sometimes governs the genitive. The Greek αἰδέομαι, "to fear," "reverence," "be ashamed," retains the old final *d*, which has been changed into *r* in the Latin *vereor*. The Chinese *wei*, "to fear," and the Mongol *aiyomoi*, have both lost the final *d*.

Beside the verb *buhu*, "be," there are also two important auxiliaries, *baihu*, "have," and *bolhu*, "become," "arrive at perfection." *Bolhu* seems to come from *bolai*, the imperfect of *buhu*, by simply treating it as a root and adding to it the usual suffixes. Thus, *bu* is "be"; *bol* is "arrived at being." In a similar way, *werden*, "to become," seems to be derived from *war, wäre*, by appending *d*, the sign of the past, which would give it the sense "already come into being." To *werd* was added the infinitive suffix *en*, and with it all the suffixes usual in the paradigm. Add to *bol* the causative *ga*, and we have *bolgahu*, "cause to become."

Perhaps *baihu*, "to have," used to assert positive

existence, is formed in a like way from the past tense, *abai*, of *aho*, "to be." But it may also possibly be connected with the Chinese verb *po*, or *pok*, "to hold," "hold in the arms or hands," etc.

On following the substantive verb root in *b* into the pronoun, we find it used in some parts only of the declension. As in English, *I* and *me* combine to make up the declension, so in Mongol *bi* and *minu* form the nominative and genitive singular, while *na*, another root, forms the dative *naded*, the ablative *nadas*, the instrumental *nadar*, the comitative *nadale*, and the substitutionary *nadat'a*.

The root *nad* or *na* I believe to be the Chinese *nga*, in Mandarin *wo*, and to be identical with the western *ego*, *aham*, *ich*, *I*, and the Hebrew *anochi*. The Tamil uses this root throughout its declension, as nominative *nân*, "I," accusative *ennei*, instrumental *ennâl*, dative *enakku*, ablative *ennil*, genitive *en*, locative *ennil*.

The Tungus and Turkish use the root *b* or *m* throughout the declension.

The Mongol plural *bida*, "we," is carried through all the cases. The root *na* does not appear at all in the plural. The suffix *da* occurs also in the plural of nouns not infrequently. The Turkish plural is *biz*, "we," where *z*, we can scarcely doubt, is a changed form of *d*, as we have found the Mongol *j* to be derived regularly from *d*. The same plural occurs in the Hebrew *aboth*, "fathers," from *ab*, "father."

But *t* in the Indo-European languages occurs not seldom for a more recent *s*. The Latin *tu*, "thou," is older than the Greek σύ, as we learn from the fact that the Sanscrit, German, Armenian, Sclavonic, and Zend (Bopp, § 340), all use *d* or *t* as the initial letter of this pronoun. We may, therefore, suppose that the original of the Indo-European plural in *s* is perhaps the Turanian and Semitic *d* and *th*. On looking for its archetype in the Chinese vocabulary, we find it in the word *ta*, "many," in Mandarin *to*, and also in the demonstrative in *t*. The Japanese plural suffix *domo* is possibly the same. Should this hypothesis of the origin of the Indo-European plural in *s* be incorrect, the Mongols still have a plural in *s*, lost from the colloquial language, but retained in books; and of this plural in *s* it may be found difficult to explain the existence in both the families without supposing an ancient connexion.

I will now place in succession those grammatical suffixes, used by the Mongols, which seem to find their prototypes in the Chinese vocabulary, and reappear in the Indo-European system of accidence and derivation.

The old Mongol nominative in *ano*, *ino*, lost from the colloquial, is the Chinese and Indo-European pronoun *i* or *in*, "he," "she," or "it"; Shanghai and Amoy dialects *i*, "he"; Latin *is, ea, id, ille, iste;* English *it;* Persian *o*, "he," *in*, "this," *àn*, "that."

The Persian accusative is *ora*, "him." This *r*, with the Latin *l* in *ille*, seems to be taken from an older Turanian form, which appears in Japanese as *are* and in Turkish as *ol*. The Tamil has masculine *ivan* and *avan*, feminine *ival* and *aval*. As *v* represents *w*, these are only the lengthened forms of the Mongol *ano, ino*. Many Mongol words ending in *n* consist of a root and a pronominal suffix *ino*, shortened into *n*, as *morin*, "horse," from the Chinese *mo*, "horse."

The Mongol book genitive in *in, u,* and *on* may have been formed from the same pronoun, just as the Indo-European genitive in *sya, s, is,* was originally the third personal pronoun *sa* (Bopp, § 134 and § 194). How this took place we see plainly enough in Chinese. Thus, the sentence "My house" in primeval speech would be "I that house." The old Chinese has *nga bung*, "my house," or *nga ti bung*, where *ti* is the old pronoun "that," "it," called in Mandarin *chï*. The natives of Amoy say *Gwa e c'hu*, where *gwa* is "I," *e* is the sign of the possessive, and *c'hu* is "house." In this instance the possessive mark is obviously our pronoun. The Shanghai people say *Ngu ku vang tsz*, literally, "I that house." In that dialect *ku* is "that." The Northern Chinese say *Wo ti fang tsï*. The old initial *ng* is lost from the pronoun "I." The third personal pronoun in *t* appears as a possessive auxiliary, and the soft *v* of Shanghai, representing the more ancient *b*, is replaced by the modern *f*. They also say, when speaking somewhat loosely, *Wo che ko fang tsï,* "I this house," where *che ko* is demonstrative "this," but also contains in itself the germ of a possessive case. Thus, in Chinese dialects the third personal pronouns in *i,* in *k,* and in *t,* are all used. The other demonstratives in *na* and *t'a* may also be expected to occur as genitive suffixes. Thus, the Japanese use *no.* The Turkish has *ning.* The Mongols, as before remarked, use *nu* in the personal pronouns. The German has a possessive *mein,* our own *mine.* The *n* may be explained in the same manner.

The dative suffix *dor, de,* "to," "in," "by," "at," is the Chinese old demonstrative pronoun *ti,* Mandarin *chï,* which is also the probable parent of the gerunds in *ju* and *d,* as explained on a former page. Just so Bopp traces dative suffixes in Indo-European languages to demonstrative pronouns (§ 164). But as *to* and *ti,* in Mandarin *tau* and *chï,* are both words meaning "to," "arrive at," the root *ti,* in its first sense demonstrative, will in its second sense have become a verb, and then, thirdly, it may have been taken by the Mongols to form a dative. So the demonstrative *i* in western languages is also a verb "to go," and then a dative, as in *regi,* "to a king," παιδί, "to a boy."

The accusative suffix in *i, gi,* is formed in a similar manner from the Chinese pronoun *gi,* "he." Compare the accusative *te, thee, me, dich, mich.*

The instrumental suffixes *ber*, *yar*, affixed to nouns to mark the thing by which an act is accomplished, are the Chinese verbs *pa*, "take hold of," "handle," and *i*, 以 "to take." Both these verbs were probably formed from demonstratives. *Pi*, "that," would originate *pa;* and *i*, "he," would give existence to *i*, "take," "by means of." What more natural for primitive man, when already furnished with demonstrative pronouns, than to use them in describing both *motion towards* the positions indicated, and *action with* or *by means of* the objects spoken of. So Bopp identifies the Sanscrit instrumental *â* with the pronominal stem *â* and with the preposition *â*, "to," "into," "reach to," sprung from the same demonstrative. (§ 158.)

The second instrumental, or, as De Castren calls it, comitative case suffix in *loga*, appears to be connected with the Chinese *dung*, "with," in Mandarin *t'ung*, and *lung*, "collect," "meet in one place." The Chinese final *ng* is usually omitted in Mongol. Here *g* seems to have taken its place.

The ablative suffix *e'che* has for its etymological equivalent *se*, which resembles the Chinese 自 *dzi*, "from," in Mandarin *tsï*. The Chinese term also means "self." The prefix *t* is probably not primeval. The old form in all words commencing in *ts* is discovered by dropping *t*. This word thus seems to be the same with the Latin *se*, "self."

The adjective suffix *t'o* is probably the demonstrative in *t* aspirated. Thus *alt'et'o*, "golden," corresponds to the Chinese Mandarin *kin ti*, where *kin* is "gold," and *ti* is the unaspirated demonstrative in *t*, here used as a termination imparting to the substantive "gold" an adjective character. So also the older Chinese *lai che*, "he who comes," is formed of *lai*, "come," and *che*, the unaspirated demonstrative in *t*, pronounced anciently *te*. The Japanese form their adjectives in the same way. Thus, they say for "golden," *kin no*, using the genitive suffix, which, as already explained, is the demonstrative in *n*. Thus, we see the adjective, the present participle, and the possessive pronoun, all proceeding from the same stem, and in the first stages of language-formation indistinguishable from each other. The demonstrative pronouns pervading all the European and Asiatic families of languages may be observed to play just as important a part in the building up of the Turanian grammatical system as they have been shown to do in that of the Indo-European family.

The adjective suffix in *hi* seems to be formed from the Chinese third personal pronoun *gi*. Thus, *dorahi*, "that which is below," English *down*.

The diminutive suffix *hen, han*, attached to adjectives, is probably the Chinese *ngan*, found in the Shanghai dialect in the sense of "a little." Thus, *holahan*, "somewhat distant." The original sense is "an eye," "a small aperture," hence "a very little."

The intensitive *b*, inserted to increase the force of the quality described, as in *c'hab c'hagan*, "exceedingly white," *ab adeli*, "exactly the same," *hab hara*, "very black," is perhaps *bit*, "to add," in Chinese *pei*, "to double," in Anglo-Saxon *botan*, "add," English *both*.

In their declension the pronouns are like the nouns, but there are some differences.

The personal pronouns have an inserted *m* in the dative and accusative of *c'hi*, "you," as in *chimador*, "to you," *chimei*, "you" (objective). This may be the dative *bi*, of *tibi* and *sibi*. As already seen, the Chinese have a verb *pet*, "to give," and *pa*, "to take hold of." These roots formed dative and instrumental suffixes in Latin and Sanscrit. Perhaps this suffixed *m* may, however, be more correctly identified with the demonstrative root *ma*, used interrogatively in Chinese and Hebrew.

The occurrence of the second personal pronoun *t'a*, "you," in Mongol, points to Semitic juxtaposition in ancient times. The existence of a Semitic element in Mongol is not impossible. Compare the Hebrew *rab*, "many," with the Mongol *airiben*, "many." The Hebrew pronoun *atta*, "thou," feminine *at*, has a plural masculine *attem*, and a plural feminine *atten*. The first syllable, *at*, is said to be a demonstrative prefix, and stands for *an*, found in the kindred dialects and in the Egyptian. The principal letter is *t*. In the Indo-European languages it appears as *t*, *d*, and *s*.

In the Mongol and other Tartar languages it is *s* (or *c'h* for *s*) in the singular, and *t* aspirated or *s* in the plural. The Turkish and Manchu prefer *s* in the singular and plural. The Mongol has *t'* in the plural. The same law which softened *t* into *s* in the Greek operated in the neighbour dialect of the Tartars, at some ancient period when the areas of the Greek and Tartar races were contiguous. The vowel *a* of the Mongol plural in *t'a*, "ye," is very suggestive of a connexion with the Greek and Latin neuter plural in *a*, e.g., in *saxa*, "stones," *ea*, "these." The distinction of gender, a Semite peculiarity, was borrowed by the Indo-Europeans subsequently to the time when they became dissociated from the ancestors of the Tartars. The neuter would precede in time the masculine and feminine forms, and this Mongol plural in *a* may be a very old linguistic relic. It is probably the demonstrative pronoun *a*. As the second person in *t* is not found in any part of Europe and Asia, except in the Semite Indo-European and Tartar areas, it need not be regarded as a primeval word, belonging to the world's first language. It may be borrowed from the demonstratives. The true primeval pronoun of the second person is the Chinese *ni* or *nu*, found in Sanscrit, Latin, and English, in the forms *yúyam, vos*, and *ye, you*. Here it is assumed that *n* has been prefixed in Chinese to the original vowel *i*, which I suppose to have been appropriated to the second person. The vowels may be imagined to have been distributed in the following manner.

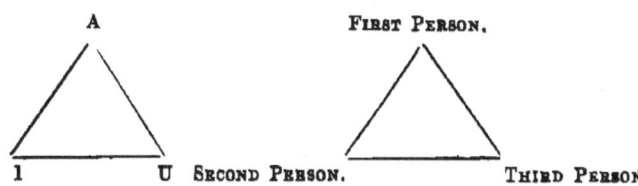

The root of the first person was *a*. This became in Chinese and Sanscrit, by prefixing certain elements, *nga* and *aham*. The Sanscrit-speaking race prefixed first *h* (for *ng*), and then *a*, and afterwards added *m*.

The root of the second person was *i*. The Chinese prefixed *n*. The Sanscrit appended *yam*.

The root of the third person was *u*, which appears in the Chinese *i*, the Turkish *ol*, the old Latin *ollus*, the later *ille*, *is*.

The Chinese use for "this" and "that," *t'sï*, *pi*, or more recently *che*, *na*. The Mongols say *ene*, *t'ere*, "this," "that," and *yim*, *t'im*, "in this way," "in that way." The Germans use the demonstrative in *d* for "this," and that commencing with *ye* for "that." The English in *this* and in *that* employ the sonant *th* Evidently it matters little which of the pronouns is used. The principle running through all is, that some one of the demonstratives shall be used when speaking of near objects, and some other when they are farther removed.

The interrogative pronoun *hen* is worth comparing with the Sanscrit forms. We find *hen*, "who?" *hanasa*, "from whence?" *heden*, "how many?" *hedui*, "how many?" *henedhi*, "whose?" The Sanscrit has *kah*, "who?" *kati*, "how many?" *kadâ*, "when?" *kat'am*, "how?" The Latin has *quot*, "how many?" *quis*, "who?" *quando*, "when?" The Mongol *heje*, "when?" is formed of the root *he* and the locative suffix *je* for *de*.

When the Turks say *kachan* for "when?" and *kach*, for "how many?" they disclose the fact that *ch* takes the place of *d* with them, as *j* does that of *d* in the Mongol. The *ti* in the Sanscrit *kati* and the *t* in the Latin *quot* are the Turanian plural in *d*, and the *do* of *quando* and *dâ* of *kadâ* are the Turanian locative suffix. The adverbial suffixes for time, place, number, and manner, in the Indo-European languages, are vestiges of the old Turanian declension. *Quis* and *kah* are the same word as the Mongol *hen* and the Turkish *kih*. The Chinese demonstrative *gi*, "he," and interrogative *ki* or *kui*, "how many?" are forms of the same root. The oldest is the demonstrative *gi*. From this sprang the Turanian interrogative *hen*, "who?" and the Chinese *ki*, "how many?" This *ki* I suppose to have lost a final *d*, which was the word *ta*, "many," in Mandarin *to*. *Ki-da* became shortened into *kid*, and the *d* was afterwards lost. There is an old interrogative *kop*, "why not?" in

Mandarin *ho*, which is compounded of *ho*, "what," and *pu*, "not." This word, there can be little doubt, has grown up in this way by the running into one of two words originally distinct. The *p* final is retained in the south-eastern dialects, but is lost from the pronunciation of the other parts of China. In Ningpo the deprecative *pu yung*, "do not," is heard *vong*. This is compounded from *veh*, "not," and *yung*, "use." Other examples might be adduced from dialects old and new. When the Pekinese say *pier* for "side," they in so doing run two words into one. The words are *pien*, "side," and *ur*, "a son," used as a suffix for substantives. The suffix loses its tone and becomes part and parcel of the word to which it is joined. Thus the flowing of the two words into one, here claimed as the origin of *kop*, is in harmony with Chinese modern practice. With regard to the assumption that a *d* or *t* has been lost from the word *ki*, I think that any one who carefully examines the characters in which it is used as a phonetic symbol, will conclude that it is so. 禨 *ki*, is "a good omen." Here we see the word *kit*, 吉 "good luck." 幾 *ki*, is "to cut asunder." Here we see *kat*, "to cut." 畿 *ki*, "a boundary," "the emperor's domain." Here appears the same root *kat*, "to cut." That which is cut off receives as its name the name of the action which cuts it off. The word 界 *kiai*, "boundary," has almost certainly the same origin, and has lost *t* in the same manner. It means "that which is cut off." The Hebrew *katsah* signifies both to "cut off" and to "end." The Mongol *hijagar*, "boundary," retains the lost *d* in the modern *j*. The phonetic 幾 having anciently the same final *d*, we may then be allowed to regard as identical with the Chinese *ki* the Mongol *heden*, and the Latin *quot*.

The origin of the Chinese *ki*, "how many?" may thus be seen to resemble that of the German compound *wie viel* and the English *how many*. *Ki, how, wie, quis,* πόσοι, are the same word. The Chinese, Mongol, Latin, and Greek forms added *da* or *ta*, "many," dropping the vowel, and in the instance of the Greek changing *t* into *s*. The Germans appended *viel* (the Greek πολλοί), and the English the word *many*. The source of the interrogative element in the Chinese word is either 其 *gi*, "he," or *ga*, "what," 何, in Mandarin *ch'i* and *ho*. Of these, I suppose the demonstrative to be the earlier, and the interrogative to be formed from it.

The Turkish has *kanda*, "where?" *kim*, "who?" *kih*, "that," "for," "who," *kach*, "how many?" *kachan*, "when?" We learn from these forms that the τε in πότε and the *do* in *quando*, "when," are the Turanian locative suffix *de*, "in" a place. The other Turkish form, *kani*, is probably formed from the root *nip*, *ni*, "in," "the inside," as in the Chinese *wei ti*, "inner land," *kung nei*, "in the palace."

Perhaps the *n* in the English *when*,[1] and German *wann* may have been derived from the same root. The *m* of *kim* may be the Chinese and Semitic interrogative *ma*, "what?" *Kih* reminds us of the Hebrew כִּי *ki*, "for," originally a demonstrative.

While the cardinal numbers in the Mongol are very different from those of China or of the Indo-European languages, there is in the syllabic addition for the ordinals a remarkable resemblance. The Chinese prefixes *de* (Mandarin *ti*). The Mongol adds *dogar*. The Sanscrit adds *tiya*, the Latin *tus*, the Greek τος, the English *th* or *d*, the German *te*. For example, Chinese *de si*, Mongol *durebdogar*, Sanscrit *chaturt'a*, Greek τέταρτος, English *fourth*, German *vierte*. The root of all these forms is the Chinese *de*, "order," "degree," found also in the form *tit*, in Mandarin *chi*, in the same sense. The Mongols say *ded ded yar* for "in succession." A *t* or *d* final has been lost in the ordinal. Since *r*, *l*, and *d* are interchangeable letters, we may expect to find the same root in the form *rod* or *lod*. Compare in Chinese *led*, in Mandarin *lie*, "to arrange," "place in order," the Greek ἀριθμός and ῥυθμός, and the Latin *ordo*, *litera* (though this may be from *lino*, "to smear"), the Russian *roda*, "a class," etc.

The Mongol verb consists of root and suffix. In

---

[1] Compare the Anglo-Saxon form in *an*, as in *niw-an*, "lately," *amidd-an* "amid."—Vernon's Anglo-Saxon Guide, p. 71.

this respect its formation is like that of other Mongol words. They are not compounds consisting of two roots, but of one only, with a servile accompaniment. This servile appendage, however, must originally have been a root having a significance of its own. There was a time in Turanian history when its long suffixes, varying from one syllable in length to four or five, were separate roots, arranged in juxtaposition like the words in Chinese sentences. Before the Dravidian and Japanese branches separated from the Tartar, many verbs had assumed servile appendages, while the right to place roots side by side without servile syllables was still retained. After the separation, the Tartar dialects gave up this privilege, and submitted to the necessity of introducing at least one servile syllable after every verb root, except when used in the imperative mood.

Most of the original roots needed to account for the servile syllables in the Mongol conjugation occur in the Chinese vocabulary. They may be arranged in groups thus :—

1. Words suitable to form past tenses are such as *bat*, "ended," *dzin*, "to end," "exhaust," *ti*, "bring to a standstill," *liau*, "decay," "end," *mot*, "end," *zeng*, "already," *wan*, "finished," *kang*, "pass through," *yi*, "already," *tse*, "past," *ka*, "passed." In Mandarin *pa, tsin, chï, liau, mo, t'seng, wan, king, i, kwo.*

2. Words suitable to be the source of future tense

MONGOL CONJUGATION. 235

suffixes, *yo*, "want," *yok*, "wish," *ngen*, "desire," *pit*, "certainly," *tsiong*, *siong*, "beside," "assist," "lead." In Mandarin *yau, yü, yuen, pi, tsiang, siang*.

3. Words suitable to form a conditional mood, *kip*, "give," *t'si, si*, "give," *shong*, "to reward," *pet*, "give," *u*, "give," *hu*, "permit," *dik*, "hand to," "present," *sung*, "to present," "accompany." In Mandarin *kei, ki, t'si, shang, pei, yü, hü, ti, sung*.

4. Permissive words are *nung, bang, hu, nim*. In Mandarin *jang, p'ing, hü, jen*.

5. Words suitable to form gerunds and present participles, *ti*, old Chinese genitive, also meaning "to," "towards," "him," "it," *gi, t'a, ui*, "he," *nei* or *nip*, "within," *dze*, "at," *le*, "within," *la, gip*, "to," *yu*, "at." In Mandarin *chï, ch'i t'a, i, nei, tsai, li, ki, yü*.

6. Causal words are, *ko*, "call," "cause," "instruct" (Mandarin *kiau*), *shi*, "use," "one who is used or sent," *ling*, "command," "cause."

7. Collectives are, *dzip*, "gather," *dzu*, "collect." Mandarin *tsi, tsü*.

In addition to this large storehouse of Chinese words, adapted to supply the necessities of the verb formation, the ancestors of the Mongols were also able to borrow from the old Turanian and Semitic vocabularies, in those departments where they happened to be fuller than the Chinese.

A Mongol Verb.

INDICATIVE PRESENT. — Book-forms, *abomoi, abon amoi, abonam,* "I take." From the substantive verb *amoi,* the English *am.* The suffix *n* is that of a gerund, and this originates the eastern colloquial *abona.*

FREQUENTATIVE PRESENT.—*Abodag,* "I am constantly taking." Perhaps from the Chinese *dung,* "constantly." Mongol *c'hang.* The Latin frequentative syllable is *ta.*

IMPERFECT.—*Alaba,* "killed." Suffix *ba* either from *pet,* "give," or from *bat,* "ended" (see chapter on Tamil). Another form for the third person is *alaron.* This suffix *ron* can only be derived from some western source. The letter *r* shows that it is not Chinese. It agrees remarkably with the Latin third person plural of the perfect tense, *amaverunt, docuerunt,* and with the third person plural middle voice of the Sanscrit potential and precative modes in *ran.* As the Mongol verb does not distinguish persons, this exceptional form must have crept in irregularly at some ancient period from an Indo-European source.

PERFECT.—*Beriloga,* "have grasped it." From *loga,* a post-position meaning "with," "at," Chinese *la,* Tibetan *la,* Semitic *al, le.*

PLUPERFECT. — *Bagoksan buloge,* "he had come down." From the past participle of *bagoho* and the preterite of *buhu,* "to be."

FUTURE.—The suffixes *sogai*, *ho*, and *ya* may be compared with the Greek future in σω and the Latin in *am*. Looking back, the most probable original roots, as found in Chinese, are *yok* and *tsiong*, "to wish," and "to lead," respectively. The form in *ho* is the infinitive, which is probably formed from the third personal pronoun *gi*.

CONDITIONAL.—Suffix *besu*. In colloquial *bel*. *Gemsibel*, "if I repent." Pluperfect conditional *ogusen bolbesu*, "if I had given," viz., the preterite participle of *oghu*, "to give," and the conditional of *bolhu*, "to become." The origin of this mood is probably to be found in the Chinese *pet*, "give," and *pi*, "compare."

POTENTIAL.—*Idemoija*, "he perhaps eats." *Ujïsen boija*, "he may have seen it." Both these verbs are familiarly used throughout Europe, *edo*, "eat," *video*, "see." *Baga* and *bija* are common in the eastern Mongol. *Ba* and *bi* are the same root *pet*, which forms the conditional. *Ja* for *da* seems to be the root *da*, "give," which perhaps lurks in the Chinese *dik*, "to present," "offer to."

PRECATIVE AND IMPERATIVE.—The simple root. *Songsa*, "hear." In the first person singular and plural the future in *ya* is used, as *yabiya*, "let us go." "Let him go" is *yaboge*. The suffix *ge* may be the Chinese *ngen*, "to desire," or *ho*, "permit."

GERUNDS.—Present in *n*. *Onggac'hi dere garan yababa*, "going out to the boat he went away." The

Greek participle in *v*, the Latin in *ns* and *nt*, the Anglo-Saxon in *nd*, the colloquial English in *n*, and the modern English in *ng*, have their origin in this Turanian form. The Chinese roots which come nearest to it in sound are *yin*, "cause," *yuen*, "cause," *nei* or *nip*, "within." I prefer to regard *yin* as the true root, and identify it with our preposition *in*, *ἐν*.

Gerund in *ju*. Old form *du*. Chinese pronoun and sign of genitive *ti*. In Mandarin *chï*. Identical with the English past tense in *ed*.

Gerund in *d*. Schmidt calls it past, but it is little more a past tense than the gerund in *ju*. Probably it is of the same origin.

Gerund in *man*. A colloquial form. *Bada idemen irebeu*, "after taking food he came."

Gerund in *tala* and *sagara*. Colloquial *sara*. They limit the verb in "time." *Tala* is "until," and *sara*, "during the time of." *Nar onatalei helchibeu*, "he conversed till the sun set." Origin, the Chinese *to* or *tau*. English *to* and *till*. *Sara* probably originates in the Chinese *dze*, "at," "to be in," or "at." Example, *uder uder ireser baina*, "daily he is in the habit of coming."

Gerund in *ltei*. A sort of passive gerund. The future participle passive of western grammar, e.g. *amandus*, "deserving to be loved." Examples, *bicheltei*, "deserving to be written," *icheltei*, "worthy to be gone to," *ene chichig ujeltei*, "this flower is worth seeing."

Formation: the *l* in *bichel* is a derivative suffix, forming a verbal noun. It may be originally *la*, "to." The syllable *tei* is an adjectival suffix, and must be referred to the pronominal root *ta*, "that." The Latin *dus* in *amandus* may in the same way be viewed as demonstrative.

SUPINE in *ra, re*. In Manchu and Latin, *re* is the infinitive suffix. In English the same preposition, "to," marks both the infinitive and the supine. We may, therefore, without hesitation, identify the supine of the Mongol written language with the Manchu and Latin infinitive. The colloquial supine in Eastern Mongolia is the infinitive construct in *hwei*, e.g. *ujihwei ichibeu*, "he went to see."

The INFINITIVE ends in *ho, hu*, and *hwei*. The Turanian conception of the verb being intensely substantive, the infinitive is regularly declined as a noun. Origin: the Chinese pronoun *gi*, Latin *hic*, English *he*. The form varies, as in *ho* or *hu*, according as the vowel of the root is *a, o,* or *e, u*. It may be called the free infinitive. The form in *hwei*, or *hoi*, is the infinitive construct, and is used in declension, and as a supine, e.g. *holda hwen t'ola garaba*, "he is gone out to sell." Here the suffix *t'ola*, "for the sake of," follows the infinitive in the genitive.

PARTICIPLE. A present in *gchi* or *chi*. As *yabokchi*, "going," "he who goes." It is used profusely for all classes of agents. Origin: demonstrative in *s*. In

Chinese *t'sï, sï*. In Sanscrit, *sah*. There is also a past participle in *gsan, san*. For example, *yabasen*, "gone," in the book-form *yabagsan*. Origin: Chinese *zeng*, "already," in Mandarin *t'seng* or *san*, "scatter," "separate." For the negative conjugation there is a form in *l*, as in *holdal ugwei irebeu*, "not having sold it he came," that is, "he came without having sold it." There is also a past negative participle in *ge*, as in *iregedei*, "he has not come."

Mongol Adverb.

In the grammar of the Turanian languages, the verb, substantive, adverb, and conjunction, are imperfectly distinguished. It was in the Indo-European system that adverbs and conjunctions first became indeclinable, and the verb began to lose its character as a noun. It was only by gradual steps that the eight parts of speech could arrive at the point of clear separation from each other. Mongol grammar presents us with a multitude of adverbs and conjunctions in the form of nouns and verbs. Much light is thrown by this part of Turanian accidence on the adverbial forms common in European speech. To show this, the following case suffixes of Mongol adverbs will be a sufficient proof.

Locative suffix *dor*, "in," "at." Eastern colloquial *de*. *Ende*, "here," *tende*, "there." As *ende* is good book Mongol, the colloquial *de* may be fully as old as the ordinary book locative *dor*. Greek οἰκόθι, "at home," ἠῶθι, "in the morning," ἔνθα, "here." English *yonder*.

Suffixes to express motion "towards," *dor* and *de*. In Chinese *tau* and *ti*. Mandarin *chï*. *Ende*, "hither," *t'ende*, "thither," *hande*, "whither." Here the coincidence with the English *ther* is remarkable. The Anglo-Saxon forms are *hider*, *þider*, *hvider*, "hither," "thither," "whither." The old Norse forms are *hëðra*, *þaðra*, *hvert*. The old Greeks used δε, as in ἅλαδε, "to the sea," θάνατόν δε, "to death." In ἐνθάδε, "thither," "hither," we have the locative suffix *dor* in θα, and that of motion towards in δε. In ἄλλοσε, "to another place," a sibilant has taken the place of *d*.

Suffix to express motion from. Mongol *ec'he*, colloquial *ese*. *Hanasa*, "whence," *enese*, "hence," *tendese*, "thence." The book forms are *hamigasa*, "whither?" *t'ende ec'he*, "from thence," *ende ec'he*, "hence." The Manchu has *c'hi* as the suffix for "from," and the Turkish *dan*. English *whence, hence, thence*. Can the English have retained the suffix *ce* by tradition from an old Turanian language? This question is difficult to answer, because the Anglo-Saxon forms were *hvonan, henan, þonan*. It may have been through the Danes, for the old Norse had *hvaðan, heðan, þaðan*, for "whence," "hence," "thence." Latham says,[1] "The *ce* in 'hence,' 'whence,' 'thence,' has still to be satis-

[1] The English Language, vol. ii., p. 320.

factorily explained. The old English is *whenn-es*, *thenn-es*." The old Norse *ʽsan* and Greek θεν being Turanian, may not the English *ce* be inherited from a Danish dialect, which has not transmitted a literature, and thus also be Turanian?

The Turkish locative suffix *dah* is the same as the Mongol *dor*. The Sanscrit *atra*, "here," *tatra*, "there," *kutra*, "there," have nearly the Mongol form. Instead of following Bopp in tracing the origin of the suffix, *tra* to the comparative suffix taken instrumentally, I would suggest that it is better to see in it a Turanian suffix *dor*, as now explained. Compare the Latin *citra*, *intra*, and (without the *r*) *quando*. The Greeks said ἔνθα and ἐνταῦθα, "here," and αὐτόθι, "in the place where he was," the old Hindoos *kadâ*, "when?" *tadâ*, "then," and *yadâ*, "when." The Zend had *had'a*, "here," the Slavish *kogda*, "when?" and *togda*, "then." The Mongol has *heje*, "when," and this is equivalent to *hede*. The Greek has ὅτε, τότε, "when," "then." The suffix in all these forms may perhaps be traced to one origin. It is ultimately a demonstrative and interrogative pronoun, and is the same with the Turanian locative in *dah* and *dor*. With the forms *when, wann, quum,* before us, there seems no reason to look elsewhere. Bopp, however, finds, as he thinks, in the *dâ* of *kadâ*, a contraction from *divâ*, "by day."[1] Perhaps the forms *here, there, dar, thar, her, hvar,* etc., have

[1] Vergleichende Grammatik, § 423.

this source also. The *t* may be omitted and the *r* left. The Sclavonic and Russian *gdye* retains the radical *ga,* "what," in the initial *g,* and the Turanian suffix *dor* in *dye.* The suffix appears in *podŭ,* "under," *mezhdŭ,* "between." The Greek derivative suffix δον, indicating the manner of an action, is probably of the same origin: ἀναφανδόν, " openly," αὐτοσχεδόν, "near at hand." This δον is often δα in Homer, as in Oδ. III. 221.

Οὐ γάρ πω ἴδον ὧδε θεοὺς ἀναφανδὰ φιλεῦντας,
Ὡς κείνῳ ἀναφανδὰ παρίστατο Παλλὰς Ἀθήνη.

"From a place" is so frequently in western languages expressed by *dan,* or equivalent forms, that we are compelled to regard the Turkish ablative suffix in *dan* as in this instance preserving a very important old Turanian type. The Greek πόθεν, "whence," corresponds to the Sanscrit *kútas,* and we may regard the Sanscrit *s* as altered from an older *n*.' The Latin has *cœlitus,* which Bopp identifies with *svargatas,* "from heaven." He also finds in the Sclavonic suffix *du,* "from," the Armenian *ti,* and the Gothic *thro,* variants from the same primary form.

The common ancient suffix for "from," in the Anglo-Saxon and German was *nana* or *nan.* Latham quotes from Grimm the Old High German *hwanana,* Old Saxon *hwanan,* Anglo-Saxon *hwonan,* all meaning " whence." The equivalents for " thence " and " hence " are similarly formed. We find in one of the Dravidian languages an ablative suffix which may explain this *nan*. The Malayalim has *ilninna* for the ablative, as in *mala-y-ilninna*, "from the mountain," where *mala* means "mountain." We have not the opportunity of examining old types of the Turanian family. We must await the decipherment of Persian cuneiform inscriptions for further light on the subject of these remarkable resemblances between the adverbial suffixes of the Turanian and Indo-European languages. The Dravidian case suffixes may perhaps be regarded as having been in use for at least two thousand years, for the Tamil writing is based on the Devanagari of the monuments. Hence the Dravidian languages were the first of the Turanian family to be committed to writing out of Persia. They were written before the Japanese or the Mongol. Any Dravidian case suffixes, therefore, which happen to agree in form with those of European languages, may easily be of very great antiquity.

Some examples of Mongol syntax will be here given with parallel examples from the Chinese language. Adjectives precede their substantives, and adverbs their verbs. Mongol *alt'en gerel*, " golden light," Chinese *kin kwang*; Mongol *saihan yaba*, " walk carefully," Chinese *hau hau er ti tseu;* Mongol *hamt'o echine*, "we will go together," Chinese *t'ung k'ü* or *i k'wai er c'hü*.

The nominative begins a sentence. Then comes the object of the verb. The verb stands last. Mongol *bi teri alaba*, "I killed him," Chinese *wo sha liau t'a*.

The Chinese verb precedes its object. But the Chinese order is not like the Mongol invariable. If an auxiliary particle be employed, the verb may stand last. Thus *pa*, "to take hold of," may be used to vary the order. *Wo pa t'a sha liau*, literally, "I taking him killed finished." This is something like the inaccurate English, "I took and killed him."

Adjectives may stand in the predicate without a substantive verb, and when a comparison is made, they may take a comparative or superlative force without its being necessary to prefix adverbs. Mongol *uge bugdege sain*, "his words are all good," Chinese *hwa tu hau*; Mongol *oseg bugdege t'odorahai*, "the letters are all in their right places," Chinese *tsï tu wen t'o*. The law of arrangement in the two languages is precisely the same. Mongol *hoyer yagomanu dot'ora ene sain*, literally, "two things amidst this good," that is, "of the two things this is the better, Chinese *liang yang tung si che ko hau*, literally, "two kinds things this one good." The comparative force is conveyed in the same manner in both languages, and that by position.

The duplication of words, to give a plural to nouns, and to denote succession in time and place, occurs frequently in Mongol and Chinese. Mongol *nig nigere hamoge ireksen*, "one by one all came," Chinese *yi ko yi ko tu lai liau*. Literally, "one" (numerative), "one" (numerative), "all come finished." The Mongol suffix *ere* or *er* or *yar*, is frequently appended to nouns and adjectives to make adverbs. It is probably the source from which the Latin adverbs in *er*, as *libenter, instanter*, have derived their last syllable. Mongol *c'hag c'hag wei wei*, "time after time," "generation after generation." Chinese *shï shï tai tai*, "age after age," "generation after generation." Compare in Latin *quisquis*, "whosoever."

These and other peculiarities show that a remarkable resemblance exists between the syntax of the Chinese and of the Mongol languages. The Tibetan in placing the adjective after its noun goes away further from the Chinese than does the Mongol. In the conjugation of the verb, and the absence of gender, the Mongol is nearer to the Chinese than the Tibetan, which prefers Semitic analogies. Thus in the order of succession perceptible among verbs when standing in juxtaposition, there is a clear likeness to the Chinese. The order is that of time. Mongol *t'ere haireju ireksen,* "he is come back," Chinese *t'a hwei lai liau*. *T'ere,* "he," is the same word as *t'a* with the suffix *r*. *Hwei,* "return," is the same word as *haireju*, to which *r* was first affixed, and then *ju*, the mark of the gerund. *Lai*, "come," is perhaps the same word as *ireksen*, the past participle of *irehu*, "come," here used as a past indicative.

CHAPTER XI.

MALAYO-POLYNESIAN.—THE MALAY THE TYPE OF A DISTINCT FAMILY. ALPHABET AND SYLLABLE.—POLYNESIAN SYLLABLE BASED ON THE OLD CHINESE SYLLABLE.—EFFECT OF MARINE CLIMATE ON THE MALAYO-POLYNESIAN SYLLABLE.—CONTINENTAL ORIGIN OF THE POLYNESIANS.— CONNEXION OF SIAMESE AND MALAY. — POST-POSITION OF THE ADJECTIVE AND GENITIVE.—PRONOUNS.—CASE PARTICLES. — SEMITIC PRINCIPLES. — CHINESE INFLUENCE ON POLYNESIA.—PRONOUNS.—VERBAL DIRECTIVES.—COMPARISON.—ARITHMETIC.—AMERICAN LANGUAGES.—THEIR MIXED CHARACTER. — THREE ELEMENTS OF AMERICAN POPULATION. — POLYNESIAN CIVILIZED IMMIGRATION.

AT the extreme south-east of the continent of Asia the Malay and Polynesian area presses upon that of the Himalaic races in the peninsula of Malacca, and meets the Chinese in Formosa. The Malaysian and Polynesian system presents to view some remarkable points of resemblance to the Chinese and Himalaic types. It is on this account that a brief chapter on this system is here introduced.

Crawfurd has condemned the opinion of Marsden, Wilhelm von Humboldt, and Sir S. Raffles, that the islands of the Indian Ocean and South Sea, from Madagascar to Easter Island, are peopled by a single race. He remarks that the population of these islands consists of brown men with lank hair (Malay), of sooty men with woolly hair, and of brown men with frizzled hair. The first of these three, the Malay race, extends over the Sandwich, the Fejee, the Society, and the Friendly Islands, with the Malayan peninsula and most of the islands of the Asiatic archipelago.

The Malay language cannot be regarded as Indo-European, because, as F. Müller has shown in a criticism on the view held by Bopp, it forms derivatives by prefixes, and not by suffixes. From *tidor*, "to sleep," is formed, by means of the prefix *per*, the word *per-tidor-an*, "a bed." In the Tagala dialect of the Philippines, from *guntin*, "shears," is formed, by the insertion of *um*, the word *g-um-untin*, "to cut with shears."

Max Müller inclines to regard the Malay as a Turanian language, and as especially allied to the Siamese. But there are some strong objections to this very extended use of the word Turanian. To class the Siamese with the Mongol and Japanese is inconvenient, because it is a monosyllabic language with tones, and like the Chinese places the verb before its object. The word Turanian can be suitably limited to languages which form derivatives by polysyllabic suffixes, make use of case endings, place the verb at the end of the sentence, and have a certain system of rules for the use of vowels.

It is better to regard the Malay as the type of a

separate family, as is done by F. Müller. The agreement between the Malay and the Siamese is indeed remarkable. The adjective follows the substantive, the genitive follows the nominative, and the demonstrative pronoun follows its noun in both languages. The personal pronouns are also alike. But the non-existence of tones in the Malay, its polysyllabic character, and its entirely new series of numerals forbid our classifying it as one with any member of the Himalaic family.

The alphabet of the Malay family is rich in letters, and in this respect resembles the Himalaic, and old Chinese, except in the want of aspirates.

A Dravidian influence is visible in the cerebral series $\underset{.}{t}, \underset{.}{d}, \underset{.}{n}$. The surd series k, t, p, s, is found both in the Malay and in the eastern or Polynesian group, but the sonants g, d, b, of the western branch (the Malay), are wanting in the eastern. There is a resemblance to the triple-branched Turanian system in the use of s and the want of sh, and to the Japanese and Dravidian divisions in the absence of the aspirated forms of k, t, and p.

The simplicity of the Malayo-Polynesian syllable shows the antiquity of the system to which it belongs. The initial consonant is usually single, and is never followed by another consonant, except sometimes by r. An initial sp, st, for example, would be impossible. In the western division of these languages, *k, t, p, ng, n, m* (as in old Chinese), terminate syllables. Also *s*, *h*, *r*, and *l* (which is not true of the old Chinese), are sometimes found at the end of syllables.

The dissyllabic character of the roots in Malay reminds us of the Semitic system. "All monosyllabic roots, with the exception of some pronominal stems and particles, are shortened from dissyllables. All words of more than two syllables have become so by phonal additions to the dissyllabic base."[1]

The possibility of terminating syllables with consonants extends eastward to the Caroline Islands. In the dialect of Ponape, sixty degrees east of Penang, and in nearly the same latitude, syllables are closed by consonants, as in the Malay.[2] In the East India Islands consonants are allowed to close syllables, and the letters used are the same which close syllables in the Turanian and old Chinese systems. The Pólynesian dialects extend south-east from the eastern termination of the Caroline Islands for seventy degrees. Here the syllables are never closed by consonants. The peculiarities in the formation of the syllable in eastern Asia are adhered to in this respect through about half the longitudinal extent of the immense island group, which reaches from Sumatra to Tahiti. Through the Australian dialects the eastern Asiatic system is still

[1] F. Müller, p. 324.

[2] Grammatical Notes on the Language of Ponape, by L. H. Gulick, M.D., Missionary on that island.

adhered to, but the final consonants are limited to *ng*, *n, m, l, r*. Australia then has, by a process of decay, lost the finals *k, t, p*. In the great cone of islands whose apex is twenty degrees east of Tahiti, and whose base is planted in the one case on the mainland of Australia, in the province of Queensland, and in the other on Ponape, in the Caroline Archipelago, the final consonants have all been lost from the syllable. In the East India Islands the finals *k, t, p*, are used in addition to those of Australia, and the resemblance to the eastern Asiatic syllable there becomes complete.

The same contrast exists in this respect between Malaysia and Polynesia as between Mongolia and Japan. The Japanese, living in a soft and luxurious climate, have dropped the final consonants, which in the cold and bracing climate of the Gobi plateau have been retained by their Mongolian cousins. So, also, the Malay syllable bears the same relation to that of Australia that the old Chinese syllable does to the modern. The Malay system admits *k, t, p*, at the end of syllables as well as *ng, n, m;* and this is also true of the old Chinese system still retained in the dialects of Amoy and Canton. The Australian system, like the modern Mandarin of China, at the end of its syllables only allows nasals or the letter *r*.[1]

In view of these facts, it may be concluded that the old Chinese closed syllable, with the finals *k, t, p*,

[1] F. Müller, p. 247.

ng, n, m, lies at the basis of, and was formerly found in, all the languages of Austral-Asia and the South Seas. Further, the additional finals, *l, s,* there existing, are such as occur in the Himalaic and Turanian systems. The want of final consonants in any of the Oceanic dialects may be accounted for by phonetic decay. They may have been simply dropped, or they may have taken vowels after them, and so become initial consonants to supplemental syllables.

In addition to the question of the finals, there is also the question of the initials. Neither the Australian nor the Polynesian dialects have the letters *g, d, b*. Yet they have sounds something like them, which, after careful consideration, the missionaries and others busied in collecting data respecting the native languages usually agree to write *k, t, p*. In the Malay region only do the letters *g, d,* and *b* occur in their full distinctness. The conclusion again seems forced upon us, that secular decay has wrought destruction in the alphabets of the more distant dialects, while the Malay, more recent in the time of its migration from the continent, has better preserved its ancient form. As in China it is only in the old middle dialect that the sonant series of the old language is well retained, so this relic of the primeval language of mankind finds a refuge in the Malay area when abandoned by all the more southern and eastern modes of speech. All this is in full harmony with the view that the Malay, and other Oceanic races of the same sisterhood, proceeded from Asia south-eastward, just as the Chinese (who drove the Miau tribes before them into the mountains of Kweicheu), and other races of Eastern Asia, all show signs of western origin. The Polynesian and Australian alphabets, now predominantly surd, were originally, as it would appear, sonant, but the Malays left the continent with the double series of letters found in Hebrew and old Chinese. It seems premature for F. Müller to say, "So much remains certain, and will never by the most brilliant and most trenchant reasonings be disproved: the Malayo-Polynesians are connected with no Asiatic people."

In the discussion which has been originated by Max Müller's views on the intimate connexion existing between the Siamese and Malay languages,—and in which Pott and F. Müller have placed themselves in opposition to that philologist,—it seems to me that reason is on the side of the Oxford professor. The resemblance is in many respects most marked. Both languages are clear of all trace of the great Turanian inversion, by which the verb is placed at the end of the sentence, and in this they are at one with the Chinese and Semitic systems. Consequently the case-marks are prefixes in Malay, as in the Siamese and its sister dialects of the eastern Himalaic family. Thus, in Malay the order is as in English, *disabrang sungei*, "beyond the river," *buka pintu*, "open the door," *dilantei*, "on the floor" (*diatas*, "upon," *lantei*, "floor").

The absence of the distinction of gender and number in nouns places the Malay in agreement with the Siamese, Chinese, and other monosyllabic languages. Thus, *orang Malayu* is "a Malay man," or "the Malays"; *orang* being "man" or "men," just as in Chinese *ta jen* is "a great man" or "the great men." The same principle underlies the Turanian languages, as in Mongol: *ende nei hwun hô aina* ("here's man all fear"), "the people of this place are all afraid." Here *hwun*, in the written language *k'umun* (Latin *homo*), is plural, though constantly used in the singular. That in such a case the regular plural form ending in *d* is not used is proof that the root without a suffix is, as in Chinese, either plural or singular. So in the Hebrew חָמֵשׁ מֵאוֹת שָׁנָה *Hhamesh meoth shana*, "500 years," *shana* is in the singular, although two plurals exist, viz., *shanoth* and *shanim*. Even in English some nouns are undefined in regard to number, e.g., *fish*, which is singular or plural. But such examples are exceptional.

A remarkable resemblance of the Malay to the Siamese and other Himalaic tongues lies in the postposition of the adjective. This principle characterizes all the Himalaic and Polynesian languages, and goes far to cut them off from any thoroughly intimate connexion with the Chinese and Turanian systems. The Semites placed the adjective after its noun, and they once occupied Persia. Persia is the western neighbour of Tibet. May not this post-position of the adjective have passed from the Semites to the Tibetians, Siamese, Malays, and Polynesians? Or did the Semites, at some date anterior to the Aryan conquest of Persia, borrow this peculiarity from the ancestors of the Polynesians?

In the parallel principle, the post-position of the genitive, the Tebetians have, under Turanian influence as it would seem, gone out of the line. But with this exception, the Semitic, Himalaic, Malay, and Polynesian systems, all agree in placing the genitive after its noun, that is, the possessor after that which is possessed. Thus the same powerful Semite influence which introduced this idiom into European languages has also made itself felt in all the eastern Himalaic languages, and in the Oceanic archipelago eastward to the Sandwich Islands, and south to New Zealand.

Another very strong proof of consanguinity between the Siamese and the Malay is found in the pronouns. The three personal pronouns are in Siamese, *ku, meung, mon*, in Khamti, *kau, mau, man*, in Malay, *ku, mu, na*. The Chinese *nga*, "I," appears in Chinese dialects under the forms *gwa* (Amoy), *ngu, nu* (Kiangsu), *wo* (Mandarin). We are not therefore surprised to find it *nad* in Mongol, *ku* in Siamese, *ego* in Greek and Latin, *ku* in Malay, *natoi* in Australian, *hau* in New Zealand, *wau* in Hawaii.

The Malay pronoun for the second person is *mu*. It is found among the Miau tribes in south-western China in the form *mu*, and among the Li tribes of the Hainan mountains under that of *mow*. The origin of this pronominal form for the second person, which is found only in the eastern Himalaic and Malay area, and does not extend into Polynesia, may be traced with great probability to an honorific use of the third personal pronoun in *m*. This pronoun is found in Siamese under the form *mon*, in Hainan as *pun*, in the Miau dialect as *men*. These forms all mean "he." In the Chinese language, the indefinite pronoun *meu*, "a certain person," is probably the same word. The Chinese and Semitic interrogative pronoun *ma*, "what?" may also be referred perhaps to the same root, for as the relative has often grown out of the interrogative, so the interrogative has quite as frequently grown out of the demonstrative. Thus the order of origin would be in Latin *hic*, *quis?* *qui*, and in English *he*, *who?* *who*.

The Malay pronoun for the third person is *na*. This we may identify with the common Chinese demonstrative *na*, "that," "which?" and with the Siamese demonstratives *ni*, "this," *non*, "that." The Malay demonstrative "this" is *ini*.

This close similarity in the personal pronouns between the Malay and Siamese does not extend to the Polynesian dialects, nor to all those of the Malay area.

The first person in *k* (*ku, ko, ki*) is found indeed in all the Malay dialects, including that of Madagascar. It also prevails in the form *ahau* and *ku* in the Tonga language and that of New Zealand.

The second person in *m* is used in Borneo, Java, and the Philippine Islands, but not in the more distant members of the Malay group; nor is it anywhere employed in Australia or Polynesia. Thus much I gather from the examples collected by Professor F. Müller, p. 342.

The argument from identity in pronouns is much stronger than F. Müller allows. The example he adduces to show that it is of little worth (p. 278), is that of the existence of similar pronouns in the Uralaltai[1] and Indo-European families. But the identity of the pronouns in these two linguistic stems is a strong support to Professor Max Müller's view. In the Tartar and Indo-European families, as has been shown, the striking resemblance noticeable in the pronouns is also found in the substantive verb, in the adverbial case suffixes, in the tense suffixes, in the gerundial and participial forms, in the signs for the plural, and in a large number of common roots. Hence, when the philological inquirer finds the pronouns identical, he may expect to discover other agreements revealing themselves on examination. The

[1] De Castren, the Finnish philologist,' proposed this term for the Tartar, Siberian, Finnish, Esthonian, and Hungarian languages.

existence of a second personal pronoun in *m*, over an area of 25° in longitude and 35° in latitude in south-eastern Asia, is parallel, on a smaller scale, to the existence of the first and second personal pronouns in *m* or *b*, and *t* or *s*, over the Ural-altai and Indo-European area, and affords good ground for expecting that many other fundamental similarities will be found to exist.

The law of position for case particles is similar in the Chinese, Semitic, Siamese, and Malay. Prepositions are used for the purpose of indicating case.

"To a place" is in Chinese *tau, to, tï, chï*, Semitic *la*, Siamese *p'eni*, Malay *datan*, Tibetan *la*, Mongol *de*.

"From a place" is in Chinese *zi, zung*, or *tsï, t'sung*, Semitic *min*, Siamese *de*, Malay *deri*, Turkish *dan*.

"With" is in Chinese *dung, t'ung*, Semitic עִם, *gim* (Latin *cum*), אֵת, *eth* (English *with*. Compare the sense of "with" in "withstand" with the meaning "against," which is the not uncommon force of the Hebrew *eth*). Siamese *kab* (connected with the Chinese *gip*, "to arrive at," "along with"), Malay *dengan*.

"In" is in Chinese *tsai*, and as a suffix, *li, tung, chung*, Semitic *be*, Siamese *mai*, Malay *di* (in some dialects *ri*), Mongol *dot'ora*.

"Towards" is in Chinese *hiang*, and in Malay *ka*.

"By means of" is in Chinese *i, tsiang, tan, yung*, Siamese *dwa*, Malay *ulih, oleh*.

Out of these six instances, there are five in which the Chinese and Malay approach each other, viz., "to," "with," "in," "towards," and "by means of."

There are three instances of agreement of the Malay with the Siamese, "from," "in," and "by means of."

The Chinese initial h is to be regarded as k, and ch as t. The Chinese l often comes from an earlier d. The final ng is commonly lost, and n occasionally.

The paucity of instances in which the Malay and Siamese approach each other in the use of prepositions is probably owing to a want of the means of comparison. Jones's "Grammatical Notices of the Siamese Language" is very brief, and contains few words.[1]

The influence of the Semitic family extends, in regard to laws of position, into Malay and the Oceanic dialects to the eastward of the Malay Archipelago, but in regard to roots it seems to stop with Tibet. So the Mongols have some Semitic principles, as the plural in d, but very few Semitic words.

In addition to the post-position of the adjective and the genitive in Malay, that of the demonstrative pronoun constitutes another striking feature. This recalls the favourite Hebrew idiom, which places the demonstrative with the article after the noun, e.g., *hammakom hahu*, "that place." The article *ha* is here prefixed to *makom*, "place," and to *hu*, "he." The Malays say, *Pikulkan peti ini*, "carry that box." *Kan* is the tran-

[1] Pallegoix' works are copious, but I have not access to them in Peking.

sitive or causative suffix to the verb *pikul*, "carry." *Ini* is the demonstrative pronoun "that." This idiom is in both languages only a particular case of the postposition of the adjective. The repetition of the article in Hebrew indicates that the order of the words is in such cases not the natural one. For, otherwise, why is the article repeated? It may, then, be concluded that in the order of nature the adjective precedes its substantive; and when the converse takes place, there is an inversion of the natural order.

The Semitic principles occurring in the Malay tongue have been adverted to, while its resemblance to the Siamese has been more fully described. I shall now illustrate the connexion of the Polynesian family with Chinese, making use of the dialect of Ponape, in the Caroline group, as described by Dr. Gulick.

The gender of nouns is distinguished by the use of special words attached to the nouns. In Chinese these words stand first. In Polynesia they come after.

In regard to the number of nouns, it is in Chinese and the Polynesian languages known from the context, *e.g.*, by that of the accompanying pronoun.

In the Ponape dialect certain numerative particles are used with nouns. Thus, *men* follows animated objects, *tun* is used with bunches of fruit, *um* with yams and bananas, *pot* with plants, sticks, and canoes. The same principle exists in Chinese and in Siamese.

Thus, the Siamese say, *luk reü sang k'on*, "two boatmen." Here *sang*, "two," is the Chinese *shwang*, "a pair." *K'on* is the numerative for "men." *Luk reü* is "boatmen." *Reü* is "boat." This in Chinese would be *shui sheu liang ko*, "water hands two." In the combination *liang ko*, "two," *ko* is the numerative of "men," *shui sheu* is "sailors."

The numerative is necessary after numerals by a common linguistic law. The law of position is, however, somewhat different in the examples. The Chinese say "water hands," and place the specific term before the generic. The Siamese and Polynesians prefer to say "men of the boat." In English we can speak in either way, but the order of nature is to place the specific word first, and there is something artificial about the inversion. When we say "sea birds," we adopt a mode of speech in genuine accordance with the spirit of our language. "Birds of the sea," on the other hand, is an expression belonging to a borrowed poetical vocabulary which is ultimately Semitic.

The Polynesian languages have a double series of some pronouns. When in addressing a person the speaker includes himself with the person addressed under one pronominal designation, it is called the inclusive pronoun. The Ponape dialect has a dual pronoun *kita*, "we," which is inclusive. So in northern Chinese *tsa-men*, "we," is distinguished from *wo-men*, "we," by the circumstance that *tsa-men* includes the person addressed, while *wo-men* does not. The origin of this inclusive pronoun for the first person is in Chinese probably the reflexive *tsï*, in old Chinese *zi*, and in Latin *se*. The Chinese write it 咱 *tsa*. This form is compounded of *keu*, "mouth," (referring to its being a common locution), and *tsï*, "self," indicating that the makers of this modern logograph felt that this was the etymology of the word. We may suppose *kita* to be the other Chinese reflexive pronoun *ki*. The Chinese of books has no inclusive pronoun, as distinct from the ordinary personal pronoun, but it may have existed in an ancient unwritten colloquial, and may have descended to the Polynesians from a common source.

The Polynesian personal pronouns agree nearly with those of China. Of the first I have already spoken. The second is in Hawaii *oe*, in Tonga *koe*, in Ponape *kowe*, in New Zealand *koe*. These I take to be the Chinese *ni*, "thou," "you." Old Chinese has 汝 *nu* and 爾 *ngi*, and the initial *ng* is easily interchangeable with *k* and *g*, as in the Turkish *ugli*, "son," Chinese *ngi*, Mongol *k'u*, "begun." Hence the Polynesian form in *k* is accounted for. But *ng* as an initial is often dropped, as in the Chinese *wo*, "I," from *ngo*, the Hebrew Ayin from an original *ng* or *g*, etc. Thus the Hawaian *oe*, "thou," is also explained. With regard to the third personal pronoun, *i*, *ya*, and *na*, are the prevailing forms. They agree with the Chinese *i*, "he," "that," and *na*, "that."

We find, therefore, the European pronouns *Ego, ich, vos, you, is, ille*, existing, not only in China, but also in the most remote Polynesian languages, at a distance from England of half the circumference of the globe, and yet capable of recognition with the help of the connecting link supplied by the old Chinese.

The verbal directives in the Ponape dialect are another example of strong Chinese influence. F. Müller has not mentioned them in his otherwise full and valuable notices of Polynesian grammar. Nor are they referred to in Jones's "Notices of Siamese." It seems to me that they must exist in all the Polynesian dialects, as in that of Ponape. We have them in English in such expressions as *go up, go down, go in, go out*, where they are adverbs following verbs, and limiting the direction of the action in space. Hence the name verbal directives. In Chinese they are verbs in apposition. *Tso hia* is "sit down." *Tso hia lai* is also to "sit down," and consists of three verbs in apposition arranged in the order of time, thus "sit-down-come." Take another example, *tseu tsin lai*, "walk in," or "he walks in," literally, "walk-enter-come." Here the law of arrangement according to time is manifest. We may expect, then, to find verbs in all the English adverbs which are connected with verbs in this way. Thus "through," in the expression "go through," in German *durch*, is in Chinese *t'ok* or *t'eu*, "to pierce through." The Chinese say of a soaking rain that it has *hia t'eu liau*, "fallen thoroughly." Here *t'eu* means that it has penetrated the soil to the full depth required by the farmer.

We find in the Ponape dialect the following prepositions and adverbs used as space directives after verbs. *La*, "from," *ta*, "upwards," *to*, "downwards," *we*, "away from," *i*, "going off," *long*, "in," *ung*, "to," *jung*, "from," *pena*, "together," *pajung*, "separate." Thus *wa la*, "take from," *tau ta*, "climb up," *ko ti*, "come down," *ko to*, "come hither," *ko long*, "go in," *ko we*, "go away," *ko ung*, "go to," *ko jung*, "go from," *ko pena*, "go together," *ko pajung*, "go separate."

Among these words may be noticed the Chinese *zung* or *ts'ung*, "from." The initial *j* is pronounced in Ponape like *dj* or *sh*, and is hard to write down. The word *to*, "down," is the Chinese *toi*, *te*, or *ti*, the Mongol *dotai*, "downwards," and the English "down." The Chinese *shang*, "above," "up," is not improbably the Ponape *ta*, "upwards," for in Cochin-Chinese *t* is the common equivalent of the Chinese *sh*. Thus in Morrone's Lexicon Cochin-Sinense the Chinese sound *shing* is detected in *thua*, "to conquer," "to remain over," "to abound." The Chinese *k'e shang*, "travelling merchants," is the basis of the disguised *kach thua*, having the same sense. Now we may naturally expect to find that in a matter of this kind, what is true of the eastern Himalaic languages will be true of Polynesian languages. They will bear a similar relation to the Chinese.

I may add that among the verb auxiliaries in the Ponape dialect is the causative prefix *ka, kau,* or *ko,* which corresponds with the Chinese *ko* or *kiau,* "to cause," used commonly as a causative in modern dialects, and identical probably with the Latin *causa.*

Such clear marks of consanguinity between the Chinese and Polynesian languages must be taken as proof, in opposition to F. Müller, that there is no room to doubt their coming from one source.

The laws of position and a common vocabulary connect the speech of the Pacific islanders with that of Siam, Cochin-China, and China. Where the law of position in the Himalaic type differs from that of China, Polynesia connects herself with Himalaya, and here, as it appears to me, is seen the action of a Semitic principle.

It is worthy of remark that the Hebrew mode of comparing by the use of the preposition "from," *min,* is parallel to that of Ponape. In the Hebrew מָתוֹק מִדְּבַשׁ "sweeter than honey," מִן *min,* "from," is inserted after *mathok,* "sweet." The Ponapean says, *met kajalel jung meteu,* "this beautiful from that," in correct English, "this is more beautiful than that." The same idiom is found in the Tartar languages, as in colloquial Mongol *enese sain,* "better than this," or literally, "this from good." Here the preposition becomes a post-position by the Turanian inversion, and *sain,* "is good," stands last as being the predicate. There appears to be little ground for doubting that the Semitic idiom is the older, and that both the Turanian and Polynesian have sprung from it. So also our English comparative degree, formed with *than,* must be referred to the same origin. This little word, which has long gone seeking in vain for a plausible parentage, is no other than the Turkish suffix *dan,* "from." Latham says, "*than* is a variety of *then;* the notions of order, sequence, and comparison being allied." If so, then the final *n* of both words is probably the Turkish post-position *ni* in *kani,* "where." This means "in," "within," "at," and is like the Chinese *nei, nip,* "within," as before remarked. It may have been originally a demonstrative pronoun.

So the English *as,* German *als,* and Greek ὡς, are perhaps the Mongol *ese,* which means "from" and "than." The Turanian form is *asa* or *ese,* according as the vowel in the noun is in the series *a, o, ö,* or in the series *e, u, ü.* In Sanscrit the root appears as the demonstrative *sa,* without the prefix. In Chinese it is demonstrative *tsi, si,* reflexive *dzi,* or prepositional *dzi,* "from." Here also it is without the prefixed vowel. In Latin the reflexive *se* also occurs without the vowel. The Turanian influence has been strong upon the Teutonic and Gothic portion of the Indo-European family, and has left its trace in the vowel initial of *as* and *als*. The English *z* in *as* agrees with the old Chinese *zi*. The written Anglo-Saxon was *swa*. Anything nearer to it I cannot find in Vernon's Guide. The unwritten dialects, if known, would throw light on the form. There can be little doubt that the Persian *ez*, "from," is the same word. We have then the sonant form *z* in English, Persian, and old Chinese, and the surd *s* in German and Mongol. The modern Chinese form is *tsï*. It appears then that in the comparison of adjectives the Ponapean dialect follows very widely spread continental models.

So far from being a savage race originally, the Ponapeans, as their language shows, are an offshoot from the continent. In addition to the above instances of linguistic connexion with Asia, which might be easily increased by comparing, for instance, the demonstrative pronoun *en*, "this," with the Mongol *ene*, "this," it may be added that the Ponapeans count to ten, but beyond that number they become bewildered. Thus, *ngavi* is with them "ten of yams," but "one hundred of eggs or cocoa-nuts"; *apuki*, "one hundred," (the Chinese *pak*) is "one hundred of men, trees, or yams," but "1,000 of eggs, cocoa-nuts, or stones." After centuries of isolation, Oceanic islanders lose the command of high numbers, and their value fluctuates or becomes lower in value. Thus, the Chinese *man* (*wan*), "10,000," retains its value among the natives of Samoa and Tonga, but when it reaches the Sandwich Islands it has already sunk to the value "4000," and in New Zealand it means "1000."[1]

F. Müller, after comparing the names of number from one to ten of the Malay and Polynesian languages, says, "From the comparison of the foregoing names of number, we plainly see that, widely as the languages which use them are separated from each other, they branched off at a time when the speakers could count at least to a hundred. This is certainly a proof of the not limited intellectual gifts and early development of these peoples." (Page 287.)

I would go a step further, and say that this fact, regarding the numbers 100 and 10,000, proves deterioration. The Polynesians could formerly use a decimal arithmetic. Whether they have adopted a quaternary or quinary arithmetic, it is probably on account of long-continued isolation, which tends to produce barbarism. The Australian tribes have already exhausted the arithmetical faculty when they have arrived at four and five. The word *kauwul-kauwul* means with them either "five" or "very many." With another

---

[1] Samoa and Tonga lie between the Sandwich Islands and New Zealand, and, if the migration of the Polynesian islanders proceeded regularly by way of the Malayan archipelago, would be populated much sooner than those two more remote localities. In F. Müller's triple grouping of the languages, as the Malay, Polynesian, and Black-race groups, the islands mentioned all belong to the second.

tribe *punku*, "four," is also "many," and *punku kalan*, "five," is "very many." Their ancestors when they left Asia could probably all count to ten. Are not the ten fingers the proper foundation of arithmetic? All human races would still practise it but for the degrading effects of long-continued isolation.

Where the arithmetical faculty is weak, the names of number easily and rapidly change. The multiplication table would be soon lost to civilization if left in the hands of the dunces. It is the bright in intellect that preserve society from lapsing into barbarism, for they transmit to coming generations the treasured discoveries of the past. Among Oceanic islanders degradation is inevitable until they are visited by the light of Christian civilization.

But easy as it is to lose the names of number, and especially those of high numbers, it is not likely that the traces of ancient knowledge will entirely disappear. Vestiges wanting in one island will be found to exist in another, and a wide recension may be expected to restore, piece by piece, the image of the buried past.

The languages of the American continent form a portion of the field to be investigated before the position and relations of the Polynesian system can be accurately determined. As Turanian languages border on North America at Behring's Strait, so the Polynesian dialects approach both North and South America by the ocean. In the valuable collection of

Lord's Prayers in more than 600 languages and dialects, published by the Imperial Printing Office at Vienna, I have searched for dialects which by their syntax might be recognized as exclusively Turanian or exclusively Polynesian. None occur. The principles of arrangement are so mixed and so evenly balanced that the principles of both families seem to be everywhere in operation. For example, in the Delaware language, alluded to in Cooper's romance, "The Last of the Mohicans," while it has case suffixes and the genitive before the nominative (Turanian), it has, on the other hand, the verb before the accusative and makes use of many prepositions (Polynesian). In the language of the Dacotahs, between the Mississippi and the Rocky Mountains, prefixes (Polynesian) predominate over suffixes (Turanian).

Among the Central American languages the Mexican is important. In *no cal*, " my house," *i cal*, " his house," the order is Chinese and Turanian, as are the roots. In the Sandwich Islands, and other parts of Polynesia, *hale* means " house " also, but there the possessive pronoun must follow its word. In Nicaragua the adjective rigidly follows its noun, which is a decidedly Polynesian feature.

The language of the Incas in Peru, in having the adjective after the substantive, is Polynesian, but in having case suffixes and the verb at the end, is Turanian. Thus, they said *Mango Capac*, while we should say in English *King Mango;* and *nocaicuman*, "to us," where *man* is "to," and is the dative case suffix.

In the language of the Caribs, whom the discoverer of the American continent found in the West India Islands, there are case suffixes, and the verb precedes the accusative. They distinguish the elder and younger brother by different words, as is done in all the Polynesian and Turanian languages. Their speech is classed with the South American division of Indian languages.

We are warranted by these linguistic data in concluding that there was a Polynesian immigration from the ocean, and a Turanian immigration by the Aleutian Islands, and by Iceland and Greenland, which united to form the population of the American continent. The influx of ocean tribes would be favoured by the former existence of extensive lands in the Pacific, now submerged. Chinese tradition speaks of a chain of large kingdoms stretching from Japan to California, through which Buddhism was zealously propagated. These notices, belonging to the fifth century of our era, should not be forgotten, though it is not safe to build much upon them.

The Polynesian element was the more civilized, and to this must be attributed the main influence in the production of the civilization of the Aztecs and Incas. The Turanian element was the more simple, and to this may be ascribed the doctrine of the Great Spirit, and the other religious views of the less civilized tribes of North America. The Polynesian element prevailed most on the western shores of the continent. The forms of science and art, national polity and belief, found there by the Spaniards, agree best with those of Southern Asia. The Turanian mould of thought and belief extended itself rather along the northern and eastern portions of the continent, and exists among the Siberian tribes in a similar way. The modern Polynesians residing on a thousand isolated points scattered over the ocean, have lost the civilization they once possessed, and have not been able, on account of their insular position, to advance in the intellectual sphere, as did the Aztecs and Incas, but their religious and mythological traditions point to India and Western Asia as their source. The tradition of a deluge and an ark follows the line of Semitic principles of language through the mountain homes of the Karens to the ocean, and proceeds by the Sandwich and other islands in the Pacific to Mexico. The belief in the divinity of serpents exists in the Fiji Islands, as it formerly did in the land of Montezuma. This is both Hindu and Babylonian, and seems to have sprung out of the narrative of the Fall in the Book of Genesis. Cycles in time terminated by a catastrophe are almost necessarily to be regarded as of Hindu or Chaldean origin. The Mexican belief in the Age of the Earth (corresponding to the Satyayuga of Hindostan, and extending to 5206 years), of Fire, of Tempests, of Water, and of the present Age,[1] may be best traced to India and Babylon. Mr. Hardwick says in regard to the American traditions of the Deluge, "So numerous, and so extremely arbitrary, are the points in which those legends are now found to have approached the sacred story, that some affinity between the two is generally recognized, except where an archæologist or schoolman is incorrigibly blinded by his love of system-building. Even the divines of Germany, beneath whose shadow every kind of mythic theory has sprung up with rank luxuriance, seem to have been almost reconciled to a belief that the traditions now and formerly current in America respecting some great deluge must have all been carried over from the old Continent."

As the proof from language proceeds side by side with that from historical and religious tradition, we are driven to the conclusion that the Polynesian and American races are Post-Diluvian, and of the same ancestry with ourselves. "Ought we not," says[1] A. von Humboldt, "to recognize the traces of a common origin wherever the cosmological ideas and first traditions of peoples offer striking analogies even in unimportant matters?"

[1] Hardwick's Christ and other Masters, part iii., p. 160.
[1] Hardwick cites this passage in p. 164 from "Vues des Cordillères."

CHAPTER XII.

THE SANSCRIT LANGUAGE. — SANSCRIT RICHNESS IN FORMS. — ITS PRINCIPLES OF DEVELOPMENT BASED ON OLDER SYSTEMS. — ALPHABET.—SYLLABLE.—PREFIX OF *S.*—INSERTION OF *R* AND *L.*— POLYSYLLABIC WORD.—DECLENSION.—CASE SUFFIXES.—PLURAL. —GENDER.—COMPARISON OF ADJECTIVES.—PRONOUNS.—DERIVATIVE VERBS.—PERSONAL ENDINGS.—TENSE MARKS.—POTENTIAL AND CONDITIONAL MOOD.—INFINITIVE.—PARTICIPLE.—AUXILIARY VERBS.—ADVERBIAL SUFFIXES.—PREPOSITIONS.—COMPOUNDS.—LAWS OF POSITION.—ZEND SYNTAX.

IN passing to the Indo-European languages, the Sanscrit first claims attention. The remarkable completeness of its grammatical forms has attracted the admiration of philologists. The same analytical genius which aided Panini in the arrangement of Indian grammar, many centuries after it attained its perfection as a language, aided his forefathers unconsciously in its gradual formation. The peculiar intellectual attributes of a nation are first recognized in the germ in their language, and afterwards in the fruit in their literature. Languages are rich, noble, and worthy of study in close proportion to the political and literary development of the people that speak them. The merit of Sanscrit consists in its richness in forms, and its orderly development.

The origin of the peculiar principles of the Sanscrit grammar must be looked for in the families of language which existed previously. Such signs of Semitic influence as appear in Sanscrit may be due to an ancient residence in Armenia, or somewhere in that region, when they were neighbours to the Semites. The traditions of Sanscrit and Zend literature point to an old national home in Bucharia. Here the tribes that spoke these languages were in proximity to Turanian races, and on the south with the occupants of Persia and Affghanistan, at that time probably speaking a Semite language. But as there was an ancient Turanian occupation of Asia Minor, the original Sanscrit type would also easily gather Turanian elements during a possible older residence west of the Caspian.

Alphabet.

The peculiar double development of the t series may be ascribed to Dravidian influence. The dental series, t, t', d, d', n, is that which Sanscrit has in common with western languages and those of Eastern Asia. The cerebral series, $ṭ$, $ṭ'$, $ḍ$, $ḍ'$, $ṇ$, links the Sanscrit with the Tamil and its sister-dialects. Let it be considered that in the Tamil there are a dental, a palatal, and a cerebral n, and a dental, palatal, and cerebral r; that there are three t sounds, and two l sounds. As these varieties do not exist north of the

Himalaya mountains, they may be supposed to be due partly to climate, and to have existed already in Dravidian languages before the speakers of Sanscrit entered the Indian peninsula.

The aspirated *k, t, p, ch*, may be traced to a Tartar origin. These letters in Mongol, Manchu, and Turkish are always aspirated. It is in that part of the world the normal way of pronouncing them. An unaspirated *t* would there be counted as *d*. Thus, in Manchu writing a dot on the right changes an aspirated *k* into *g*.

The aspirated series, *gh, dh, bh, jh*, has perhaps been originated by the Hindoos, from an unconscious tendency to make the sonants as complete as the surds.

The unaspirated surd series, *k, t, p, ch*, seems to have been formed by the common ancestors of the Indo-European languages from the older series, *g, d, b*.

The Mongol *gar*, "hand," is in Sanscrit *kara*, and in Greek χείρ. Thus Grimm's law is the Indo-European expression of a wider law embracing all the Asiatic families, by which unaspirated and aspirated surds are both formed from an older sonant series existing in Turanian, Semitic, and old Chinese.

No family has ever been so creative in politics, in literature, in the arts, and in language, as the Indo-European. It was suitable that they should start on their wonderful career with a more perfect alphabet than had hitherto satisfied the wants of nations. The

Turanian alphabet was deficient in surd sounds. The Indo-Europeans developed them by the exercise of a powerful instinct, and thus succeeded in so widening the bounds of the alphabet as to adapt it for embracing the vast variety of new grammatical forms, and new names of things and actions, which Sanscrit, Greek, Latin, German, and English require. In this they appear to have been assisted by the Semites, who at a very ancient period added *k*, *p*, and *t* to the still older *b*, *g*, and *d*. The Semites, however, never arrived at the evolution of so copious an alphabet as their younger brothers, the descendants of Japheth.

The Sanscrit *ch* corresponds to the Chinese *k*. In the Indo-European languages generally *k* has shown a tendency to change into *ch*. In Italian *Cicero* became *Chichero*. In English κυριακή, or *kirche*, became *church*. In Russian *castus*, "pure," is *chisto*. This law of change, belonging to all the languages, must have commenced before the separation into dialects. It does not affect the eastern Asiatic languages. Very recently, however, it has made its appearance in Chinese. Thus, in Northern and Western China *king*, "to honour," is now pronounced *ching*. The law of change which usually corresponds in Eastern Asia to that of *k* to *ch* in Europe, is that of *t* to *ch*. This exists alike in Chinese and in the Turanian languages.

Example. *Chitra*, "paint," "wonder," Chinese *hwei*, *git*, "paint," *k'i*, *gi*, "to wonder," *kwai*, *kat*, "strange."

The Sanscrit *v* corresponds to the Chinese *w*. In Chinese, for instance, 圍 *wei, wat*, is " to place round," "inclose." The round covering of a cart, a tent, a curtain, and a low circumscribing wall, are called *wei*. The Tamil has *vaṭṭam*, "circle," "revolution in an orbit," "halo." The Sanscrit has *vaḍ*, "surround," *vaḍa*, "circle"; Latin *verto*, "turn," *volvo*, "revolve."

The consonant *f*, wanting in Sanscrit, was probably also unknown to the old Turanian language, on which it was based, for it is not found in Mongol, or in the old Chinese.

The Syllable.

The inherency of *a* in all consonants having no other vowel mark coming after them means that the Sanscrit-speaking people lost the habit of ending a syllable with a consonant. There need be no hesitation on this account in ascribing to the mother-tongue of the Indo-European family a syllabary of which one characteristic was the possession of final consonants. The Sanscrit roots are represented by the Indian grammarians as ending in many instances with consonants. Also many syllables actually end with the consonants *n, m, t, d, k, r*, etc. Hence the law of Sanscrit grammar here referred to is not strictly true. It is certain, however, that the tendency of ancient Hindoo pronunciation was towards vowel endings, just as is found to be the case with the Japanese syllabary as compared with the Mongol. This may be due to the enervation consequent on change to a warmer climate. The Greeks and Latins had much fewer consonantal endings than the English and Germans now use.

The Semites and Turanians agreed in introducing *r, l, s*, among the final consonants of their syllabaries. They were followed by the speakers of Sanscrit. When words belonging to these languages are compared with the Chinese roots, such finals seem to be phonetic additions rather than changed finals. The Chinese *he*, "black," in the old language *kek*, appears in Sanscrit as *kâla* and *kâka*, and in Mongol as *hara* or *k'ara*. The *l* and *r* are here introduced in place of a lost *k*. But it would be improper to say that *k* had become metamorphosed into either of these letters. With *t* and *d* final the case is different. These letters have a natural affinity for *r* and *l*, and interchange is not uncommon. Thus, the Cochin-Chinese *dat*, "earth," suggests that there was once an appendage consisting of *t* or *d* to the Chinese 地 *ti*, in the old language *da*. The Sanscrit form is *dhara* and the Latin *terra*. The Hebrew *arets* and the English *earth* seem to be connected by a change from *d* to *r*, and the prefixing of the vowel *a*. The *r* of the Sanscrit and Latin forms may be changed from the old final *d* or *t*.

That the connexion between the Chinese syllable and the Indo-European syllable is to be brought to light through intermediate Turanian links cannot be doubted, when it is observed that these final *r*'s and *l*'s, coming in place of the Chinese *t*, occur not infrequently in Indo-European and Tartar languages. Chinese *sat*, "scatter," "sow," Mongol *sargigolhu*, "scatter," Latin *sero*, "sow," Tamil *sidaru*, "scatter."

One of the most striking differences observable between the Sanscrit and Mongol syllable is the prefixing of *s* to other consonants in the former. As this is a permanent feature in all the Indo-European languages, it must have originated before their separation. It was probably an intensitive. The Semitic roots which appear to have received *s* or *sh* as a prefix modify their sense so as to be in harmony with the idea that the sibilant was intensitive. East of the Sanscrit and Persian there are absolutely no examples of an *s* prefixed to the root. In comparing western words, it is necessary, therefore, to strip them first of this appendage. Thus, *stand*, *sto*, ἵστημι, in Sanscrit *st'al*, "to stand," *st'âna*, "a place," "situation," may be be referred to the Chinese equivalent by removing *s*. The final *t* of the Chinese word 翯 *dat*, "to tread upon," is found in the Sanscrit *st'ita*, "steady," and in the English *stead*, *steady*. The Arabic has *dâsa*, "tread," and the Hebrew *nathan*, "to place," where the *n* does not seem to be radical. Compare in Tamil *tandu*, *tâl*, "stand," Tibetan *ten*, "to halt." The root *tat* or *dad*, *tan* or *dan*, is probably imitated from the natural sound of the foot striking the ground.

Another example is 觸 c'hu, old form tok, "to pierce," stechen, stick, stigo, stingo, sting, στίζω, Anglo-Saxon stechen, "to stick in," sticcels, German stachel, English stickle. The Sanscrit is stak.[1]

A change of almost equal importance, as adding greatly to the number of syllables, was the introduction of r and l between the initial consonant and the vowel. Thus, krit, "to cut," krishna, "black," kri, "to do," in Mongol hadahu, "to reap," hara, "black," hihu, "to do." Compare cut, culter, cædo, Hebrew gadang, גָּדַע and קָטַף, Tamil katti, "knife," and for kri, "do," the Chinese hing, old form gang, "to do," "to go," recollecting that the loss of final ng is a common circumstance in Chinese words.

As an example of the insertion of l may be mentioned kapála, "skull," also karpara, Latin calva, Sclavonic glava and golova, "head," German Kopf, Haupt, "head." We have dropped the p in our word head, but the German restores it to view. Greek κεφαλή, Latin caput. The Chinese is 甲 kap, "head of a series," "shell of a tortoise," "coat of mail," "a cover," "to

---

[1] Compare σμύρνα, myrrh, darben, "starve," nose, sneeze, pike, spike, as examples where the prefix of s has been so recent that it exists in some languages and is wanting in others. Observe also that sh is prefixed in Sanscrit and German, while English, Latin, and Greek refuse to admit it. Schmerzen, smart, Schmidt, smith. Compare amarus, "bitter," müde, "toil."

cover." In this last sense the Sanscrit has *kub* and *kubh*, "to cover," which may be compared with the Greek κρύπτω, "hide," and καλύπτω, "cover." In Mongol we find *hobc'his*, "clothing," and *habhan*, "a covering." The Hebrew has כָּפַר, "he covered," "expiated," and the Arabic *ghufran*, "pardon," *ghayb*, "hidden."

The occurrence of καλύπτω with a vowel preceding the inserted *l* shows how the syllabary may acquire a new extension. The monosyllabic root thus becomes dissyllabic without either prefix or suffix. Instances, however, of this sort of extension among European roots are comparatively rare.

Another mode of extending the primitive syllable is to insert *r* and *l* before the final consonant, as in *karpara*, "the skull," from the root *kap*; *kart*, "to cut," from the root *cut*. Compare the English *work* with the Latin *ago, actus*.

The Polysyllabic Word.

The monosyllable needed to be lengthened and endowed with a more perfect and beautiful form. Just as among the works of the Creator are found first ferns and mosses, and afterwards grasses and trees and all the rich variety of flowering plants, so the plain and unattractive words of the most ancient men were destined to expand into the ever-changing abundance and beauty of the Indo-European vocabulary.

FORMATION OF THE POLYSYLLABLE. 283

With the expansion of the monosyllabic root into a polysyllable by prefixes, suffixes, and inserted letters, the subject of derivation is inseparably connected. Take an example from the Sanscrit vocabulary.

The old English *quoth* is in Sanscrit *kat'*, "to speak." From this is formed *kat'aka*, "a speaker," by appending a demonstrative pronoun *ka*, the English *he*, and the Chinese *gi*, "he," *ku*, "that." The Chinese *hwa*, "words," "to speak," is the same word, the old form being *gat*. In Mongol *helhu*, "to speak," takes *c'hi* in place of *hu*, to express the agent. In *helchi*, "the speaker," or "he who speaks," the syllable *c'hi* is also a demonstrative, the Chinese *t'sï*, "this," and the Sanscrit *sa*, "he."

Another suffix which presents itself is *n*, as in *kat'ana*, "saying," a neuter noun. In Mongol we have *helen*, occurring as one of those substantive forms of the verb which we call infinitive or gerund.

The same suffix meets us in the participles, as in *kârin*, "a doer," from *kri*; *ghâtin*, "a killer," from *han*; *sâyin*, "a sleeper," from *si*[1] (Chinese *shui*). In these cases the word in *n* is either a noun of agency or a present participle. The English participle in *ing*, formerly *in* (Latham's English Language), limits itself to the sense of a participle and infinitive, leaving the expression of agency to the suffix *r*, as in *lover*,[2] *loving*.

[1] Williams's Sanscrit Grammar.
[2] The suffix *r* for agency may be changed from *s*, as *was* is called in the west of England *war*. It may then be regarded as the demonstrative in *s*.

Other forms from *kat* are *katʻangkatʻika*, "an interrogator," *katʻangkatʻikatʻâ*, "question," *katʻangkatʻita*, "questioner," *katʻaniya*, "that may be told," *katʻantâ*, "inquiry," *katʻâ*, "word," "tale," *katʻânurâga*, "attentive to what is said," *katʻika*, "story-teller," *katʻita*, "said."

Among them the suffix *ta* or *tâ*, used of an agent or participially, is found in the Chinese 的 *ti*, 者 *che* (old form *ta*), and in the Mongol gerund or past participle *heled*.

The Sanscrit *chitra*, "painting," "to paint," forms *chitraka*, "a painter." This word is lengthened into *chitrakara* and *chitrakâra*, both meaning "painter." *Chitratala* is "painted like a floor." *Chitralikh* and *chitrakrit* mean "painter." *Chitragata* is "painted." *Chitrala* is "variegated." *Chitralekhâ* is a "picture." Compare with this family of words the Chinese *hwei* or *gat*, "to paint," the Tibetan *ṣkud*, "to smear," "to mark," *kud-pa-po*, "a marker," "painter," *kus-pa*, "smeared," and the Russian *chertit*, "to paint," *cherta*, "a line," *ocherk*, "a line."

The suffixes *raga*, *rege*, are quite common in Mongol. So also are *lig*, *al*, *el*, *del*, *ga*. Thus, *tʻerege*, "a cart," is formed from the Chinese *cʻhe*, formerly *tʻe*; *cʻhicʻhiglig*, "a garden," is formed from *cʻhicʻhig*, "a flower"; *ujel*, "a mode of viewing things," comes from *ujihu*, "to see"; *sigudel*, "judgment," comes from *siguhu*, "to judge."

The Tamil derivatives from *kâtu*, "to kill," are *kâtakam, kâtam,* "killing," *kâtakan,* "a killer," *kâtal,* "act of killing," *kâtei,* "killing."

It appears, then, that the Sanscrit derivative nouns are formed by appending syllables which bear a strong resemblance to similar syllables in Mongol. Forms are, however, more numerous in Sanscrit, which admits compounds, than in Mongol, which does not. Thus, *chitrakrit* is formed from *kri*, "make," joined with *chitra,* " painting."

Declension. Case.

The Turanian languages had formed cases of nouns before they were known in the Indo-European family. All the best Turanian types have them. The Sanscrit shows a more close kinship with its Turanian cousins in this respect than any other Indo-European language, because it does not use prepositions at all to express the relations of nouns to each other. The words for *from, to, in, out, by,* etc., come after the noun, as they do in all true members of the Turanian family. The other Indo-European languages use these prepositions plentifully before their nouns. The Sanscrit has come, therefore, more fully under the control of Turanian principles than any other member of the family. Yet a distinction remains to the Sanscrit which forbids our classing it among Turanian languages. It uses prepositions copiously as inseparable prefixes to roots, just as did the Greeks and Latins. But it is contrary to the nature of the Turanian system to do this.

The resemblances noticeable between the Sanscrit case suffixes and those of the Turanian system have already been examined. Obvious as they are, it would be wrong to say that the only influence at work in the formation of the declension was the Turanian. The Semitic system has had an effect of its own peculiar kind. It has given genders to the nouns and perhaps the accusative case in *m*. It has also added a dual number.

The letter *m* plays an important part in Semitic grammar. It serves to form a plural *im* for the masculine gender, and is then a suffix. It is also a prefix to denote participles in *Piel, Hiphil,* etc. It marks an infinitive or supine in Numbers x. 2, לִמְקְרָא "to call," said of the use to which the silver trumpets, ordered to be made by Moses, were to be applied—"to call the assembly." Then it is further used as a prefix in verbal nouns, as *mishpat*, "judgment," *moday*, "acquaintance," from *shaphat*, "to judge," and *yaday*, "to know." It is also met with in the dual, where *ayim* is used instead of the plural *im.*

As a common interrogative in Hebrew, *ma* would, it is likely, be originally demonstrative, and in that state it might originate the Dravidian plural suffix *mâr* and the Sanscrit accusative in *m*, as well as the Semitic plural suffix and the participial prefix just described. This explanation of the Sanscrit accusative is the more probable, seeing that neuter nouns take *am* in the nominative, as well as in the accusative; and in Tamil and Mongol[1] *m* is a very common suffix to nouns, and makes a plural in Tamil.

Bopp refers all case suffixes to a pronominal origin, and points to the pronoun *imau*, "these two," *ime*, "these," as the source of the accusative ending in *m*. His view of the origin of the cases appears to me to be wanting in convincing evidence in some respects. Thus, the instrumental and some other suffixes must, if viewed under the light of Chinese grammar, be regarded as true verbs. Bopp, however, was not willing to allow them to be other than pronouns. I believe them to have been both. The following are reasons for this opinion. First, it is more natural when *motion towards* or *from*, *making use of* or *giving to*, have to be spoken of, to employ verbs to express these ideas. They are really verbs, and no word could easily be employed to describe them without its having a verb sense. Secondly, if pronouns are employed as dative, instrumental, and ablative case suffixes, it should be allowed that, since they are used with such a force, they have already a signification as verbs. Thirdly, the Chinese demonstratives agree in form with certain common verbs meaning "follow," "give to," "carry," "bring," "do," "be."

[1] Compare *hugjim*, "music," the Chinese *gak*; also the pronouns *t'im*, *yim*, "that sort of," "this sort of."

從 zung, "follow," "from."

自 sï, "from," "self," "spontaneously."

此 t'sï, 斯 sï, "this," 賜 t'sï, "give," 錫 sik, "give."

那 na, "that," 拿 nap, "carry," "capture."

伊 i, "he," 以 i, "make use of," "other," eo, ibam, ivit, "go."

彼 pi, "he," "that," pet, "give," "go away," "another."

他 t'a, "other," "he," "to draw," "drag."

伊 i, "that," 爲 wei, "be," "become," "do," "action," "that."

是 zhi, "this," "is," "be."

The ideas of *existence, transitive action, self, other, carrying, following, moving*, are all mixed in confusion in these words.[1]

Probably the verb sense was the earliest, for to this a name would be most easily applied. The notion of the demonstrative pronoun would be a little more abstract, and therefore less easy for primitive man to grasp. He would see motion. He would hear a sound. The motion would be named from the sound. Thus the verb would first obtain a name. Early names for "walk," "move," "go," "carry," would thus come into use. With a small stock of verbs primitive man would be prepared to fix on his demonstrative and other pronouns. The name of an action

[1] For some criticisms on Bopp's views on this subject, see article on Language in the English Cyclopædia.

would be applied to the actor who was seen performing it, or to the place or time in which he performed it. As the actor is not always known, the pronoun thus acquired would also naturally be assigned to positions in space and time. Thus true pronouns, prepositions, and adverbs would be formed to express all spatial relations. This seems to be the true reason of the fact, that some of the commonest Chinese verbs coincide in sound (though usually differing in tone) from the most ancient and widely spread pronouns.

Since Bopp's time all philologists seem to agree in accepting the view that case suffixes are of pronominal origin. Yet it may not be considered superfluous to remark, in proof of the pronominal origin of the accusative in *m*, so widely spread in Sanscrit, Latin, German, and English,[1] that the corresponding Turanian accusative suffixes *gi, i, ni, a*, etc., are all easily reduced to demonstrative roots.

The Greek, Zend, and Sanscrit languages were spoken by nations in very near relations with Semitic peoples, and none of the other Indo-European races have had so full a development of the dual as these three. We can then only regard the dual number as of Semitic origin. It does not appear in the Hamite languages. Thus we are shut up to this hypothesis.

The Sanscrit mark of the nominative plural is *h*, corresponding to the Greek, Latin, and English *s*.

[1] Compare the English *him, whom, them*.

The Mongol has *s* and *d*. Perhaps all meet in the Hebrew *th*. For *s* and *t* are interchangeable letters. The genitive plural in *m*, so extensively used in Sanscrit, Zend, and Latin, may be referred to the Hebrew plural in *im*, and ultimately to the demonstrative in *m*. Bopp finds the demonstrative *ma* in the Greek μεν and the old Latin *emem*. I would add the Chinese *meu*, "some one," the Siamese and Malay second personal pronoun *meu, mu*, and the European words *multi, much, many, magnus*. So the Chinese *ta*, "many," *da*, "great,"[1] may be referred, with some probability, to the demonstrative root *t*.

As the Semitic dual is formed from the plural by slightly altering the suffix, that is, by changing *im* to *áyim*, or *th* to *tháyim*, so the Sanscrit dual is formed from the plural by changing, e.g., *as* to *au* (Bopp, § 206) in the nominative, *am* to *oh* in the genitive, and so on.

Gender.

The triple distinction of gender, as masculine, feminine, or neuter, found in Sanscrit and other Indo-European languages, we may suppose to have originated among a Semitic or Hamitic people, and to have been carried on to its completion by the Indo-Europeans. If the Hamites were not sufficiently imaginative to personify natural objects, the credit of this creation

[1] In Mandarin *to* and *ta*.

GENDER OF NOUNS. 291

must be allowed to the Semites, of whose tendencies to view nature with a poetic eye we have such abundant proofs. But the mythological creations of the Egyptian mind (unless they sprang from Shemite teaching) may well suggest that the gift of imagination was shared by some at least of the Hamites. The mark of the feminine in old Egyptian was *t*, and this agrees with the Hebrew feminine-ending *th*, sometimes shortened to *h*. (See Ges. Heb. Gr., § 79.)

The Indo-Europeans were likewise highly imaginative, and they adopted with avidity from both Hamites and Semites their personifications, alike in grammar and in mythology. They also carried forward the distinction of genders to its completion by adding a third form, the neuter.

To the ancient Hebrew, while his language was in course of formation, inanimate objects were by the poetic faculty endowed with life and distinguished as masculine or feminine. Strong and powerful objects appeared as masculine. Those which are easily associated with weakness and timidity were regarded as feminine (Ges. Heb. Gr., § 105). But strength and power can be attributed to few things, and consequently the majority of the names of inanimate objects are feminine. Abstract ideas, offices, and collectives are usually feminine.

Objects seized upon by the imaginative nations as suitable for mythological personification are in Hebrew nearly all masculine. *Cloud, rain, morning, tree, heaven, sun, moon, river, mountain, light,* are examples.

Among words occasionally feminine are *evening, sun, fire, cloud, wind.* Of these the last is rarely masculine. *Name, blood, city,* are masculine.

In Sanscrit *sun, moon, soul* (âtman), *head, mountain, tree, evening,* are masculine. *Earth, night, light, life, heaven, river,* are feminine. *Dawn, mind* (manas), *blood, honey, deed, water, gift,* are neuter.

When the Greek and Latin languages made the *moon* feminine, they departed from the usage of the Hebrew and Sanscrit. In all the four languages *life* is feminine. *River* is masculine in Hebrew, Greek, and Latin. In Sanscrit it is feminine. *Wind* is feminine in Hebrew, but masculine in Greek ($\mathring{\alpha}\nu\epsilon\mu o\varsigma$) and Latin. The Greek has also a neuter word, $\pi\nu\epsilon\hat{\upsilon}\mu\alpha$.

Comparison of Adjectives.

If Bopp's explanation of the Sanscrit comparative degree in *tara*, as derived from *tar*, "to pass beyond," is open to any doubt, I would suggest that it should be considered whether the Mongol demonstrative *t'ere* may not have originated it. It has its source in the primitive root *t'a*, "other," "he." Its force would be, after the word *good*, for instance, "that other is good." The Manchu *ere*, "this," would furnish an explanation of the Latin *or*, in *melior*, "better," and the Mongol *ene* might be adduced to throw light on the Greek comparative ων, in καλλίων, "more beautiful."

The Mongols say t'imu, for "such," t'uilin bogda, for "extremely wise and holy," and demile airiben baina, for "there are very many." Here demile means "very," baina, "to be," and airiben, "many." Perhaps an explanation of the Sanscrit superlative in tama may be found in this last form. In Latin the sim in carissimus, "most dear," and pessimus, "the worst," may be the same word with the t changed to s.

Personal Pronouns.

First Person. *Aham*, "I." The Chinese *nga*, and Mongol *na* in *namai*, "me," etc. The forms in *m* are identical with the Mongol *bi*, "I," *minu*, "of me," but instead of being limited to the nominative and genitive, they are extended to all the cases. The accusative *mâm* has the demonstrative in *m* for its final letter. The instrumental *mayâ* has the Chinese 以 *yi*, "to take," as its suffix, or, in other words, the demonstrative in *i*. The dative *mahyam* has the Chinese *yü* 與 "give to," and the demonstrative *m* for its suffix. The ablative *mat* has the demonstrative in *t* for its ending. The genitive *mama* and locative *mayi* have respectively the demonstrative in *m* and the Chinese 於 *yü*, "at," "in," for their ending.

The plural *vayam* is apparently the Chinese 予 *yü*, "I," and the English *we*. The oblique cases in the plural are, accusative *asmân*, indicative *asmâbhih*, dative *asmabhyam*, ablative *asmat*, genitive *asmâkam*, locative *asmâsu*. Bopp regards the initial *a* as meaning "I," and the whole of the remainder as demonstrative.[1] I would draw attention to the modern Chinese plural suffix 們 *men* in *women*, "we," the causative *pet*, the dative *pet*, the demonstrative elements *k, t, m,* and the preposition 在 *tsai, ze,* as throwing light on these forms.

SECOND PERSON.—As in the first person, there is a mixture of three roots, *aha, ma, wa,* corresponding to the *na, bi, mi,* of Mongol, so in the second we have *twa, yu,* corresponding to the Mongol *c'hi, t'a*. In the first person the speakers of Sanscrit selected *na* and *mi,* and made no use of *bi,* except in the substantive verb. In the second they neglected *c'hi,* and made use of *t'a* in the singular and the Chinese *nu* in the plural. The *n* is lost, as is the case in the Latin *vos* and English *we*.

THIRD PERSON.—The nominative *sah* is found in the Chinese 此 *tsï* and 斯 *sï*, "this." The old form of both these words was *si*. The *ta* of the accusative *tam,* instrumental *tena,* dative *tasmai,* ablative *tasmât,* genitive *tasya,* locative *tasmin,* is the Chinese 第 *di,* 之 *ti,* 的 *ti,* 這 *te,* "this," and 他 *t'a,* "that," "other," with the Mongol *t'ere,* "that." The inserted *m* in

[1] In the Shanghai dialect "we" is *ngu ni,* "I you"; "you" is *nung na,* "you he."

three of the oblique cases resembles that of the Mongol second person, which has in the dative and locative *c'himador*, accusative *c'himai*, indicative *c'himaber*, *c'himaloga*, ablative *c'hima ec'he*. This similarity becomes still closer when it is remembered that the second person usually takes origin from the third. The Greek σύ and Mongol *si* (old form of *c'hi*) help to connect the Sanscrit *tvam*, Latin *tu*, English *thou*, with the Chinese *si* and *ti*, "this," "him."

Demonstrative and Relative.

The demonstrative *ayam*, "this," accusative *imam*, is the Chinese 伊 *i*, and Mongol *ino*, *ano*, and *ene*. Compare also the Mongol *im*, "such a," "so," as in *im yehe*, "so large."

The Sanscrit relative is formed from this demonstrative, as the Latin *qui* and the English *who* are derived from the demonstrative in *k*. The Turanians, like the Chinese, are without a full relative, and the appearance of this feature in the Indo-European languages must be attributed to Semite influence.

The Hebrew *asher*, "who," "which," may be compared with the Chinese 唯 *shui*, "who?" "whoever," 是 *shi*, "this." The old forms of these words would be *zhi* and perhaps *zhid*. They are found in the oldest remains of Chinese literature. I suppose the demonstrative to have been first, then the interrogative, and lastly the relative. Since the demonstrative and interrogative are paired together, as words alike in form in so many languages, there can be no doubt of their identity of origin. How easy is the transition from the one to the other may be seen, for instance, in *that?* as distinguished from *that*. But when the interrogatives *that?* and *who?* and *which?* are formed from the demonstratives *that* and *he*, a transition just as easy changes the interrogative into a relative, and advances language on the path of progress another stage. A tone of the voice divides the word *that?* when it asks a question, from *that*, when it points to some object; and a change to another position in the sentence distinguishes the relative *that* from the demonstrative *that, e.g.*, That watch, That watch? and The watch that he made. The history of the formation of all relatives was very much like this. The Hebrew relative *asher*, then, may be supposed to have come out of the Chinese demonstrative and interrogative root in *zhi*, unless it be formed from the demonstrative in *t*, by change of *t* to *sh*.

The reason why the Eastern Asiatic nations did not adopt a relative with full powers is found in the nature of their grammar. The subordinate sentence must in their languages come before the principal one. A sentence whose nominative is a relative pronoun is with them a subordinate sentence, and speech cannot in their languages expand itself by a series of subordinate or circumstantial clauses coming after that which contains the nominative and principal verb.

It was the triumph of Semitic grammar, by simply drawing back the verb to the beginning of the sentence, to leave the way open for a concatenation of clauses to follow, which might commence at discretion with conjunctions or the relative pronoun. This afforded a facility and easy sequence to the expression of thought, which is unknown in Eastern Asia.

The Indo-Europeans took from the Semites this feature, and hence the origin of the relative pronoun in their grammar.

Interrogative Pronoun.

The interrogative *kah, kam, kena,* etc., is the same word as the Mongol *hen,* "who?" This is proved by the related interrogative adverbs, viz., *kati,* "how many?" *kadâ,* "when?" corresponding to the Mongol *heden,* "how many?" *hejiye (j* for *d),* "when?"

The Sanscrit relative *yah* appears in Mongol as one of the interrogatives, and is conjugated like other adverbs. We find the forms *yambar,* "what?" *yago,* "what?" *yagahin, yagahinem, yagahihu, yagonhihu,* "how?" *yagahiju,* "how?"

Reflexive Pronoun.

The Sanscrit reflexive pronoun *swa* is the Latin *se,*

sui, suus, and our *self.* It agrees with the Chinese 自 *tsï, zi,* "self," "spontaneously," "from." The Chinese have another reflexive, 己 *ki,* which seems to be connected with the demonstrative in *g* and *k,* viz., *gi* and *kit.*

VERBS. DERIVATIVES.

The desiderative and intensive forms of verbs reduplicate the first letter of the root. This is a principle we find in Mongol and Turkish. The Sanscrit *śuśobhish* is "to desire to shine," and *śośuby,* "to shine very brightly." In Mongol *c'habc'hagan* is "very white," *habhara* is "very black." The resemblance, though only partial, is worth attention. Complete similarity in all points is not required in order to prove consanguinity of language. Else why is the conjugation of the Greek verb so different from the Sanscrit in many respects?

As the Sanscrit has a causal, a passive, a desiderative, and an intensive, among its derivatives, so the Mongol has a causal and a collective. When Sanscrit grammar was formed, the passive had not become a voice, but was, as in Mongol, simply a derivative. Here is evidence of consanguinity.

Derivative syllables immediately follow the root, after them come the marks of mood or tense, and finally those of person. Consequently derivatives are the oldest, then come the mood and tense marks, and the personal endings, the most recent in formation, stand last.

Personal Endings.

The personal endings in Sanscrit verbs, as in the present *mi, si, ti*, may be compared with those belonging to certain Tartar languages which border on the Indo-European area, viz., the Turkish and the Buriat-Mongol. The more distant languages, such as Mongol Proper, Japanese, Tamil, have not personal endings. We conclude, therefore, that the marks for the persons sprang into existence after the Mongol and other older branches of the Turanian family had left their original seats in Western Asia, and before they were followed by the Turks. The Turks did not leave the vicinity of the Arian mother-stem till the principle of the relative pronoun had been introduced into their language from the Semitic, and they themselves had communicated the personal endings to the Arians, or received them from that race. The Turkish relative is the interrogative in *k*, and as such it agrees with the Hebrew כִּי, occasionally used as a relative, and with the Latin and English relative *qui* and *who*.

In the Turkish personal endings, as they are at present (Davids' Grammar), we find the elements *um*, first person; *sen*, second person. In the third person of the present tense we find nothing. The syllables *um, un, i*, are the marks used in the preterite.

TURKISH PRESENT TENSE.

SINGULAR.
1. *deugurum*, I strike.
2. *deugursen*, thou strikest.
3. *deugur*, he strikes.

PLURAL
deuguruz, we strike.
deugursiz, you strike.
deugurler, they strike.

The antiquity of the Turkish is shown in the absence of the initial *s* and inserted *r* found in the English equivalent *strike*.

SANSCRIT PRESENT TENSE.

SINGULAR.	DUAL.	PLURAL.
1. *karomi*, I do	*kurvah*	*kurmah*.
2. *karoshi*	*kuruthah*	*kurutha*.
3. *karoti*	*kurutah*	*kurvanti*.

Where the original elements are not too much decayed, we see in these two examples the identity of the marks of person. In the first person singular and plural *m* is the distinguishing mark. It is dropped, however, in the Turkish plural, where the suffix *iz* of *biz*, "we," alone remains. In the second person *s* stands in the Turkish singular and plural. It has changed to *t'* in the Sanscrit plural, reminding us of the Mongol *t'a*, "ye." In the third person the Sanscrit prefers the demonstrative root *t*, while the Turkish adopts that in *i* or *o*, as in the preterite *deugdi*, "he struck," where the second *d* marks past time. The Turkish plural *ler* is probably formed from *ol*, "he," equivalent to the Latin *ille*. An *r* is added and the initial *o* is dropped.

The idea of marking past time by a prefixed *a* in Sanscrit and *e* in Greek, having no prototype in Turanian languages, may with probability be traced to Semitic influence. The creative power of Semitic grammar is centred on the beginning of the word and sentence, and in Turanian grammar on the end. The vowel in the Semitic past tense is *a*, as in *bara*, "he created." The two Sanscrit preterites of *bhû*, "to become," are *abhavam* and *babhûva*. *Kartum*, "to do," has three preterites, all having the vowel *a*, viz., *akaravam*, *chakâra* (*ch* for *k*), *akârsham*. I suppose, therefore, that *a* has in it a past force, and it may be compared with the Chinese 已 *i*, "already," which seems to be the root of Turanian and Indo-European preterites in *u* (Tamil), and *ui* (Latin),[1] since *a* sometimes changes to *i*.

[1] Bopp regards the augment in *a* as *a privativum*, and views it as an expression of the denial of presence. This view has involved him in some difficulties, and brought him into collision with more than one philologist. For example, how shall we explain the Greek augment in *e*, which bears no likeness to the *a* of negation? Bopp says the *a* in the Sanscrit augment had already lost its negative force, and had become a sign of past time, before it passed into Greek as the augment in *e*. Buttmann supposes it to be a broken-down form of the consonantal augment, regarding ἔτυπτον as a shortened form from τέτυπτον. This, however, does not look very probable, and, in respect to Bopp's opinion, it is surely better first to make wider researches in kindred families of language, in hope of discovering the true origin of the augment. To explain it as the *a* of negation should be only a *dernier ressort*.

The Sanscrit future in *tá* is probably connected with the infinitive in *tum*, and the Latin supine in *tum*, *tu*. I suppose its origin to be in the preposition *to*, the mark of the English infinitive, and the Chinese *chi*, "to a place," in old Chinese *ti*. If this be true, it is also formed ultimately from the demonstrative root in *t*, if at least that be not rather regarded as itself previously a verb of motion *towards*.

The Sanscrit future in *sya* is conveniently referred to the Chinese 將 *tsiang*, *siung*, an auxiliary word used in giving a future tense to verbs. It means primarily, "starting from the side of," "side," hence "to lead a division." The Mongols have indeed a future in *sogai*, used for the first person singular and plural, which may be formed from the old Chinese *sik*, "give," first used as a precative and then as a future. The former etymology is the more probable in appearance.

The future participles seem to have connexion with the Turanian conjugation. They are formed with the suffixes (1) *tavya*, (2) *aniya*, (3) *ya*. Thus, from *bhuj*, "to eat," is formed *bhoktavya*, "edible." *Bhojaniya*, *bhojya*, mean the same thing. We are strongly inclined here to identify the first of these forms with the Mongol suffix *t'o*, *t'ai*, *t'ei*, in *heregt'ei*, "necessary," *idelt'ei*, "to be eaten," *dort'ai*, "willing," *johist'ai*, "ought to be." The Latin gerund *dicendus*, "to be said," also bears features of resemblance. In Manchu the similar form ends in *rangga*, e.g., *ararangga*, "that which is to be written," from *arare*, "to write." The form in *ya* seems to be connected with the future indicative of the Mongol verb, which is formed by the same syllable.

The potential in *ya* may be compared with the Mongol future in *ya*. The Sanscrit potential has usually the idea of fitness (Williams' Sans. Gram., p. 199), and is sometimes a softened imperative. The Mongol future is also used imperatively, as in *yabiya*, "let us go." So the Latin potential in *e* or *i*, as in *amem*, "I may love," *sis*, "thou mayst be," may also be explained.

The Sanscrit conditional in *sya* seems to be identical with the Mongol conditional suffix *so*, as in *bolbeso*, "if it be so." There can be little doubt that it is the Chinese *sik*, "to give." The Latin conditional conjunction *si* finds also here a convenient etymology, and is then seen to be parallel to our own word *if*, derived from *give*. I see no reason why we should not hope to be able at some time to go further back and identify the conditional in *s* ultimately with the demonstrative in *s*. Such simple ideas as *giving, going, coming, carrying*, have attached to them sounds which are like the common demonstratives. Thus, in addition to examples mentioned on a former page, *ti* is used for "to arrive at a place," "him," "to." *Gip* is "to give," and it is also "to arrive at a place." *Ded*, "this," "that," is also "to carry in the hand." *Kit*, *gid*, "he," is perhaps the European verb *gad*, "to go," Russian *chod*, Sanscrit *gati*, "going," *gata*, "gone." *Si*, "this," is in old Chinese "to move from one place to another," and in Mongol, under the form *ac'hiraho*, it means "to carry," and under that of *ec'hihu* "to go." It is also in the West the verb of existence *sum*, *asmi*, *esse*. Further, the demonstrative *zhi*, *zhet*, "this," may be compared with *shed*, "to let go," *shoot*, and such like verbs.

Verb as Substantive. Infinitive. Participles.

As the Sanscrit infinitive in *tum* is apparently formed of the demonstrative in *t*, and the accusative in *m*, so in Mongol the infinitive in *hu* resembles the accusative in *gi*, and in Turkish the infinitive in *mek* seems to be formed from the demonstrative in *m*.

The participle in *t*, as in *bodhat*, "knowing," is like the Mongol gerund in *ged*, which in colloquial is pronounced *ed*, thus, *medeged* or *meded*, "knowing." The two roots, *budh*, *med*, are, there can be little doubt, the same word.

The participle in *amâna* may be compared with the Mongol colloquial gerund in *man*. This form is not given in Schmidt's Grammar. Its use is parallel to that of the gerunds in *ged* and *ju*.

The passive past participle in *ta* may be compared with the Mongol gerund in *ju*, of which the equivalent old form is *du*. As the Sanscrit form is often used indicatively as a perfect, so is it with the Mongol. The substantive comes first, and then the indicative. The verb is fundamentally a substantive, and gerunds, participles, and infinitives, lie at the base and constitute the foundation of the Turanian verb, e.g., *ochogder medeji*, "I knew it yesterday," where the Chinese *tsok*, "yesterday," is seen in the first of the words, and *ji*, the colloquial form of the gerund *ju*, in the second.

It may be objected that this Mongol gerund is active, and the Sanscrit form *ta*, now compared with it, passive. I would then suggest a comparison with the Mongol adjective in *t'o*, *t'ai*, as in *heregt'ei*, "necessary," *morit'ai*, "possessed of a horse." Bopp states that the passive participial suffix *ta* forms in Sanscrit possessive adjectives out of substantives, as *p'alitás*, "gifted with fruit" (§ 835). So in English we say "horned cattle," forming a possessive adjective from "horn," just as the Mongols would say *uburt'ei*, "horned," from *ebur* or *ubur*, "horn."

Auxiliary Verbs.

The substantive verb *as*, "to be," in English *am*, *art*, *are*, *was*, appears in Mongol without *s*. The root therefore is *a*; which means "being," and is also the ultimate root of *aham*, the first personal pronoun. The idea of being is derived from that of personality, and the oldest expression of personality is found in this pronoun *a*.

The second Sanscrit auxiliary verb is *kri*, "do," *karomi*, "I do." In Mongol a very common verb is *hi*, "do," *himoi*, "I do," or "he does," *hibe*, "he did," etc.

The third Sanscrit auxiliary verb is *bhû*, "become," "be," *bhavitum*, "to become," *bhava*, "become," *abhavam*, "I was," or "I was becoming." This verb is in its Mongol form distinguished as neuter and causative. The root *bu* is neuter, "be." The insertion of *l* makes it equivalent to our word "do," taken intransitively as in *bolomoi*, "it will do." The past participle *bologsen* means "completed," and is used as an auxiliary to express the accomplishment of the action of any verb.

What proof can be more convincing than the existence of these auxiliary verbs of the essential identity in origin of the Sanscrit and Mongol languages? But the same proof holds good also for the Turkish and Tungusic stocks. It is only when we come to the Japanese and Dravidian branches that this system of identical auxiliary verbs diminishes from three to one. The verb *a* for existence keeps its place everywhere. Hence it appears that the original Tartar language, which was split into Turk, Mongol, Manchu, Finnish, etc., immediately preceded the Sanscrit in the linguistic development of the world.

Adverbial Suffixes.

T in Sanscrit is *d* in Mongolian. Thus among

the adverbs of place, *atra*, "here," *tatra*, "there," correspond to the Mongol *ende*, "here," *t'ende*,[1] "there." The suffix in the two languages is identical.

D in Sanscrit is equivalent to *j* or *d* in Mongol. Thus *kadâ*, "when?" is the Mongol *hejiye*, "when?" *Ekadâ*, "once," is in Mongol *nigodaga* or *nigodâ*, "once," from *nig*, "one." *Tadâ*, "then," is in Mongol *t'eduile*, "then."

The suffix *vat* in *sûryavat*, "like the sun," from *sûrya*, "sun," may possibly be the Mongol *adeli*, "like." The initial *v* was originally not consonantal. The Latin is *idem*.

Negative Adverbs.

The negative *na, ne, nehi*, is derived from the same source as the Japanese negative. That source will have been some Turanian language in South-western Asia.

The negative *mâ* is found in Chinese, in the Tartar languages, in Tibetan, and in the Semitic family. It is used over nearly the whole of Asia, but, except in Greek, is little employed in Europe.

Time, Manner, Comparison, Place.

Adya, "to-day," "now," may be compared with the Mongol *edoge*, "now." *Evam, eva*, "so," "thus," are suggestive of identity with the Mongol *yim*, "thus," "so." *Kwa*, "where," is the Mongol *hamiga*.

[1] The Mongol *e* is the same in sound as the Sanscrit *a*.

Prepositions.

The absence of prepositions to mark the relations of nouns is peculiar, among the Indo-European languages, to the Sanscrit branch. The Romans used "in," "ex," "ab," etc., as the English now use "from," "in," "to," etc. It is a specialty of the Sanscrit, and of the triple-branched Turanian system, to employ case suffixes instead of the more ancient prepositions found in the Chinese, the Semitic, and the Himalaic systems. The Greeks, loving freedom, early threw off the yoke of this Turanian law. The speakers of Sanskrit never did so. In Homer the adverbial case suffixes are used with the prepositions. In later Greek the adverbial case suffixes are not found. They have given place to prepositions, as afterwards the cases of nouns also became needless over much of the European area, and were exchanged for the primeval prepositions which seem to be ever engaged in recovering their long lost dominion. In Sanscrit the prepositions are only used in compounds as inseparable prefixes, and here the nearest Turanian type to which in this respect it can be compared is the Dravidian.

Compounds.

When in Sanscrit words are compounded, connective letters are not used, and the resulting whole is treated as a single word. Thus, for "moonlight" *chandraprabhâ* is used. In Mongol it would be *saranu gerel*, where *nu* is the genitive case. The Tartar languages have an aversion to naked compounds, and prefer to introduce, as here, the genitive suffix. This I believe to be a comparatively modern tendency. The Sanscrit acts here according to the true ancient principle for the compounding of words by simple juxtaposition, as found in Chinese. The Tartar languages appear to have acquired the habit of inserting case suffixes, and other particles, between words which would otherwise coalesce into compounds, since they were separated from the Japanese and Dravidian branches. Hence, in regard to the way of forming compounds, the Hindoo principle must be compared with that existing in older stems, *e.g.*, in Chinese *yue liang*, "moon light." In Japanese and the Dravidian languages the crude forms or roots are likewise placed side by side without connecting particles. Japanese *tsuki akara*, " moon light." In the Greek and Latin languages, as in *lunæ lumen*, the genitive suffix is, as in Mongol, carefully inserted. Hence the Tartar race remained in juxtaposition with the forefathers of the Greeks and Latins later than the time when the speakers of the Sanscrit and Dravidian idioms were in a position to exercise an influence upon each other.

The compound *guruśishyau* means " master and scholar." There is no conjunction. *Au* is the sign of the dual. *Guru*, "teacher," and *śishya*, " scholar," are co-ordinate nouns—roots standing together without connective, as *bakshi*, "teacher," *shabi*, "scholar," might do in Mongol. But the Mongol is without the dual mark, unless *hoyol*, "the two," be added, as is sometimes done.

The want of a conjunction is in accordance with the custom in all eastern Asiatic languages.

In the compound *maranavyâdhiśokâh*, *marana* is "death," *vyâdhi* is "sickness," and *śokâh* is "sorrow." These three nouns are written together without a conjunction, forming one huge word, which in Sanscrit syntax is treated as a single substantive. It may be compared with the Chinese *sheng lau ping sï*, "birth, old age, sickness, and death," in Mongol *t'urehu, ot'olhu, obc'hinhu, uhuhu*. The four Chinese substantives become in the Tartar idiom four infinitives. How thoroughly they are regarded as substantives appears from the fact, that in the Buddhistic language common in Mongolia they are known as the *durben dalai*, "four seas."

The addition of the connecting conjunction in more western languages is proof of the influence of Semitic grammar. The aggregation of substantives without conjunctions is a circumstance in Sanscrit which shows how completely that language rests, in regard to its linguistic principles, on the speech of more eastern races.

The resemblance may be noticed in all sorts of compounds. In this part of grammar Sanscrit looks like an old Mongol using but sparingly its apparatus of case particles. *E.g.*, *svarga gata*, "gone to heaven," *svargang gā*, "the Ganges of heaven." In Mongol *T'engri dor garaksan*, *Tengrin Gangga murun*, where *dor* and *n* are locative and possessive. In Chinese, ancient or modern, the position of the verb, as standing before its noun, weakens the resemblance to Sanscrit, and throws into more prominent relief the essential identity of Sanscrit and Turanian syntax.

The Sanscrit *manda gata*, "going slowly," is in Chinese *man tseu*, and in Mongol *odan yabahu*. In the last two of these languages this compound may take a genitive suffix and another noun, for instance, *man*, after it. The Sanscrit form is an adjective, of which the syntax is the same as if it were simple.

When such compounds occur as *râjagâmin*, "that which goes to the king" (*e.g.*, revenue), *râja guru*, "king's instructor"; *râjakula*, "king's family," from *kula*, "family," "caste," the Chinese *kia* or *ko*, "house," "family"; *râjaghna*, "regicide," from *ghnat*, "killing"; *râjadanda*, "punishment by a king," from *danda*, "punishment;" Chinese analogy seems to require that the relation should in all cases be regarded as *possessive*. Even where the English rendering requires *from* or *by*, as if the relation were ablative or instrumental, it is better to hold to the simplicity of primeval grammar, and explain all such instances on the principle of possessive dependence. Thus, "punishment by a king" is also rendered by "king's punishment," without much forcing.

By regarding the relation as possessive in all cases where in a compound the second noun depends upon the first, the analogy with Chinese grammar becomes perfect. Thus, *wang tsï,* "king's son," *wang tsung,* "king's family," *wang fa,* "punishment by the king," *wang ki,* "land appropriated to the use of the king."

The same law rules in all the languages from the Hindoo area eastward to the Japanese Islands, except in the eastern Himalaic and Malay region, where the Semitic inversion, which transposes the genitive, holds sway. The true reason why this inversion is impossible in Sanscrit is, that this language is in fact controlled by the same laws of position as the Turanian idioms.

The modern Pekinese speaks of *fu fu lia,* for "husband and wife." Here *fu,* "husband," takes one intonation, and *fu,* "wife," another, while *lia* is a contraction for *liang,* "two," and corresponds to the dual suffix, which would by the Sanscrit grammarian be placed here. Could analogy be closer? But compare the words themselves; *fu,* "husband," is *bharu, fu,* "wife," is *bháryá,* and in Greek πόσις is "husband." The proof of original connexion in language thus becomes still more clear.

Examples may easily be collected from Mongol to show that the inserted particles are often omitted, and that the analogy thus brought to view may also be extended to the use of dual and plural suffixes. Thus c'has c'hagan, means "white as snow." If written in full, met'u or adeli would be added after c'has, "snow." This is exactly the Chinese siuet bak, "white as snow," and the Sanscrit himaśítala, "ice-cold." So also echige ehe hoiyogola, "the father and mother both."

The resemblance to Chinese and Turanian idiom is carried also into what are called the relative compounds. Thus in mahâdhanah purushah, "a man who has great wealth," mahâ is "great," dhanah is an adjectival form of dhanam, "wealth." Native Sanscrit authors explain this usage as equivalent to the employment of the relative in the genitive case.[1] With this may be compared in Chinese a sentence such as ta hio wen chï shï, "a scholar who has great learning," consisting of ta, "great," hio-wen, ("learning and heard") "learning," chï, the possessive particle, shï, "scholar." In Mandarin the possessive ti is also used after adjectives, as in hau ti, "good." Compare also the Mongol yehe gabiya t'ai humun, or yeheu gabiyan humun, "a man who has great merit." Gabiya, "merit," is here made into an adjective by the suffix t'ai, which thus corresponds to the Sanscrit adjective suffix h.

Laws of Position.

In the Sanscrit and the Turanian languages, the

[1] Williams' Sanscrit Grammar, p. 166.

laws of position are the same in several of the most important particulars.

If we take the sentence, "And the children of Israel dwelt among the Canaanites," in Jud. iii. 5, we find the Hebrew order the same with the English. The Sanscrit and Mongol both read, "Israel people Canaanites among dwelt." The Chinese would be "Israel people at Canaanite people midst lived," or "Israel people lived Canaanite people among." Thus the translators of the scriptures at Calcutta (edition 1852) have adopted an order for the words exactly agreeing with the Mongol.

Another example is, "Jabin king of Canaan, that reigned in Hazor" (Jud. iv. 2). As before, the Semitic order is as in English. The Sanscrit reads *Hatsoranivâsinah kinâniyarâjasya yâvinasya haste.* Here *nivâsinah* is an adjective, "residing in." *Râja* is "king." *Sya* is the possessive suffix. *Haste* is "hand" in the locative. Omitting the word "hand" and the possessive case preceding it, the Sanscrit reads, "Hazor residing Canaanite king's Jabin." The Mongol reads, "Hazor in ruling Canaanites' Jabin king," *Hajor t'or ejelegsan Hanayan t'anu Jabin hagan.* The translators have adopted in Calcutta the same order nearly as those who performed their work on the eastern shore of Lake Baikal in Siberia. The Mongol introduces the case suffix after Hazor, and gives the name Jabin before his title. These are the variations; otherwise the laws of position are identical. *T'anu* is the genitive plural.

Hence the Sanscrit language has peculiar laws. The Greek and English both have the Hebrew order. In this part of grammar the Sanscrit is cut off from its proper relationship, and bears no close resemblance to any western language. It is in agreement with the eastern idiom of the Asiatic continent, with that of China and Japan, Mongolia, and Dravidia.

This general agreement in syntax between the Sanscrit and Turanian types is subject to numberless exceptions. To make this plain, I here give two sentences out of the Hitopadeśa, taken from Williams' Grammar. *Asti,* "there is," *gautamasya munes tapovane,* "in the sage Gautama's grove of penance," *Mahātapā nāma munih,* "a sage named Mahātapāh." *Tena,* "by him," *āśramasannidhāne,* "in the neighbourhood of his hermitage," *mūshika śāvakah,* "a young mouse," *kāka mukhād bhrashṭo,* "fallen from the mouth of a crow," *dṛishṭah,* "was seen."

Turanian syntax would require the verb *asti,* "there is," to be at the end of the first sentence, and the descriptive clause, "crow's mouth from fallen," to precede the noun "mouse little one," to which it refers.

These two things excepted, the laws of arrangement are Turanian, as in "Gautama sage's penance garden in," "a Mahatapah named sage," "hermitage neighbourhood in," "mouse's little one," "crow mouth from fallen," and the position of the verb "was seen" at the end of the second sentence. The resemblance is still closer, inasmuch as *drishtah* is a participle used indicatively, which is a common phenomenon in Mongol grammar.

Judged by syntax alone, Sanscrit and Mongol are sisters, just as Hebrew, Greek, and English, if tested in the same way, might, though the similarity is somewhat less close, also be called sisters.

It was after the separation of the Chinese from the primitive stock, that the great Turanian inversion occurred, which placed the verb last, and thus originated the declension of nouns. The Turanians remained long enough in the west to bring with them in their wanderings the declension of substantives, the conjugation of verbs, and a syntax which places them in a midway position between China and the western world. And then the Sanscrit, the most easterly member of the Indo-European family, by its peculiar syntax, its principle of agglutination in compounds, and its use of the participle, conveniently occupies the interval between Turania and Europe.

A word upon the Zend. The absence of the Turanian order in Zend syntax is a sure indication of Semitic influence. Bopp gives the following sentence in Zend. *Staumi*, "I praise," *maig'emcha*, "the clouds," *varemcha*, "and rain," *ya te kehr pem*, "which thy body," *vak'sayato*, "make to grow," *baresnus paiti gairinanm*, "on the heights of the mountains." Here *gairi*, the Sanscrit *giri*, and Mongol *agola*, "mountain," occurs last, after its nominative. This is Semitic order, which is also prominent in the whole sentence. The Zend, in fact, has an accidence and vocabulary like the Sanscrit, but a syntax like the Hebrew. As in the modern Persian, Semitic words had also pushed their way into the Zend. Thus *athr*, "fire," is the Hebrew *esh* by the common change which takes place between *sh* and *t*.

A few Zend words with old Chinese and Mongol equivalents are here appended.

"Bad," Zend *eghe*, Chinese *ak*.

"Flesh," Zend *machshe*, Mongol *maha*, Persian *maso*.

"Not," Zend *ma*, Mongol *bishi*, *bu*, Chinese *mo*.

"Ear," Zend *goshte*, Chinese *ngi*, Sanscrit *ghosha*, Persian *gosh*.

CHAPTER XIII.

European Languages. — Latest and Grandest Development of Language. — The Alphabet. — Common Radical Syllabary of Chinese and European Languages. — European Radical Syllabary. — The European Word. — Semite Influence seen in Conjugational Vowel Changes, in Doubled Consonants, in Masculine and Feminine Terminations, and in Dual and Plural Numbers. — Turanian Influence seen in Moods and Tenses, and in Compounds. — European Syntax. — Chinese Element. — Semitic and Turanian Elements. — Greek. — Tones in Chinese are Accents in Greek. — Common Words in Greek and Mongol. — Latin. — Resemblance of Latin Gerund and Supine to those of Tartar Languages. — List of Roots Common to Latin, Chinese, and Mongol. — Latin Syntax more Turanian than the Greek. — Roman Family Relationships Suggestive of Connexion with Eastern Ideas. — Resemblance between Roman and Old Chinese Religious Beliefs. — Russian: The Best New Type of the Sclavonic Family. — Full Alphabet. — Abounds in Prefixes to Roots. — Examples of Syntax. — Anglo-Saxon. — The Syntax Turanian. — Anglo-Saxon and German have more of the Turanian Element than is seen in the English. — English Returns to Chinese and Primeval Syntax. — Cause of these Variations. — Resemblance of Anglo-Saxon Poetry to that of the Mongols. — Alliteration: Exchanged for Rhyme; Cause of this Change. — English. — List of Common Words, Chinese and English.

Old as are the European languages, evidenced by an unbroken series of literary works, dating from about the ninth century before Christ, they bear in their structure the marks of youth, if compared with the

Turanian and Semitic families. Principles of grammar seem to have been early borrowed from both these families, and incorporated in European speech at a time when language was still plastic. Destined themselves to be the dominant powers in the world's history, from the conquest of Babylon by Cyrus, they were before that epoch living as independent nations, occasionally subject to the Semitic rulers who from time to time were able to reduce some of the nearer among them under their sway. Semitic and Turanian conquest at a very ancient date would impart Semitic and Turanian elements to the language of the conquered, and when these nations themselves invaded regions occupied previously by Semite and Turanian peoples, similar results would ensue.

The Indo-European system, with the Chinese, Semitic, and Turanian, would each branch directly out of the primeval trunk of language. Each would develope its special characteristics with a varying rate of rapidity. Civilization, the invention of writing, maturity in arts, and in political institutions, would soon harden the Chinese and the Semitic families into a distinctive moulded form. The Turanian and Indo-European would take a longer time to harden, and in them the language-forming power would continue for a longer period. They would remain in a plastic state till the polysyllable and the paradigms of substantive and verb forms were completed.

Rapidity of change in language is in proportion to the civilization of the people speaking it. In early times languages changed more quickly than now. Not many centuries would be required for the primeval development of the existing families. But once formed they would last for thousands of years. Yet there is a sense in which they may be said to stand in chronological succession.

As in geology it has been shown that the lesser ranges of mountains were first elevated and the highest last, so it has been in the history of language. Monosyllabic speech preceded the dissyllable, as the dissyllable preceded the polysyllable. The Alps, Andes, and Himalayas, were not thrown up till the lesser mountain systems were complete. They are more aspiring, they pierce the region of the clouds, they possess a greater variety of vegetation, present to the eye richer landscapes, originate larger rivers, and promote the fertility of wider tracts of land than lesser mountain chains. So it has been with the Indo-European languages. They have aimed high in thought, enlarged the field of poetic feeling, advanced scientific inquiry, and led the human race forward on the path of civilized progress to an unequalled degree. The greatest thinkers in philosophy, the creative intellects of science, the most noteworthy conquerors and legislators, have been those whose speech was Indo-European.

As the cause of the greater elevation and magnitude of the more recent mountain chains may be probably referred to the increased thickness of the earth's crust, and the consequent increased pressure on the liquid materials beneath, so the richness in forms and in capability for expressing human thought which marks the Indo-European languages, is due to the united action of the older linguistic families upon this last and noblest creation of the language-forming power.

It is necessary, therefore, to review briefly the traces presented to view in European languages of the presence in a long distant time of strong Turanian and Semitic influence. The German, Russian, French, and English of the present day are descended from older forms of speech, which assumed their peculiar shape under this double formative influence.

THE ALPHABET.

A.

The broad *a* in *father* belongs to all languages. It has been replaced in modern Chinese by *o*. In western vocabularies it occupies less space in those which are modern than in those which are ancient. Hence it abounds in Hebrew and Sanscrit. It has become *u* in some Chinese words, as in *fu, mu,* "father," "mother," from the primeval *ba, ma.* It belongs to the pronouns, and represents the first person. As a suffix it is common in Greek and Sanscrit, as in the Greek names of the Phœnician letters. *Beth, caph, teth,* etc., became *beta, kappa, theta,* etc. In the inevitable softening down of language the consonantal finals *t, p,* took after them in Greek the vowel *a*. *A* has become *o* in Hebrew, so that *lo,* "not," is written לֹא, with *aleph*. In Tamil, Japanese, and Mongol, *a* is much prefixed to roots, as in Japanese *ame,* "rain," Tamil *mazhei,* Latin *madeo,* "moisten."

The short *a* of Sanscrit is understood whenever no vowel mark is used. This is an indication of the extensive ancient use of this vowel.

B.

The consonant *b* was the old representative of the Chinese *p* and *f* in the lower or sonant series. It is interchanged with *m*, as in Persian and Mongol *boron,* "rain," Japanese *ame,* Hebrew *mayim,* "water," Hebrew *matar,* "it rained." Also Mongol *bi,* "I," Turanian *min,* Latin *me, mihi*. Also *bal,* "honey," Latin *mel*. It is sometimes used in Greek for *w*, as in βούλομαι, "I wish," Latin *volo, velle*.

In Sanscrit it also took an aspirate occasionally like *d* and *g*, as it probably did in old Chinese in the first sonant tone, which in Mandarin has become aspirated *p*.

CH.

The compound letter *ch* is the modern equivalent of *t* in the eastern Asiatic languages, and of *k* in the

Indo-European. In modern Chinese we also see *ch* originated from *k*, when standing before the letters *ü* and *i*. All Chinese words in *ch* not thus formed recently from *k*, are derived from *t* or *d*, according as they belong to the surd or sonant series.

The Sanscrit *ch*, aspirated and unaspirated, are both from *k*. The Tibetan *ch*, *ch'*, is from *s* or *sh*. The Mongol *ch* aspirated is from *t's*, and this again from *s* or *sh*, as *c'hag*, "time," Chinese *shi*, *c'hilagon*, "stone," Chinese *shiag*. The same thing occurs in Fuhkien, where *shui*, "water," is *chui*, also in Tibetan, as *c'hu*, "water," *c'hi*, "die," Chinese *sï*. Perhaps a part of the Chinese words in *sh* formerly had *c'h* for *sh*. The guttural *ch*, as in *loch*, "a lake," in Europe, represents *k* in Chinese. Thus *wechseln*, "to change," may be seen to agree with the Chinese *yik*, "to change."

The Turkish *ch* corresponds to the Mongol *d*. Thus *kach*, "how many," is in Mongol *heden*. The Chinese *ch* is also found to be *j* in Mongol, both having sprung out of an older *d* or *t*. The Japanese *ch* is in Mongol *s*, and is, strictly speaking, *tsi*.

D.

The letter *d* is in old Chinese the equivalent of the modern *ch* in the lower series, and of the modern Mongol *j*. Compare the Sanscrit *kadâ*, "when?" Mongol *hejiye*.

The lost final *d* of many Chinese roots is recovered

in Japanese, as *kudari*, "to descend," in Chinese *hia*, *ge*, κατά, *sadzki*, "to receive;" 受 *sheu, zhud.*

D is often interchangeable with *l*, as in *lacryma*, δάκρυον, "tear," *longus*, "long," Chinese 長 *dung*, "long."

D sometimes becomes *t* in western languages, as Chinese *da*, "earth," Latin *terra*.

Dj takes the place of *g* in the Shanghai dialect before the vowels *i*, *ü*. The same occurs in English, as in "bridge," from "brig," and several other words where *g* is final.

E.

The vowel *e* in "then," "there," is derived in Chinese from *ya*, and is scarcely used except as a modern final.

In Mongol *e* is classed with *u* and *ü* as female, while *a, o*, are male. These terms mean that when the root has, for instance, *e* for its vowel, the vowel of the added syllables shall be of the same class. The Mongol *e* is now enunciated as the Sanscrit short *a*, but in Hindoo words whose sound is transferred, as in *Ganges*, *a* is used by the Mongols for the short *a*; thus they write *Gangga* (not *Gengge*).

The European *e* is usually the Chinese *i*, as in *yit*, "one," Sclavonic *yedin*, Chinese *nyit*, "hot," Scotch *het*, German *heiss*.

The English *e*, as in *be, see, me*, we all pronounce in

open syllables with the sound *i*. The modern Chinese medial *e*, as in *p'ei*, "to be fit for," "to match," is found in European languages to be *i*, as in *fit*. But in this case the old form in Chinese is usually *p'it*. The Chinese *i* has changed to *e*, while the English *e* has changed to *i*.

The Sanscrit *e* is found late in the series of vowels, forming with *o* a supplement to the three chief vowels, *a, i, u*. Similarly, the Greeks adopting the three leading vowels of the Phœnician alphabet *a, u, i, aleph, vav, yod*, proceeded to apply an aspirate *he* to represent the vowel *e*, as they used a guttural sign *ayin* for the vowel *o*. The Semites were content with three vowels. The Indo-Europeans needed five. The Greeks did with the Semitic alphabet in the west what the inventors of the Devanagari did in the east. They took the chief vowels as they found them, and used new signs for vowels not represented. That at both ends of the Semitic area, which once probably reached from the Mediterranean to the Indus, the three letters *aleph, vav*, and *yod*, should have been regarded as vowels, may be appealed to in proof that they were not originally consonantal signs, as some grammarians maintain, but true vowels.

F.

F is a new letter in Chinese. It proceeds from *b, p*, and *p'*. It is wanting in Mongol and Tamil, as it is also in Sanscrit. In Greek it crept in as an aspirated *p*, gliding afterwards into *φ*, pronounced like the Latin *f*. The Latin *f* came from *p*, as did the English. The Semitic *f* probably also came from *p*. One sign ב is used for *p* and *f* in Hebrew, and the Greeks, adopting the Phœnician alphabet, used the same sign for the value *p*, which shows that at about the time B.C. 1000, this was its usual force. *F* is inserted in a few German words after a radical initial *p*, as in *pflegen* (*pledge*, *pignus*). In Japanese *f* is used for *h* when standing before *u*, and proceeds ultimately from *p*, *b*.

G.

The letter *g* is the old form of the modern *k* and *k'* in the lower series. In Mongol the old Chinese *g* is found as *g* or *h*, e.g. *hwun delehu*, "to honour," from Chinese *king*. In Hebrew and in European alphabets, it precedes the corresponding surd letter *k*. In Latin *g* changed to *dj* before *e*, and this again became *zh* in French.

The Mongol *g* sometimes corresponds to the Sanscrit *k* and the Greek *χ*, as in *gar*, *kara*, *χείρ*, but also to the Sanscrit *g* and *gh*.

The Persian *g* sometimes corresponds to the Chinese *ni*, as in *gao*, "cow," *gosh*, "meat," "flesh," "ear," as does the Greek in *γύνη*, "woman," if compared with 女 *nio*.

An initial *g* is often dropped, as in *if* from *give*, and in the Platt Deutsch, where *gewesen*, "been," becomes *yevesen*.

H.

The Chinese *h* seems to be a modern letter formed from *k*, *k'*, and *g*. For example, 喜 *hi*, "joy," Latin *gaudium*. The final *d* is recovered from the phonetic, 吉 *kit*, "luck," forming the upper part of the character.

The Japanese *h* represents *p* or *b*. The Mongol *h* represents *k*, *k'*, *g*. In Greek it stands for *s*. In Latin it corresponds to the Chinese *k* and *g*, as *hic*, "this," Chinese 其 *gi*. The same is true in German and English, as *kok* 高, "high," *hoch*, "high."

In the old middle dialect of China, as still spoken in the Sucheu and Hangcheu region, *h* is subdivided into a strong and weak aspirate. In the Mandarin dialect of north and west China, it coincides with *s* when it precedes *i* and *ü*. In Zend and Persian, *h* occurs for *s* in *hapta*, "seven," etc.

The Semitic *heth*, the Scotch *ch* in *loch*, is not used in the eastern Asiatic languages. The Semitic *heth* and *he* both correspond to *g*, and probably derived their origin from that letter.

I.

I is one of the three primitive vowels. In modern Chinese it sometimes becomes *wei*. This we learn from the Japanese, who call *wei*, "a seat," *i*. It is a prefix in Japanese and Tamil, as in *iku*, "how many," from *ki*, "how many?" The changes of vowels are too rapid to allow any general correspondence to be traced between the Chinese *i* and the European equivalent, or *vice versâ*.

J.

The Chinese modern *j* is from *ni*, the Mongol from *d*. The Chinese *j* is *zh*, the Mongol is *dj*. The Sanscrit *j* is *dj*, and is derived from *g*, as *ch* from *k*. The Latin *j* was *y*, and sometimes *dj*, and has changed into *zh* in French, and into *dj* in English. The Mongol *ujihu*, "to see," *jirehe*, "heart," are the Latin *videre* and the Persian *dili*. The Semitic *y* is pronounced *j* by Europeans, as in Jehovah. The Sanscrit *yuj*, "join," in Chinese *yok*, is in Latin *jung*, and in Greek ζευγ, where *dz* is the Greek equivalent of *dj*. The Greeks could not pronounce *ch* or *sh*. The Arabic *j*, pronounced *dj*, is altered from an older *g*, as in *jahannam*, from *Gehenna*, "hell," just as *dj* has replaced *g* in the English words *gender*, *genitive*, etc., derived through the French from the Latin. Thus it appears that *dj* is primitive in no alphabet, but, like *f* and *ch*, is of recent origin, and was perhaps quite unknown in the early languages of the world.

K.

In modern Chinese, *k* before *i* and *ü* has changed to *ch*. In the European languages, *k* changes to *ch* before all vowels, except *o* and *u*. In ancient Chinese, *k* changed to *h*, but was also itself changed from *g*. There are not wanting indications that the true primeval source of *k* was *g*. The original of the Hebrew כִּי, *ki*, "for," "that," and כֹּה, *ko*, "thus," is found in the Chinese 其 *gi*, "he." The Sanscrit *k* corresponds to the Mongol *g*, as *kara*, "hand," Mongol *gar*. The Japanese *k* also corresponds to the Mongol *g*, as in *kado*, "gate," Mongol *egude*, Chinese *hu, gud*. In Sanscrit, *s´* occurs for *k*, as in *s´ata*, "a hundred," as compared with *centum*. The Chinese change from *k* to *h* exists in Mongol, where the Sanscrit *kaṭ'ara*, "hard," is found *hat'o*, Japanese *kataku;* and in Europe, where *collis* became "hill," and *collum*, "neck," *hals*. These two words are in Chinese *ngok*, "hill," and *kang*, "neck," where the old finals both appear. In Russian, *ch* occurs commonly for *k*, as in *chistiye*, "pure," *castus*, the Chinese *kit*, "pure," "clean." In Tamil, the old *k* appears for the Chinese and Mongol *h*, as in *karumei*, "darkness," Mongol *harangwei*, Chinese *hek*.

Kt appears as initial in the Greek κτείνω, "kill." Here the intermediate vowel has been dropped. The Hebrew is *katal*, "he killed," and the true root is *kat*, "to cut."

The aspirated form of *k* appears in Sanscrit, Chinese, the Himalaic languages, in Coorean, and in Mongol and Turkish. Pronounced as the *k* and *h* in the word *inkhorn,* but brought closer together. In Eastern Asia the aspirated and unaspirated *k* are separate letters. In Europe, on the other hand, if *k* is aspirated, it is the consequence of local or individual habit, and embraces all the instances. In the province where *card* is called *k'ard, cold* will also be called *k'old,* and so on.

L.

The Latin *l* is found in Chinese usually as *ch,* coming down from an older *d,* as in 長 *ch'ang,* "long," old sound *dung,* Latin *longus.* So the Hebrew *l,* as in *lakach,* "to take," Greek λαγχάνω, seems to be found in the Chinese *t,* as in *tek,* "to get." Compare also לָבֵשׁ, "clothe," "put on," with the Mongol *debel,* "clothes." The frequent change of *d* to *l* perhaps indicates that the true origin of the letter is *d.*

It is sometimes changed to *n,* as in the Mongol *nogon,* "green," Chinese *lok,* and the Latin *nemus,* "grove," Chinese *lim,* Hebrew *lo,* "not," *non, na.*

L is frequently inserted after an initial *k, t, p, g, d, b,* as in *flat, pledge, black,* as compared with *patina, pactum,* and the Sanscrit *bahula,* "black," and the Chinese *bed,* "spread out," *bang,* "pledge," *mek,* "black."

If *l* occurs after an initial *s* in European languages it is radical, and the *s* not so. Thus, *sloe,* "a wild plum," is in Chinese *li,* "plum," and *slachten,* slay, are in Chinese *lok,* "kill."[1]

---

[1] *Slip,* Latin *labor, lapsus,* German *schleifen.*

THE ALPHABET. 331

Sometimes a connecting vowel is introduced between the initial and the inserted *l*, as in καλύπτω, "hide," "cover," Sanscrit *kub*, Chinese *kap*. For *caput*, "head," the Russians have *glava* and *golova*.

The insertion of *l* is common in some of the Himalaic languages, in Semitic, and in Indo-European languages. It is avoided in Chinese and the triple-branched Turanian system. Hence in comparing roots it must be omitted from the European word before the Chinese or Mongol equivalent can be found.

L is a favourite suffix in Turanian words, and a common third letter in Semitic triliteral roots; as in Mongol *gol*, "river," Chinese *ga*. Hebrew גָּעַל, *ngagal*, "revolved," from a biliteral root *gak*, which appears in *circulus*, *circle*, κύκλος, etc.

L is sometimes inserted between the final consonant and the preceding vowel, as in our word *old*, Mongol *ot'olju*, "old," Latin *vetus*. It then sometimes takes a vowel, as in the Russian *zoloto*, "gold," where *z* is *g*.

In the Cochin-Chinese and Siamese languages *l* takes the place of *h*. So also in the Malayo-Polynesian.[1]

The Chinese *l* is usually *r* in the west, as *rota*, "wheel," Chinese *lut*, "a round thing."

M.

The letter *m* in Chinese corresponds to the *m* of western languages, as in *mel*, "honey," Chinese *mit*;

[1] Thus, *lima*, "five," may agree with the Hebrew *hhamesh*.

miles, "soldier," Chinese *mo,* "military." The final *m* of some European roots is represented by *ng* in Chinese, as κάμπτω, "bend," Chinese 弓 *kung,* "bow," "to bow." The Hebrew final *m* seems to correspond in the same manner to the Chinese final *ng,* as *ram,* "high," Chinese *lung.* The Greek *m* sometimes corresponds to the Mongol *b* and the Chinese *p,* as μακάριος, "blessed," Mongol *boyint'o,* "happy," Chinese *pok,* "happiness."

The Chinese *m* occasionally agrees with the English *b,* as in *black,* Greek μέλας, Chinese *mek,* "ink," Mongol *behe.*

Final *m* has in modern Chinese become *n.*

N.

The letter *n* is frequently interchanged with *t* as in εἷς, ἴδιος, "one," *unus,* Chinese *yit,* "one." Final *n* in Chinese corresponds to final *n* in the west. *Fundo,* to "found," may be compared with the Chinese 本 *pen,* "root," "foundation." Chinese *lun,* "wheel," English "round," Chinese *tan,* "that which is stretched out," Latin *tendo,* "stretch."

Final *n* is often dropped in Tamil, as in *kuzhal,* "tube," Chinese *kwan*; Tamil *kuri, kól,* "stick," Chinese *kan*; Tamil *tâl,* "sheet of paper," Chinese *tan.*

The Tamil *n* final sometimes represents the Chinese *t* final, as in *tan,* "stand," Chinese *dat,* Indo-European *stan, stad.*

What we write *ng* is a separate letter related to *k* and *g*, as *n* is to *t* and *d*. It is initial in Chinese and Tibetan.

The Chinese initial *ng* is apt to be omitted, as in *wo*, "I," formerly *nga*. The final is also often dropped, as in *kwang*, "light," Mongol *gerel*, Japanese *akari*, Latin *gloria*. So also *neng*, "able," Tibetan *nupo*, "one who is able."

In Latin roots *ng* often replaces the final *k*, as in *pingo, pinxi, pictum, pango, pepigi*, etc.

What we write *ni*, is in Sanscrit and old Chinese regarded as a distinct letter belonging to the *ch* and *j* series. It has changed in modern Chinese to *j*. In Turkish and Mongol it is found as *k'* or *g*. For example, *nin*, "man," Turkish *k'ishi*, Mongol *humun*, *ni*, "two," Turkish *ik'i*, *niok*, "flesh," Turkish *gosh*, *ni*, "ear," Turkish *gosh*, *niok*, "if," Turkish *eger*. The European ἀνήρ, and *homo*, "man," seem to belong to this little knot of words. Compare also *gleich*, "like," "if," *gracilis*, "tender," γύνη, "woman," γάλα, "milk," with the Chinese *niok*, "like," "if," *niok*, "weak," "tender," *niu*, "woman," *niu*, "milk."

The Chinese *n*, *ng*, and *ni*, are on the whole usually found *k*, *g*, *h*, in Tartar and European languages. Compare *ngu*, "cow," Mongol *uher*, Latin *vacca*, German *kuh*. *Nga*, "I," *ego*, *niuen*, "origin," γένος, *genus*. *Ngan*, "eye," *oculus*.

Some examples exist of *n* unaltered, as *nehmen*,

nimm, "take," Chinese *nim,* "carry," "burden," "responsibility," in modern Chinese *jen.* For the Hebrew *ayin* see *o.*

O.

The letter *o,* like the other vowels, is often prefixed to roots. Chinese *tʻi,* "tooth," ὀδούς, ὀδόντος, *dens.* Compare in Malay *orang,* "man," with the Polynesian *rang,* "man," and the Chinese *lang,* "man." The Japanese say *obui,* "carry on the back," Chinese *pei.* In Turanian languages the prefixed vowel is the same as that of the root syllable. Mongol *olos,* "people," λαός, *leute.* So in Chinese the colloquial word for "elder brother," is *aka,* where the prefixed vowel takes its quality from that of the root *ka,* the old word for "brother." This is a very old law of change, for it appears also in the Semitic *ahh,* "brother," *ab,* "father."

In the triangle of the three primeval vowels *a, i, u,* the letter *o* stands between *a* and *u,* and is liable to change into either of these vowels, or into the intermediate values *ō, e,* and the *o* in "gone." The old Chinese *o* has become *u* in the modern language. The modern Chinese *o* has come out of *a.*

The Mongol *o* has in the eastern dialect the values *ö* and the *o* in "gone." The Chinese *o* is usually the *o* in "go."

The old Chinese *o* agrees with the European *o,* as in

rota, rotation, Chinese *lon,* "wheel," "revolve," *lot,* "anything round," now changed to *lun, lu.*

The Greek letter *o* was taken from the Phœnician *ayin,* of which the old sound was *ng* and *g*. Thus ענה, "he sang," "he answered," "he spoke," is by Gesenius identified with *cano,* "I sing," but may as probably be compared with the Chinese 言 *ngen,* "words," "to speak." So עמם "congregate," must have been anciently pronounced *gamam.* It is identified by the same grammarian with the root in γάμος, *cum, cumulus,* which is the same with the Chinese 咸 *gam,* "collected." Thus the Hebrew *ayin* was first *g,* then it became *ng,* and was afterwards dropped or changed for a vowel, usually *o.*

P.

P in Chinese rests upon *b* as its base. No widely extended roots with the initial *p* are without representatives in the old sonant series. Thus *pang,* "to tie," has *bog* among the sonants, with the same meaning. Compare the European *pack* and *pango.* In the Mongol syllabary *b* is the normal form of this labial. The aspirated and unaspirated *p* grew out of *b* in the Chinese, Tibetan, and Sanscrit syllabaries. In the Semitic languages *p, v,* and *f,* appeared on the base of *b.* The Greeks, however, assigned the values *b* and *p* to the second and seventeenth Hebrew letters. We must therefore suppose *b* to be older in Hebrew than *v*, and *p* than *f*. All Latin, Teutonic, and Persian words in *f*, can in Chinese and Mongol only have equivalents in *p*. Thus *fugio*, *fliehen*, φεύγω, are in Chinese *bik*, in Mandarin *pi*. The Japanese equivalent for the European and Chinese *p* is *h*. The Egyptian has *p* for the Hebrew *f* in *apta*, "bird," Hebrew צִיפ.

Q.

The letter *q* is *ku* or *kw*, and its existence is a proof that the Phœnician alphabet was once syllabic, and perhaps it may be concluded that Cadmus made use of that alphabet partly at least as syllabic.[1] The Chinese *kwa* comes from an older *ku*, *kwo* from *kok*, and so on. Hence *kw* is modern, and of no use in tracing etymologies on the Chinese side.

R.

This letter has appeared recently in Chinese. It shares with *j* the possession of the inheritance of words once belonging to the lost initial *ni*, as 兒 *ni*, "son," now called *ur*, or *er*, or *rh*, as it is differently written, Turkish *ugli*, Mongol *hubegun*. In Japanese *r* represents the Chinese *l*. In Mongol and Tibetan as an initial it seems to indicate a Semitic origin; for the

[1] Professor Key, in English Cyclopædia, Art. Q. Yet this hypothesis fails to explain why the Hebrew *kuph* is used as a final, as in מָתַק, "was sweet." It may be remarked here that *kuph* in this example is a suffix, the root being *mat*, "honey," "sweet," the Chinese *mit*, and Greek μεθυ.

words in which it is found, e.g., Tibetan *rab*, "high," Mongol *airiben*, "many," Mongol *oregen*, "broad," Mongol *orosiyahu*, "to be pitiful," as compared with רָב, *rab*, "high," "great," "many"; רחב, *rahab*, "broad"; רצה, *ratsa*, "treat kindly."

R is inserted commonly in roots after the initial in the Himalaic, Semitic, and Indo-European languages, and before the final in the latter of these families, as in *crow*, Latin *corvus*, Sanscrit *kâka*, *umbrella* from *umbella*, *sprache* from *speech*, *world* from *welt*. Before comparing roots, this inserted *r* must be everywhere first eliminated. The comparison can then be conveniently made. Thus *sprache*, *speech*. Omit the prefix *s* and the inserted *r*. Change the guttural *ch* into the *k* or *g* from which it sprang. The root is then *pak*, which in old Chinese means "to speak," and is so used in the modern Shanghai dialect.

R is also a common suffix in Himalaic, Turanian, Semitic, and Indo-European languages, as in Tibetan *charpa*, "rain," from *c'hu*, "water," Hebrew *kaphar*, "to cover," Chinese *kap*.

R and *l* are in many respects much alike. The European prefix *r* is in Chinese *l*. Thus, *ros*, *regen*, *rain*, are in Chinese *lu*, "dew," in old times *lok*.

As *l* came from *d*, so also did *r* derive its origin from that letter. The Hebrew ארג, "weave," is *texo* in Latin and *tek* in old Chinese. I suppose both these words to have had formerly an initial *d*. Thus, רֹאשׁ,

rosh, "head," is Chinese *dud*, in modern times *t'eu*. The Semitic *sh* is commonly convertible with *t*, and was perhaps derived from it. The change, however, might be the other way. The Aramean, which used *tam* for "there," is usually supposed to be newer than the Hebrew, which used *sham*. To judge from Chinese analogy, the most widely spread at the present time should be regarded as the newest of the Semitic languages. Further, as Abraham came from the land of the Chaldees, the language-forms preserved in the Nineveh and Babylon inscriptions should be regarded as older than the Hebrew. If so, *t* might be the older form.

R is also introduced as a second letter in Semitic roots. Thus, *baruch*, "the blessed," where the root *bak* agrees with the Chinese *pok*, "happiness."

S.

The letter *s* is freely introduced as a prefix before the radical initials *k, t, p, l, m, n*. Thus, *small* is the same word as *minus*, μικρός, and the Chinese *mi*, "little."

It sometimes comes in place of *e*, as *squire* from *equerry*, the Latin *equites*.

In Sanscrit and Zend *s* stands for *k*, as in the old name *Massagetqe*, where *Massa* is *Mahâ*, or *magnus*, "the great Getae." In Latin *s* final stands for *t*, as in *patior, passus*. In Russian *s* final stands for *k*, as in *sosat*, "to suck." In German it represents *t*, as in *beissen*, "to bite."

In Hebrew both *samech* and *sin* (having each the value *s*) interchange with *t*. Thus, פסס, *pasas*, "diffuse," is in Arabic *basat*. The older form is *t*.

The Chinese *s* corresponds to that of Europe in words such as *su*, in *kau su*, "to tell," old form *sok*, as compared with *sagen*, *say*. So also Chinese *sat*, "scatter," "sow," Latin *sero*, *satus*. This root is in Persian *zed*, as in *ghemzeda*, "heaviness-dispelling." So also Chinese *sok*, English *seek*.

Sometimes the European *s* is recognized in the Chinese *ts* or *t's*. Thus *sot*, "a drunkard," is *tsui* or *tsot*, "intoxicated."

The Chinese *s* becomes *t* in Cochin-Chinese, and generally in the Eastern Himalaic and Malay system.

SH.

This sound was not employed by the Greeks and Romans, and they did not, therefore, need an alphabetic sign to represent it. In the Turanian languages it is also very sparingly used. As it is fully developed in the Chinese, Semitic, and Himalaic families, the cause of its non-appearance in Greek and Latin may be probably traced to Turanian influence.

It has struggled back into existence in the French, where it appears as the representative of the Latin *k*, as in *calor*, French *chaleur*.

The Chinese *sh* is *sh* in Teutonic, Sanscrit, and Sclavonic languages, and *s* in Greek, Latin, and

Mongol. Thus, *schiessen*, "to shoot," is the old Chinese *shet*, "an arrow." 矢, 舍, and 捨, in Mandarin, *shï*, *shè*, *shè*, and meaning "arrow," "shed," "let go." How many summers and winters have passed since the ancestors of the Teutons and of the Chinese parted from each other, each with their vocabulary of common words, such as *to shed, to shoot, a shed,* etc.? It is marvellous that, after so many ages, Time's defacing fingers have not yet destroyed the traces of original identity.

The German *sch* is often softened down from *sk*, as in *schreiben*, the equivalent of *scribo* and γράφω. So the English *sh* comes often from an older *k*, as in "wash," Chinese *ok*, Mongol *ogahu*, "to wash," and perhaps the Greek ὑγρός, ὑγραίνω, "moist," "wet," "to wet," unless that comes from *sok*, our "soak."

The Chinese *sh* is sometimes represented by the European *k*, as in *cado*, "to fall," in Chinese *shwai*, in the old form *shat*, and probably the same as the word "to let go," *shè*, given above. For all verb-roots are capable of assuming the causative, transitive, intransitive, passive, and reflexive modes.

In Semitic languages and in Chinese dialects, *sh* is apt to change to *s* and to *t*. The affinity of *sh* for *k* appears first in Sanscrit and then in Europe generally. At present, however, in the Mandarin change now gradually taking place of *ki* and *kü*, to *chi* and *chü*, as also in that of *hi* and *hü*, to *shi* and *shü*, we see the budding of a similar principle.

We also see *sh* pushing its conquests in the Turanian area, as in Manchu, where it represents the Mongol aspirated *ch*. This *ch* aspirated is in the Mongol area the eastern representative of the northern and western *ts*. For the Buriats, Kalkas, and Kalmucks, all prefer *ts*, which appears to be the older and typical form. The eastern *c'h* may therefore be regarded as a sign of a tendency to introduce *sh*, appearing at the east end of Mongolia. *Sh* proper also occurs in Mongol words commencing with *si*, which are softened into *shi*, as *shidorogo*,[1] "honest." Such is the law in Japanese also. The letter *sh* is thus seen in these three languages asserting its lost existence, and winning back its ancient dominion, as in France, Spain, and other portions of the Latin area it has also been seen to do.

T.

The letter *t* comes in very many cases from *d*. Thus the Japanese *kita*, "north," is in Mongol *hotai*, "behind," "north," *hejem*, "behind," "after." Here *j* is *d*, and the old Chinese word would be *gud*, in the modern clipped form *heu*. So *treten*, "to tread," is in Chinese *dat*. The modern *ti*, "brother," *tau*, "reason," are from older words *de*, *do*. The letter *t* occurs for the Chinese *sh* and *s* in the eastern Himalaic languages.

[1] The Chinese *shih*, "real," old form *shit*.

This letter early became *t'*, a form which probably appeared in the transition from *d*. The Sanscrit, Tibetan, and Chinese, have it in addition to *t* and *d*. In Turkish, Mongol, and Manchu, it is the normal form of *t*; that is, every *t* is aspirated, and sounds like the union of *h* with *t* in "anthill."

The Semitic form of this letter was *th*, as in our "thin," "thick," and the Greek θ in τίθημι, "I place," which occurs for the Mongol *d*, as in θαλάσση, *dalai*, "the sea."

T often precedes *s* in Japanese and Chinese, and in such cases is often aspirated. This compound letter, when not aspirated, is the German *z* in *zeit*, "time," and when aspirated it is the Mongol *t's* softened by the eastern tribes into *c'h*.

The German *z* or *ts* is derived from *t*, as is the Hebrew. For example, צור, *tsor*, Tyre, was by the Greeks, Latins, and Arameans, known as Τύρος, Tyre. Probably in this case *t* was the original sound, but this is not certain.

U.

The letter *u*, like the other vowels, is prefixed in Mongol to roots. In modern Mongol it takes the place of *e*, as in *umun*, "before," in old Mongol *emun*. It corresponds to the Greek ει, as *ujihu*, "to see," εἶδον, εἴδομαι. Here *j* stands for *d*, and *hu* is the sign of the infinitive.

In Japanese and Tamil *u* is prefixed to roots, as in *uma*, "horse."

The modern Chinese *u* (*wu*) has lost *m* from before it in many instances, as in *mo*, "not," now *wu*. It has also taken a prefix before it very frequently; for example, *e* in *du*, "sorrowful," modern sound *ch'eu*, Latin *dolor*, *doleo*.

The old equivalent of the modern Chinese *u* was *o*. The modern diphthongs *au, eu, iau, ieu*, were formerly *o, u, o, u*.

A modern form of *u* is *ü*. This vowel appears in no ancient alphabet, so far as can be known. Its place in the triangle of which the angles are the three primitive vowels, is between *u* and *i*. As it has replaced *u* in some Chinese and Mongol words, so has it done in many French words of Latin derivation.

V.

The letter *v* has taken the place of *u* in many Latin words, as *vereor*, "to fear," Chinese *wei*, Mongol *aimoi*. The Romans, however, pronounced it *w*. The Germans have also changed initial *w* to *v*, retaining the written symbol unaltered. The English are right to keep *w* in "was," "were," "will," for the equivalent words in Chinese and Mongol have no trace of *v*. The Germans write *werden, wollen, was*, correctly, but they are wrong in the sound they give to the initial *w*.

The Greek *digamma* was *v* or *w*, as in Ϝεικοσι, *viginti*, "twenty." Here the *d* of the full form *duikosi* was dropped, and *u* became F, and was afterwards lost.

That the Sanscrit *v* was a vowel seems to be deducible from facts such as that the suffix of the dative case was *ye* or *ve*.

The old Chinese *v* was the sonant form of *f*, and as such came from *b*. In modern Chinese it has become *f*. Its equivalent in western alphabets is *b* or *p*.

In Hebrew, *beth* took *v* as one of its values. This was followed by the Greeks, who used their *beta* for words written by the Romans with *v*. So at present the Russians for the sound *v* write the sign в, herein imitating the Greeks. The Hebrew *vav* was formerly *w*.

The Tamil *v*, like that of Sanscrit, represents the *w* of old Chinese, and the *ui* of Mongolian.

The German *v* is an *f*, as in *Vogel*, "bird," *Vater*, "father." The English *v* is a German *b*, as in *eben*, *even*.

Thus it appears that in Hebrew, old Chinese, English, and German, *v* rests on *b* and *f*. In Latin, Sanscrit, Tamil, and Russian, it is a mispronunciation of the primitive *w*.

W.

The letter *w* belongs as an initial to the old and new Chinese. In the old Hebrew alphabet it was *vav*, afterwards pronounced *v*. In Greek the Chinese *w* appears as a vowel. The root *wan*, "to bend," appears in the

THE ALPHABET. 345

Latin *vinum* and Greek οἶνος, "wine," from *vinea*, "a vine," "that which bends." The English and Greek keep the primeval *w*. In Latin as now pronounced, and in French, it is changed to *v*.

The European *w*, as preserved in the Saxon part of the English language, and in the ancient Latin, is represented in Chinese and Mongol by a vowel initial, which may be *a, o, i,* or one of the corresponding consonantal values, *w, y.* Thus *vulgus,* "the people," is in Mongol *olos*; *vacca,* "cow," is *uher*; *video,* "see," is *ujimoi,* etc. So also *wail* is in Mongol *weilehu*; "was," "were," are in Mongol *aho,* "to be," *weiledhu,* "to do," (the substantive verb here assuming an active character,) and in Chinese *wei,* "to do," or "to be." The German *wechseln,* "to change," is in Chinese *yik.* Here the *y* is a modern prefix. A form still more modern is *l*, as in Mandarin. The Latins had *vicis,* "change," *vix, vicissim,* etc. In the Greek ακις of πεντάκις, "five times," we have the same root meaning "times," and it may be the origin of the Latin *es* in *vicies,* "twenty times," and the English *ce* in *once, twice.*

The letter *w* is inserted after the initial of a root. This seems to occur through a tendency in the vowel *u* to become a consonant. Thus *ku,* "a melon," in Europe "cucumber," "gourd," etc., is in modern Chinese *kwa.* The vowel *a* is an addition, and *u* appears as *w.* So in our word *sweat, w* represents the vowel *u* of *sudor* and *sudo*, and *ea* is inserted. The same thing takes place when the first letter is *u*, as in *uge*, the Mongol for "word." This corresponds to *voco* and *vox* in Latin. The vowel *u* becomes a consonant *v*, and *o* is inserted. So in the Chinese *yue*, "say," in the old form *wat*, the English equivalent is *word*, where *r* is inserted. The Latin is *aio*, "I say," the Greek αὐδή, "voice." The Hebrew *yadah*, "praise," may be the same word. The original primeval root was probably *ad* or *ud*. From this the Chinese formed 曰 and 謂, *yue* and *wei*, both anciently called, we may suppose, *ud*, and afterwards *yet* and *wat*. In the mediæval dictionaries they are read *yet*, *wei*.

A similar change took place in Semitic words. Thus the city *Erech*, in the old Hebrew *Ark* (where the initial vowel was perhaps intended to be repeated in the second syllable, so that it would read *Arak*), is now *Waraka*. The Arabs have prefixed *w*. The Latin form was *Areca*. It means "the long" city. The pointing of the grammarians, directing it to be read *Erech*, cannot represent a very ancient pronunciation.

X.

The letter *x* and the *ksh* of Sanscrit represent combinations of *k* and a sibilant. They are unknown in the languages of Eastern Asia. The Greek ξ took the place of the Hebrew *Samech* between *n* and *o*. Hence we learn that the base was looked on as *s*, and *k* as an addition. But its real value was nearer to *k* than to *s*. This is shown by such words as ξυνός, " common," which is the same as κοινός. If, then, Palamedes and his associates, who are said in the time of the Trojan War to have added θ, ξ, φ, χ, to the alphabet, proceeded to give this letter its position on the supposition that it is modified from *s*, they were mistaken. It is, in fact, formed by inserting *s* after *k*. Thus, ξηρός, " dry," is convertible with σχερός, σκηρός, and χέρσος, all meaning " dry." In a similar way ψ, *psi*, is formed from *p* by inserting *s*, and in Hebrew *ts* from *t* in the same manner. Thus, ψυχή, " the breath," " soul," is the Chinese *p'ak*, "the corporeal soul," which is distinct from the *hwun* or *gun*, " the immaterial soul." This last word by interchange of final *n* with final *p* becomes *gut*, and may be identified with *kwei* or *ket*, " ghost," " geist." So also ψυχρός, " cold," is the Latin *frigidus*, *r* being inserted in place of *s* in the more western form.

The Chinese and Tibetan are like the Semitic family in not taking *s* after *k* or *p*, but only after *t*.

Y.

The letter *y* is *i* viewed as a consonant. Vowel initials have a tendency to assume a consonantal form. Of the three prime vowels, *i* takes *y*, *u* takes *w*, and *a* takes either *y*, as in the Tibetan *yab*, "father," from the

Semitic *ab*, or *w*, as in the Chinese *wan*, "bend," "circle," when compared with *annus*, "a year," or *ng*, as in Mandarin *ngan*, "rest," from *an*, the old form.

The Chinese *y* is *j* in Latin, as *yik*, "to throw," *jacio*, English *jerk*. In Greek it agrees with the unaspirated *i*, as ἴδιος, "alone," Chinese *yit*, "one." Here, too, we see the probable origin of *idem*, "the same," "identical." It is the Mongol *adeli*, "same," and the Chinese *yit*, "one."

The vowel *o* also is apt to take *y* before it. The Mongol *ogahu*, "wash," is in Chinese *yok*.

The Chinese *y* and Latin *j* are in Sanscrit *y* and in Greek ζ. This makes some confusion, for one of the most common values of *j* is *d* + *zh*, and it is formed from an older *d* with *zh* inserted, as *Jupiter* from *Diu*. In Σδεύς, a dialectic form of Ζεύς, the sibilant is placed before the initial *d*, instead of after. Hence *j* in Latin and *z* in Greek sometimes come from *d*, and at other times from *y*. In German *j* has the value *y*. In English *y* is used as in *yoke*, German *joch*, except in words of Latin derivation, as *juvenile*, which in Chinese is *yeu*, old form *yu* or *u*.

Z.

The letter *z* may be connected with *s*, *d*, *y*, *t*, or *k*.

Old Chinese words in *z* (that is, in the sonant series of *s*) have now become *s*.

In the Hebrew vocabulary words with *samech*, *tsade*, and *shin* sometimes take *zayin*. Thus, *zûr*, *sûr*, are both used for "to return."

In Hebrew the occasional origin of *z* from *d*, like that of *s*, *ts*, *sh*, from *d* and *t*, may be shown by examples. Thus, בזא, *baza*, "cut in two," is by Gesenius compared with the Sanscrit *bhidh*, "to cut." Compare also the Greek ρίζα, "root," with *radix*.

In Tibetan *zang*, "copper," *zab*, "deep," *zar*, "fork," seem to be allied with the Chinese *dung*, "copper," the European *deep*, and the Chinese *t'a*, "fork."

The connexion of *z* with *y* has been already noticed in speaking of the Greek *zeta* under *y*.

In German *t* has become *z*, and is then pronounced *ts*.

In Russian final *k* in a root often becomes *z*, as in *lizat*, "to lick," German *lecken*.

The letter *zh* is otherwise written *j*, as in the French *jamais*, *jour*.

In Chinese it has grown from an older *ni*.

It must be looked for in European vocabularies as *n*, *h*, *k*, etc., as stated under *j*.

Common Radical Syllabary.

The common roots of the Chinese and European languages consist of monosyllables. That all roots are monosyllabic was known by philologists as the result of the comparison made, in the first half of the present century, of European languages with those of Western

Asia and India. But when the roots of European speech are compared with those of China, they assume a definite shape, at the knowledge of which philologists, while they hesitated to cross in their researches the Imaus and the Himalayas, could scarcely arrive.

Roots may be first arranged in two groups, those which end in vowels and those which end in consonants. Among examples of the first are words such as *a*, used as "I," and as a verb "to be," *ba*, "father," *ma*, "mother." Of the second are *bad*, "divide," "other," *kab*, "cover," "head," *nig*, "hide," "black," *dak*, "cover," *bang*, "strike," "noise of slamming," *kan*, "tube," "straight stick," *om*, "dark," "shade."

All the vowels interchange, but the chief lines of distinction are between *a, i, u*. Thus we have among the open syllables a triple division made by these primary vowels.

The closed syllables in ultimate roots are chiefly formed by the six consonants *g, d, b, ng, n, m*.

The initials are the three vowels, the six consonants just mentioned, with *l, z*, and *zh*.

The syllabary, with these elements, would consist of, (1) three vowels; (2) eighteen biliteral syllables with consonant finals; (3) twenty-seven biliteral combinations with vowel finals; (4) 162 triliteral combinations with consonant initials, vowel medials, and consonant finals. In all there would, with these elements, be 210 combinations.

This is the smallest number of syllables that we can allow for the common syllabary, unless we also eliminate *l*, by deducing it from *d*.

If we add to the initials *k, t, p, s, z, w, y*, there will be twenty-one more biliteral combinations, and 126 more triliteral. In all 357. These are perhaps the most probable and convenient limits for the common syllabary.

It would be unwise to extend the finals by adding *k, t, p*, for although in European roots the difference between *k, t, p*, and *g, d, b*, is recognized, it is not so in any Chinese dialect. The Shanghai people pronounce *g* final before a sonant and *k* before a surd. The difference depends on position, but the fact indicates the possibility of *g, d, b*, having once occupied an important place in the Chinese syllabary which was afterwards lost to *k, t, p*, as these have in their turn resigned their position at the ends of words in favour of the vowels.

Examples will be here given tending to show that it cannot be learned from the European roots whether *k, t, p*, and *g, d, b*, all belonged to the primeval syllabary or not.

The English *reed*, German *rohr*, is in Chinese *lu* and *lut*. The Latin *rota, rotundus*, and the Greek ῥυθμός, ἀριθμός, with the English *round* and Latin *arundo*, "reed," all come from the same root. The finals *t, d, nd*, are found interchanging in European languages, while in Chinese, where *lun* is "wheel," and *lut* "anything round," *n* and *t* interchange. A fair inference is, that we cannot tell whether *t* or *d* was the original final, but that *n* and that final were interchangeable before the Chinese language separated from the Indo-European.

So with the Chinese *yok*, "to desire," when compared with the Latin *acer*, French *aigre*, and English *eager*, we cannot tell if *k* or *g* is the older.

The arts of life had sufficiently advanced, when the Chinese separated from the Indo-Europeans, for the names of boats, of agricultural processes, of weaving, of houses, of the physician and the necromancer, to be the same.

Take *texo*, "to weave," Chinese *tak*, meaning "to weave cloth," or "to weave a hedge" of willow branches or bamboos. The corresponding European words do not appear ever to have *d* or *g* in them. Hence it may be inferred that in this case *t* was the form of the initial previous to the separation of the races. The Russian is *tikat* or *tkat*, "to weave." The Greek has τεῦχος, "a wall."

At that distant time wooden cups were in use, which were called *pat*, 杯 the Sanscrit *pátra*, the Latin *patera*. "A boat" was *bat*, and "an oar" was *lut*, ἐρετμόν. "A house" was *ok*, οἶκος. "To heal," and "a physician" were both *it*, ἰατρός, ἰάομαι. "A magician" was *ma*, the Mongol *bo*, Persian *magus*, and Dravidian *bagai*. "A dog" was *k'on*, "a cow," *gu*. "A coverlid" and "to cover" were *bed*, the Latin *pallium*, and English *bed*. "To clothe" and "clothing" were *wit*, the Latin *vestio*, *vestis*. If *boat* and *paddle* (Latin *batillus*), and *bowl* and *patera*, are connected, it seems hopeless to expect that the original form of the initial, whether *b* or *p*, can now be ascertained with certainty.

European Radical Syllabary.

The European families while still one with the Hindoo prefixed *s* and *sh* to the initial consonant of many roots, and also inserted *r* or *l* after the initial in many more. To the six final consonants of the roots, which were originally *k, t, p, ng, n, m*, were added *s, sh, r, l*. Further, *r* and *l* were often inserted before the final consonant of the root.

These processes were common to the Semitic and Indo-European systems. In the Semitic system the result was a vast formation of dissyllabic roots consisting of three letters each. Sibilant prefixes, the insertion of *r* and *l*, the duplication of certain letters, and the addition of *r, l, s, sh, p, m, k, h*, and perhaps others at the end, made that formation what it is. There is no trace of sibilant prefixes in the Turanian languages, nor of the insertion of *r* and *l* after the initial consonants of roots. In Eastern Asia sibilant prefixes occur only in Tibetan and Burmese, and the insertion of *r* and *l* only in these languages and in the eastern Himalaic family. We may, therefore, refer the sibilant prefixes and the insertion of *r* and *l* to Semitic influence. At least, these phenomena first make their appearance in that family, and the example was followed in the Indo-European and Himalaic systems. Examples: Hebrew *shakab*,[1] "he reclined," κύπτω, *cubo, cumbo*, English *scoop*. Hebrew *sagab*, "was high," *gabab*, "was high," *shafat*, "he judged," from *pat* or *bad*, "divide."

Turanian influence on the European root appears in the finals, where *r*, *l*, *s*, are found as in Semitic. Examples: Mongol *agola*, Manchu *alin* (where the *g* of the root is dropped, as in colloquial Mongol), Sanscrit *giri*, Greek ὄρος, German *Hügel*, English *hill*. The Greek has dropped the initial *g*. For the Turanian *l* we find the English and German *l* corresponding. The Semitic is *har*, which has been followed by the Sanscrit and Greek. The Latin *collis* joins the Teutonic group. The Sclavonic *gora* is in agreement with the Semitic and Greek. The German medial *g*, which might seem to be an intruder, is found in the Chinese root *gok*, "mountain." It has been lost in all the other languages. Hence the European root is *gor* or *gol*, while the ultimate root is *gok*, with the sense "high," as in the words *high* and *hoch*.

[1] For the prefix of the sibilant in Hebrew to biliteral roots, see Gesenius, Lex. Man., 954, under the letter שׁ.

Greek εὐρύς, "broad," Sanscrit *uru*, Mongol *oregun*, "wide." Here *ur* seems to be the root.

Greek ἄρρην, ἄρσην, "male," Mongol *ere*.

Greek πόλις, German *burgh*, *berg*. Mongol *balgasun* and *balig*. Here the root is *balg* or *balig*, and the insertion of *l* is of Turanian origin. *Khanbalik*, the Turkish name of Peking in the time of Polo, means "the city of the Khan."

The European root shows a special and independent activity in its great extension of the sibilant prefixes and of inflexions, and in the great variety of its initials and finals.

The European Word.

In assuming the polysyllabic form, the European word followed the Turanian analogy rather than the Semitic. This is signally manifest in the formation of derivatives, of case suffixes, of the polysyllabic tenses and moods of verbs, and of the greater portion of the particles.

Yet the Semitic influence is very apparent in the introduction of strong preterites, doubled consonants, and all tense forms where the change of the vowel is a characteristic. The English preterite in *oo*, *u*, *e*, *ou*, or *o*, etc., from a present in *a*, *i*, etc., may be accounted for most satisfactorily in this way. This principle of change in the vowel—as in *seethe, sodden, stand, stood, senden, gesandt*—occurs less prominently in Greek and Latin, where λείπω becomes ἔλιπον, and *spargo* becomes *spergo* in *dispergo* and other compounds. In the first of these examples the change fixes the tense, in the other it depends on laws of accent and quantity. In the Hebrew such changes distinguish tenses and moods, and so we find it in the Tibetan. We must suppose, then, that the ancestors of the Germans, Greeks, English, and Tibetians, adopted this mode of marking tense, mood, and conjugation, from the Semites.

The distinction of masculine and feminine is also of Semite origin, and with it the idea of dual and plural numbers.

The conception of mood and tense is chiefly Turanian. To this the Indo-European has, as its own contribution, added the distinction of voice, the augments of the past tenses, an increased number of tenses, and a very full development of the personal endings.

A Greek verb has in its imperative the simple root, as found in all languages. Its particles and infinitive, past, future, conjunctive, and other forms, are Turanian. They are made by verbal and pronominal suffixes, in many cases identical with those used in Turanian languages. The theory of the conjugation of verbs rests on the mode of viewing the verb. It is regarded as a substantive, and the infinitive and participles were apparently first formed, the verb being here more concrete. From them came the past tenses of the indicative, in the manner already described in preceding chapters.

The formation of compounds reveals to us the principle of juxtaposition, as in the oldest stems. Thus, in λευκόστολος, "white-robed," the law of order is as in Chinese and Turanian. Where a preposition combines with a verb or noun to form a compound, the principle of order is Turanian, and not Chinese. Thus, καταπατέω, "to trample down," is in Chinese *chai hia*, or, as the ancient sages would have pronounced it, *dat ge*, where *ge*, the equivalent of κατά, comes last. The English agrees with the Chinese, and the principle of arrangement is that of the juxtaposition of two verbs in the order of time. But in English the word *down*, originally a verb, has become an adverb. In the Greek compound the principle of arrangement is Turanian. The word κατά, originally a verb, "to go down," and the same with the Chinese *ge*, or *hia*, and the Japanese *kudaru*, "go down," is here found in the position of the adverbs of space and direction, as in Mongol *dôtai tebi*, "place below." So in English *understand*, in German *verstehen*. So in Russian *nishodit*, "to go down," where *ni*, "down," is connected with *nijnie*, "lower," as in the name *Nijnie Novgorod*, literally "the lower new city." The English *down* is the Latin *de*, the Chinese *ti*, "bottom," and the Mongol *do*, "below." Thus the Indo-European languages in their prepositional verb compounds use a Turanian law of arrangement, while giving to the preposition a verb force which is peculiar to those languages.

EUROPEAN SYNTAX.

The syntax of the European languages is a mixture. It contains Chinese, Semitic, and Turanian principles. The order of words is either natural or inverted. Where it is natural, as in "William's son," "tall man," "William struck Thomas," "quickly fly," "with a stick William struck Thomas," the order is usually Chinese and primeval. Where it is inverted, as in "the son of William," "un ouvrier industrieux," "du sollst Gott, deinen Herrn, anbeten,"[1] "thou shalt worship God thy Lord," it is by principles derived from the more ancient Semitic and Turanian families. The post-position of the adjective, genitive, and adverb, is Semitic; that of the verb is Turanian.

The effect of Semitic influence is seen at its maximum in the translations of the Scriptures made in the sixteenth and seventeenth centuries, *e.g.*, in Luther's we read, "Aller Augen, die in der Schule, sahen auf ihn." The English version reads, "And the eyes of all them that were in the synagogue were fastened on him." The relative clause in both cases is thoroughly Semitic. The only feature not Semitic is in the German, in the order of the words *aller Augen*, "eyes of all." The Mongol would be *horal on dotora baiksan hwun bugudeger nidun yer teguni sirtabai*, which might be translated word for word thus, "Synagogue's within being men all eyes-with him observed." *All* refers to

[1] Luther's Bible, Luke iv. 8.

men, and *with* to *eyes*. *Him* is the accusative after *observed*. The participle *being* is in the past tense, and here performs the duty of the relative.

The same Semitic influence, however, appears in Homer. Thus, in ἄναξ ἀνδρῶν, "king of men," the genitive comes last, and the adjective in δουρί τε μακρῷ, "with a long spear."

GREEK.

The Greek seems to be specially founded on the Chinese in regard to tones. For what are the acute, grave, and circumflex accents but Chinese tones? Yet we have found tones existing in the Himalaic languages and also in a dialect of the Mongol. It is, therefore, uncertain from what source in particular the Greek accents are derived.

Vocal sounds are necessarily either emphasized or slurred, even or inflected, high or low, long or short, or, in other words, admit of distinctions in emphasis, tone, pitch and quantity. In modern Europe the quick rising inflexion or tone is appropriated to questions. When and where this began it is difficult to say. It would not be much needed in ancient Greek, for in that language very commonly interrogative words were placed at the beginning of sentences, and this inflexion was probably the proper sound of the acute accent. The grave accent would then be the quick descending inflexion heard in modern Europe as the tone of commands. The circumflex would be a combination of the rising and falling inflexion.

Long and short quantity may be illustrated in Eastern Asia by the distinction between long and short tones in the south-eastern dialects of China, and that between long and short vowels in Sanscrit.

The Greek circumflex was attached only to syllables long by nature. The Chinese circumflex or double inflexion may be applied to any word, according as it happens in the local habit of any dialect to be appropriated to this or that tone class to which the word in question belongs.

The occurrence of a long vowel in the last syllable of a Greek word necessitated the change of a circumflex to an acute accent in the penultimate. Thus, φεῦγε became φεύγω, and οἶνος became οἴνου. This change resembles the change of inflexion noticed sometimes in Chinese compounds. In the Peking pronunciation of *shui sheu,* "sailor," the application of the lower slow rising inflexion (which properly belongs to them) to both words would be unpleasant to the ear. The first word takes instead the upper quick rising inflexion. In Pekinese, as in the ancient Greek, it is easier to pronounce a long inflexion before a short syllable than before a long one.

Prefixes threw the accent back. Thus, τύπτω, "I strike," became ἔτυπτε, "he struck." παιδευτός "taught," became ἀπαίδευτος, "untaught." So in the

LIST OF GREEK AND MONGOL COMMON WORDS. 361

Pekinese dialect, composition often deprives the last word of its emphasis. Thus, *Yamen,* "public office for despatch of business," which originally means "flag door," is emphasized on the first syllable, which keeps its proper tone, the upper quick rising inflexion, while the last syllable, requiring the same inflexion, is slurred over. A prefix in this instance deprives the word *men,* "door," of its tone.

The special resemblance of Greek to Chinese and Mongol may be judged of by the following examples:

αὐτός, "he," "same," "himself," Mongol *adeli,* "same," Latin *idem.*
οἶκος, "house," Latin *vicus,* "village," Chinese *ok,* "house."
ὁράω, "see," Mongol *harahu,* "see," "look at steadily."
θάλασσα, "sea," Mongol *dalai,* "sea."
ψεῦδος, "lie," Chinese *put,* "not," Latin *falsus,* English *false.*
σύ, "thou," Latin *tu,* Mongol *chi,* Mandarin *si,* Doric τύ.
οὐκ, "not," Mongol *ugei,* "there is none."
ἀνοίγω, "to open," Mongol *nehehu,* "to open."
πόλις, "city," German *burg,* Mongol *balgasun,* "fortified place," "city."
ἄρσην, "male," Mongol *ere,* "male," Latin *vir.*
θύω, "to sacrifice," Mongol *tehihu,* "to sacrifice."
κύανος, "dark blue," Chinese *hiuen, gun,* "dark."
σίδηρος, "iron," Chinese *t'it,* Mongol *tumur.*
κύων, "dog," Latin *canis,* Chinese *k'iuen,* English *hound.*
ψυχή, "soul," "life," Chinese *p'ak,* "animal soul."
κελαινός, "black," Mongol *hara,* Chinese *kek.*
πενθός, "grief," Chinese *pei, pit,* "grieved."
γῆ, "earth," Mongol *gajir,* "earth."

On these words the following observations are offered.
1. As the Mongol *adeli* is nearer to αὐτός than to *idem,* and *chi* and *si,* "thou," are nearer to the Ionic σύ than the Latin and Doric, it may be inferred that the old

Turanian colony, whose language influenced the Greek, would be in juxtaposition with the Ionian Greeks in Asia Minor.

2. The same supposed Turanian colony would add the second syllable *ga* to the root *bal*, "city," after separation from the Greeks, but while still in the neighbourhood of the Gothic stem. For instance, this may have taken place on the east of the Caspian Sea, where the Goths were long settled.

3. The addition of the favourite sibilant suffix in most of these words would take place after the epoch of Turanian influence, and therefore after the time when the infinitive in $\epsilon\iota\nu$, the participles in $\omega\nu$, $\mu\epsilon\nu$, and σ, the past tenses in κ and σ, etc., were formed. Thus, $\beta o \nu \lambda \epsilon \nu o \mu \epsilon \nu$ was formed before $\beta o \nu \lambda \epsilon \nu \acute{o} \mu \epsilon \nu o \varsigma$, and *aman*, "loving," before *amans*.

4. The change of *t* to *s* is specially prominent in Greek, Hebrew, and Mongol. It is greater in Hebrew and Greek than in Mongol. It may be regarded then as a characteristic of Western Asia, where the Turanians seem to have been settled before they were in Tartary. The existence of a law like this goes far to show that these three language-stems have one origin.

LATIN.

The resemblance of the Latin verb to that of the Tartar dialects is most remarkably seen in the gerund and supine. In this part of the verb the Latin is peculiarly old, and reveals a special affinity for that Turanian characteristic which views the verb as predominantly a substantive. Only in Sanscrit, where the use of the participle is specially extended, is the influence of the Turanian idea equally prominent. In the pronouns and adverbs some remarkable similarities to Latin words in Turkish, Mongol, and Japanese, have been already pointed out. The following examples will help to give an enlarged idea of the number of such resemblances:—

homo, "man," Mongol *humun*, Chinese *nin*.
vulgus, "people," Greek ὄχλος, Mongol *olos*.
vetus, "old," Mongol *otolji*, "old."
egeo, "to be in want," Mongol *ugei*, "there is none."
os, ossis, "bone," Greek ὀστέον, Mongol *yesa*.
aurum, "gold," Mongol *alte*, "gold."
puto, "think," Mongol *bodaho*, "think," "compute."
odi, "hate," Mongol *usihu*, "hate."
pauci, "few," *baga*, "small," English *few*.
emo, "buy," Chinese *mai*, English *buy*.
alter, alius, "other," Mongol *ore*, German *oder*, Greek ἄλλος.
oppidum, "town," Chinese *ip*, "city." Compare *urbs*.
jus, justus, "just," Mongol *yoso*, "right."
quæro, "seek," *quæso*, "pray," Mongol *goyoho*, "pray," Chinese *gu*, "seek," "pray."
ambulo, "walk," Mongol *yabahu*.
altus, "high," Mongol *undur*.
mille, "thousand," Mongol *minggen*.
decet, "it is becoming," Mongol *johistai*, Chinese *tong, tok*, "ought."
peto, "seek," Mongol *badaraho*, "seek."

The old form *ollus* for *ille*, "he," is the Turkish *ol*, "he." Examples of resemblance to Turkish, Manchu,

Mongol, and Chinese words occur in all parts of speech in the Latin vocabulary. So with the Tibetan, as in *nig,* "black," which is the same with *niger.*

This similarity in words and in the conjugation of the verb is well borne out by the syntax. Compared with Greek, the Latin syntax shows more of Turanian influence. The greater freedom and flow noticed in the Greek arrangement of words is due to a more thorough and prolonged intercourse with Phœnicians, Assyrians, and other ancient Semite races. The different spirit of Greek and Latin syntax finds its solution here.

The Turanian element in Latin syntax may be noticed in the favourite position of the verb. In Livy's First Book the following sentences occur: "Nondum maturus imperio Ascanius Æneæ filius erat." A Greek would not put the little verb *erat,* "was," last in the sentence. A Turanian could place it nowhere else. "Tamen id imperium ei ad puberem ætatem incolume mansit." The arrangement is Turanian, except that the preposition *ad,* "till," should take the place of a suffix after *ætatem.* "Tantisper tutela muliebri (tanta indoles in Lavinia erat) res Latina et regnum avitum paternumque puero stetit." In this sentence the Turanian element operating on the syntax keeps the verb in its place at the end, in the parenthesis, and in the principal sentence. The position of four adjectives after their nouns is evidence of Semitic influence, and this principle is retained in the French language to the present time. The natural place of the adjective is, however, retained by *tanta* before *indoles*.

"Ab eo coloniæ aliquot deductæ, Prisci Latini appellati." The first of the two participles in this sentence corresponds in position to the Turanian gerund occurring at the end of a subordinate clause. The last participle, used here as a perfect indicative, corresponds to the Mongol past participle in *ksan*, which is also constantly used as a perfect indicative, terminating the principal clause. The introduction of the parenthesis is impossible in Eastern Asiatic syntax. Western freedom originated this phenomenon.

The Latin seems to stand further back in time than the other European languages, and possesses an air of antique dignity which has been derived from the east. Roman solemnity and power appear in marked contrast to Greek poetry and life. Among the causes which produced this variety in the language, as in the history and literature of these two races, probably none was more powerful than the intimate intercourse they had in a long distant antiquity with Turanian and Semitic peoples. The character of the Roman family relationships is strongly suggestive of connexion with China and Tartary. The Latin *gens* and the Celtic *clan* are the counterpart of the Chinese *sok* (Latin *socius*) and the Mongol *turul*. The Latin *patruus* and *avunculus*, uncle on the father's, and on the mother's side, respectively, agree in sense with the Mongol *abaga* and *nagacho*, and with the Chinese *pak* and *gu*. The resemblance of Mongol and Roman usage is here the more observable, because the Chinese subdivides the relationship on the father's side into two classes. The uncles who are older than the father are called *pak*, and those who are younger are known as *shok*. The Manchu *amji* and *echig* correspond with the Chinese. The Mongol calls both kinds of uncles *abaga*.

Other remarkable agreements between Chinese and Roman customs exist. For example, the Romans used raised altars of earth or stone for the worship of heavenly divinities, and scooped a hollow in which to place offerings to those that are terrestrial. The Chinese offerings of bullocks and silk at the Temple of Heaven are presented on an elevated altar, while at that of Earth they are, both silk and bullock, buried in the ground. The belief in the presence of spiritual beings in the woods, streams, trees, cultivated fields, and mountains, and the worship of them, was very similar among the ancient Romans and the ancient Chinese, so much so as frequently to impress the reader of passages in the Chinese classics bearing on these subjects with the idea of ancient connexion with the old Latin religion. The whole argument for the common origin of eastern and western nations might perhaps securely rest alone on the institution of sacrifices and

THE RUSSIAN SYLLABLE REDUCED. 367

religious ideas. No one can deny the remarkable similarities between the religions of the old western world and China, which spring up to view on making special inquiry. But the main scope of our investigation is philological, and it is well to attend chiefly to that branch of evidence.

RUSSIAN.

The Russian language shows what the Sclavonic type of European speech has arrived at in its most modern form. It has a very full alphabet, including *s, z, j, sh, ts, ch,* and an aspirated *ch* among its sibilants. The old final *g* or *k* of a root syllable is often found in Russian changed to *j* or *ch.* Thus *Bog,* "God,"[1] becomes *bojie,* "divine." The compound *ts* represents an old *t,* as *tsel,* in German *Ziel,* in Greek τέλος, "end," "aim."

The letter *v* represents the *w* of Chinese and English, and the *v* of Latin and German, as in *voda,* "water," *volya,* "will."

As an initial, *z* represents an old *g,* as *zoloto,* for "gold," *zina* for *hyems,* "winter," *znanie,* "knowledge," γνῶσις.

The Russian language is fond of prefixing several consonants to the root, as in *vskochit, vsklochit,* "to clot," "entangle." *Klochit* means the same thing. The prefixed *s* is the usual Indo-European sibilant prefix, and

[1] Supposed to come from the Sanscrit *bhagavat,* "the blessed," "the glorious," "the adorable."

the initial *v* is an old *u* placed before the word in the Greek and Mongol fashion. The *l* is inserted, as in the English word, after the initial consonant of the root.

Sometimes a concourse of consonants is caused by a vowel dropping out, as in *mnogie*, "many," where the English word shows that an *a* has been lost. The word for "prince" is *knyaz*, and is the same as the German *König*, "king." The *g* is softened into a sibilant, but is retained in the feminine *knyaginya*, "princess." The Chinese is *kiün* or *kon*, "chief," "leader."

The Russian declension of nouns and verb paradigm are very full, and in this respect the language wears an old aspect.

The syntax is simple and modern, and seems to have fewer inversions than the Sclavonic, from which it has sprung. A few examples here follow, taken from the ecclesiastical Sclavonic version of the New Testament, now about seven centuries old, and the modern Russian version published in 1862 by order of the Synod of Moscow. Acts i. 7. Sclavonic: *Muja dva stasta pred nimi bo odejdi byelye*. In English, translated word for word, this reads, "men two stood by them in clothing white." The Russian is *vdrug predstali ime dva muja ve byeloi odejdye*, "suddenly stood by them two men in white clothing." The Russian restores the adjective to its place before the noun. It uses a compound *predstali* for "stood by." It is formed by prefixing the preposition *pred*, "near," as our word *bystander*, from *by*.

Acts ii. 31. Sclavonic: *I budet ve poslyedniya dni*, *glagolete Gospod izliyo o Duha moigo na vsyaku plot.* "And shall be in last days, saith Lord, I will pour of Spirit my on all flesh." The Russian is almost identical with the Sclavonic. *I budet ve poslyetnie dni, govorite Boge izliyo ote Duhe Moego na vsyakuyo plot.* A new word, *govorit*, is introduced for "saith." The Sclavonic and Russian word *Boge*, "God," is substituted for *Gospode*, "Lord," which seems to have come into the Sclavonic version through inadvertence. The word *plot* in Sclavonic and Russian is our "flesh," the consonant *f* not being used in the Sclavonic. *Duhe*, "Spirit," is the Hebrew *ruahh*, "spirit," "wind." The preposition *ve*, "in," is also Semitic.

Acts iii. 15. Sclavonic: *Nachalnika je jizni ubili.* Literal English: "Prince and of life they killed." Russian: *A nachalnika jizni ubili*, "And prince of life they killed." The Russian restores "and" to its place at the beginning of the sentence. The Sclavonic *je*, "and," like its etymological equivalent *que* in Latin, is placed after its noun. In this example, so nearly the same in both languages, there seems to be no sufficient reason for placing the verb last, except the presence of a Turanian element, the same which we have found powerfully operating in Sanscrit and in Latin.

ANGLO-SAXON.

The following sentences are taken from Vernon's

Anglo-Saxon Guide. "He cannot help him," is rendered by *He him helpan ne maeg,* "He him help not may." "How she may escape from the hostile spirits," is translated, *Hu heo tham feondlicum gastum othfleon mage,* "How she the hostile spirits escape may."

The syntax is Turanian. "May" is here to be regarded as the indicative verb closing the sentence. Immediately before it comes the infinitive "fly." The adjective "hostile" preceds its noun, *gastum.* These words in the ablative case constitute with the initial pronoun a circumstantial clause preceding the clause which contains the principal verb. Before this circumstantial parenthesis stands the nominative. All so far is Turanian. Only the adverb "how" is out of its place. It should immediately precede the verb "escape." This is the single exception to Turanian order.

So frequently does the verb occur at the end of the sentence, after its accusative, or following some circumstantial clause, that it may be concluded, respecting the Anglo-Saxon as compared with modern English, that it was much more pervaded by the Turanian spirit. The same thing may be said of German when compared with English.

The Anglo-Saxon, like the Latin and German, broke partially free from this law, which in Sanscrit and in the three Turanian families ties the verb to the end of the sentence. The modern English has escaped from it entirely.

With this instance of the gradual abandonment of Turanian grammar in the modern European languages agrees the ever-advancing decay of the marks of declension and conjugation. Our ancestors a thousand years ago declined the word *guma*, "man," which is also, when slightly modified, good Mongol and Latin, with four variations of the suffix, namely, nominative *a*, accusative, ablative, and genitive *an*, ablative and dative plural *um*, and genitive plural *ena*. The adjective *soth*, "true," our *sooth*, the Chinese *zhet*, "real," and the Mongol *sidorago*, "honest," has applied to it the suffixes *ne*, *e*, *um*, *es*, *re*, *ra*, which supply it with five cases, two numbers, and three genders. Just as this more complex system of suffixes used in the days of Alfred connects our modern English with the original Indo-European mother-language, so the deeper tinge of Turanian influence in the syntax of the same age forms a midway link between the English of the nineteenth century and a still older Turanian model.

But behind the Turanian influence there is a still older one, that of the language of which Chinese is the type. Turania cannot furnish a satisfactory solution of the problem of the origin of language. In a still earlier age nature was true to herself, and inversions were still unknown. Chinese syntax is much more natural than the Turanian; and the English of modern days, and the Greek of two thousand years ago, are found returning to the more simple laws of arrangement which were familiar both to the ancient Chinese and to the language of the Antediluvians. China throws light on the problem by showing that the Turanian and Sanscrit awkwardness in syntax is in truth not primeval, but an inversion of natural laws, introduced contemporaneously with the growth of cases, tenses, and moods.

Language in its developments has been always controlled by the desire to arrive at a measured and elevated expression. What is attempted at a later period in poetry is sought at an earlier time in language. There is discernible in all speech an unconscious longing after internal harmony and symmetry. The desire for ideal beauty which God has implanted in the soul must be satisfied as far as possible in the creations of the language-forming faculties. The poet, seeking this ideal, voluntarily places himself under the limitations of art. Language is, although unconsciously, always doing the same thing. The Semite, fond of bold imagery, imagined the objects of nature to possess the distinctions of sex. A few centuries passed and his language became thoroughly permeated with this idea. A few more, and a male and female mythology grew into popular belief. The Indo-Europeans adopted both the idea of gender in language and of sex in mythology which they found among those to whom they then looked as teachers and examples.

On the other side, the Turanian race left the Chinese

freedom, and adopted a certain rigid law in syntax. The verb, relegated to the end of the sentence, gave origin in great part to case suffixes, and the moods and tenses of Turanian grammar. These became the fruitful source of an abundance of word-forms imitated by those who first used Indo-European speech, then in the time of its youth and its greatest susceptibility of impression. After many generations, language became weary of these strict rules, of a long array of cases, and a complex system of moods. She is now throwing away these encumbrances as fast as she can, and has, in the English language at least, already attained to an almost entire freedom from them.

The Anglo-Saxon poetry and that of ancient Germany was alliterative for the same reason that Mongol poetry is so. It was partly because words having polysyllabic suffixes are unsuitable for rhyme or metre, and also, probably, on account of both these schools having received the laws of their versification from some unknown race which originated alliteration in poetry. Rhyming was not practised by the Germans in their poetry till the Christian period.[1] Alliteration characterized all their oldest heathen versification, such as was used, for instance, in the war-songs of which Tacitus speaks.

The Anglo-Saxon alliteration is less regular than the Mongol. In Mongol, a poem may begin, for example,

[1] Weber's Weltgeschichte, 6th edit. Vol. ii. Geschichte der Deutschen Literatur.

with *a*. Each principal word in the first, second, third, and fourth lines will also begin with *a*. In the next stanza another letter will be used in the same manner. In the third stanza, a third, and so on. Thus the system is more like that of the old Hebrew alliteration, as in Psalm cxix., where the letter Aleph occurs at the beginning of each of the eight verses, Beth at the beginning of each of the second eight, and so on to the end of the alphabet. In Anglo-Saxon the irregular repetition of the alliterated initial in two or three principal words is enough. The poet does not attempt to carry the alliteration through more than two lines.[1] He prefers to begin a new alliteration with some other letter.

Rhyme is best suited for languages where monosyllabic roots abound. Polysyllabic suffixes render it impossible, or not agreeable to the ear. There would be no pleasure felt by the Mongol ear in the repetition at the end of several consecutive lines of three or four past tenses, such as *yababa*, "went," *taraba*, "agreed," *sanaba*, "thought," *hairaba*, "returned." For the same reason the Greeks and Latins used no rhymes, because they had few words without suffixes, and the repetition of mere suffixes in rhyme would have been wearisome and inharmonious. Rhyme came into use in Europe when derivative suffixes began to decay. In the Chinese language rhyme was always used. It is found in the most ancient portions of the Book of History. It suits

[1] Vernon's Anglo-Saxon Guide.

LIST OF ENGLISH AND CHINESE COMMON WORDS. 375

a monosyllabic language, because the emphasis and the rhyme fall together on radical syllables. In English and German the number of monosyllabic words is large, and hence the rhyme can be so arranged as to fall on roots, and not on servile syllables. It is this circumstance that renders the device of rhyme pleasing, and a suitable ornament of poetry.

ENGLISH.

A list of identical words will now be given, to show the extent to which the Chinese and English vocabularies agree. After the Chinese new and old pronunciations will be added a few examples of the forms assumed by the same roots in some select languages.

Avoid, 違 *wei, wit,* Latin *veto, vito, divido.*

Augment, 益 *yi, yik,* Latin *augeo,* Greek αὐξάνω, German *wachsen,* English *wax.*

Back, 背 *pei, pok,* Persian *pusht,* Greek ὀπίσω.

Baggage, 縛 *fu, bok,* Russian *poklaja.*

Bake, 炰 *p'au, bok,* Persian *pochtan,* Latin *frigo,* Greek φρύγω.

Bang, 磾 *p'eng, bang.*

Bear 負 *fu, bu, be,* Latin *fero, porto,* Greek φέρω.

Beat, 伐 *fa, bat,* Latin *batuo,* Russian *bit.*

Bed, 被 *pei, bi, bit,* "to spread," "a covering."

Black, 墨 *me, mek,* "ink," "coal," "that which is black," Greek μέλας, Sanscrit *malina.*

Boat, 筏 *fa, bat,* Anglo-Saxon *bat,* Russian *bot.*

Bow, 伏 *fu, bok,* German *bogen.*

Break, 劈 p'i, p'ik, "cleave with a hatchet," Latin *frango, fractus*, Sanscrit *bhagna*, "broken," Hebrew בקע, "cleave."

Bright, 白 pe, bak, Sanscrit *bhaj*, "shine," Latin *fulgeo*.

Burn, 焚 fen, bun, Latin *pruna*, Greek πῦρ.

But, boot (to add), 裨 pei, pi, pit, Anglo-Saxon *botan*.

Buy, bought, 買 mai, mui, muk, Latin *emo*.

Call, 叫 kiau, ko, kok, Greek καλέω.

Can, "a cylindrical drinking vessel," 罐 kwan, kan, 管 kan, "a pipe." Hence anything long and round, as *channel*, through the Latin *canalis*, and *cane*, from *canna*, in Chinese 稈 kan, "a stalk."

Certain, 決 kiue, kit, Latin *certus*.

Chaste, 潔 kie, kit, "clean," Latin *castus*, Greek καθαρός.

Cough, 咳 k'o, k'ok, German *keiche*, Greek κοίζω.

Cow, 牛 nieu, gnu, Sanscrit *go*.

Crooked, 曲 k'iü, k'ok, Latin *curvus*.

Crow, kwa, ku, Sanscrit *kâka*, Latin *corvus*.

Cut, 割 ko, kat, Latin *cædo*, Hebrew גרע.

Day, 晝 cheu, tok, German *tag*, Latin *dies*.

Deem, 忱 c'hen, dim, Russian *doomali*, "think."

Dew, 露 lu, lok, Sanscrit *dai*, German *thau*, Latin *ros*.

Din, 闐 chen, din, "noise of war drums."

Dong, ding-dong, 鐘 chung, tang, "bell."

Down, 低 ti, "low," "bottom," Latin *deorsum*, Mongol *dôra*.

LIST OF ENGLISH AND CHINESE COMMON WORDS. 377

Drag, draw, dray, 拖 t'o, t'a, Latin *traho, tracto*, German *ziehen*.

Eager, 欲 yü, yok, "to desire," Latin *acer*.

Ear, hear, 耳 rh, ngi, Persian *gosh*, Sanscrit *ghosha*, Turkish *kulak*, Latin *auris*, German *ohr, hören*.

Eat, 喂 wei, wid, wat, Sanscrit *annam*, "food," Mongol *idehu*, "eat," Latin *vescor*.

Elk, 鹿 lu, lok, Russian *los*, German *elch*.

Embrace, 包 pau, pok, Latin *amplector, brachium*, "arm," Greek πῆχυς.

Fast, 必 pi, pit, Mongol *bedu*, "firm," Greek πίστος, Latin *fides*, Sanscrit *bad*, "to be steady," Hebrew בָּטַל, "he trusted."

Father, 父 fu, bo, Latin, *pater*, Hebrew *ab*, Turkish *baba*.

Flee, 避 pi, bi, bik, Latin *fugio*, Greek φεύγω, German *fliehen*, Russian *biegat*, "avoid," Hebrew בָּרַח.

Fly, flit, 飛 fei, pi, pit, Sanscrit *patat*, "bird," Greek πέτεινος.

Fœtus, 胚 p'ei, p'i, p'it, Latin *fœtus*.

Fold (as in *two-fold*), 倍 pei, bei, bit (as in *saṅ pei*, "three-fold").

Forth, 發 fa, pat, "express," "go forth."

Foundation, 本 pen, pun, Latin *fundamentum*.

Gather, 會 hwei, git.

Give, 給 ki, kip, German *geben*.

Glad, 喜 hi, kit, Latin *gaudeo, gratus*, Greek γήθω.

Go, gang, 行 hing, gang.

Goose, 鵝 ngo, Russian *gus*, Mongol *galagad*.

Grip, grasp, 夾 *kia, kap*, "take under the arm or with tweezers," Latin *capio, habeo.*

Gullet, 喉 *heu, gu*, Sanscrit *gola*, Latin *gula*, German *hals*, "neck."

Hate, 憎 *hwei, git.*

He, 其 *k'i, gi*, Latin *hic*, Hebrew הוא.

Head, 甲 *kia, kap*, "coat of mail," "first in rank," "cover," 蓋 *kai, kap*, "covering on the top," *caput*, κεφαλή, *kopf, haupt.*

Hem (as a substantive), 襟 *kin, kim*, "hem of a garment," "a boundary"; (as a verb) 禁 *kin, kim*, "to prohibit," "restrain," Russian *kaima.*

High, 高 *kau, kok*, Latin *celsus*, German *hoch.*

Hollow, 虛 *hü, ku*, Latin *cavus*, German κοῖλος.

Hook, 鈎 *keu, kok.*

Hoop (cooper), 箍 *ku, kup.*

Horn, 角 *kio, kak*, Latin *cornu*, Greek κέρας, Hebrew קרן, Sanscrit *śringa*, Persian *shag.*

Hot, 熱 *je, nyit*, Mongol *halon*, Latin *calidus*, German *heiss.*

House, 家 *kia, ke*, Latin *casa*, Mongol *gere.*

Humble, 謙 *k'ien, k'im*, Latin *humilis.*

Hymn, 吟 *yin, gim*, "to chant," Greek ὕμνος.

I, 我 *ngo, nga*, Latin *ego*, German *ich.*

Kick, 脚 *kio, kak*, "foot," Welsh *cic*, "foot," *ciciaw*, "kick."

King, 君 *kiün, kun*, Welsh *kun*, "a chief," German *König.*

Lake, 澤 che, dak, Latin lacus.
Lamp, 燈 lan, lam, Greek λαμπάς.
Lath, 裂 lie, lit, "to split," "a rent," or "slit."
Law, 理 li, li, leg, Latin lex, Greek λόγος.
Leaf, 蝶 tie, dip, "butterfly," (so called from its leaf-like wings,) 疊 tie, dip, "fold one thing over another," Mongol lapc'hi, "leaf."
Lick, 嘗 c'hang, dong, Latin lingo, linxi, Greek λείχω.
Long, 長 c'hang, dong, Latin longus.
Mill, 磨 mo, ma, "grind," Latin mola.
Mother, 母 mu, mo, Greek μήτηρ.
Much, 莫 mo, mok, "abundant" (used in poetry).
Muck, 墳 mo, mok, "dust."
Paint, 票彡 piau, pik, "to draw," "to adorn," Latin pictor, pix, pingo.
Pair, 配 p'ei, p'i, Latin par.
Part, 別 pie, pit, bit, "to part from," "different," Latin pars, portio, partio, Hebrew בָּרַד, "he divided."
Paunch, 腹 fu, bok, German bauch.
Peace, 平 p'ing, bang, "even," "peace," Latin pax.
Peel, 皮 p'i, ba, Latin pellis.
Peg, pierce, 剽 "to pierce by setting on a spear." Compare the words prick, pick, spoke, poke, pike, with the Sanscrit pij, "kill," Greek πικρός, Latin pungo, pugno, German fechten.
Pledge, 憑 p'ing, bang, "lean on," "proof," Latin pignus, German pflegen.
Pot, 杯 pei, put, "cup," Sanscrit pâtra.

Prepare, 備 *pei, bi*, Mongol *belehu*, Latin *paro*.
Put (in *put forth*), 發 *fa, pat*, "go forth," or "be put forth."
Quiet, 歇 *hie, kit*, Latin *quies, quietis*.
Quoth, 話 *hwa, gwat*, "say," "words," Sanscrit *kath*, Latin *cedo*.
Reed, rod, 蘆 *lu, lut*, German *rohr*, Latin *arundo*.
Right, 直 *chï, dik*, "straight," Latin *rectus*, Greek δίκαιος, Sanscrit *dakshina*, "right."
Ring, 領 *ling, ling*, "collar."
Round, 輪 *lun*, "revolve," "a wheel."
Row, 櫓 *lu, lo, lot*, "a scull," German *ruder*, "oar," Latin *remus, remigo*, Greek ἐρετμός.
Rude, 魯 *lu, lod*, Latin *rudis*.
Rule, 理 *li*, "to govern," *leg*, Latin *regula, rego, rex*.
Sad, 悴 *tsui, dzot*, "sorry."
Same, 參 *t'san, t'sam, sam*, "blend with," "be one with," Latin *similis*.
Satisfy, 實 *shï, zhit*, "full," "real," Latin *satis*.
Say, 訴 *su, sok*, "tell," German *sagen, saga*.
Seed, 撒 *sa, sat*, Latin *sero, sator*, Sclavonic *syet*, "sow."
Seek, 索 *so, sok*, "seek," German *suchen*. Compare *search*.
Self, 自 *tsï, dzi, zi*, Latin *se*, German *selbst*.
Serve, 事 *shï, zhi*, Latin *servo, servus*, Sanscrit *shach*, "to serve," *śri*, "to serve."
Set, 設 *she, shet*, Latin *sisto, sedeo*, Hebrew שִׁית.
Shed, 舍 *she, shed*, "cottage," 室 *shï, shed*, "house."

To shed, 捨 she, shed, "let go," "forgive."

Shine, 烜 shen, shin, German *scheinen*, Latin *candeo*.

Shoot, 矢 shï, shed, "arrow," "to swear," German *schiessen*.

Sigh, 息 si, sik, German *sorge*, Sanscrit *suka*, "air," "wind."

Sing, 誦 sung, zung, "to chant," 頌 sung, song, "to praise."

Sister, 姊 tsï, tsi, Latin *soror*.

Slay, 戮 lu, lok, German *schlachten*, Anglo-Saxon *sleahan*.

Small, 微 wei, mi, Latin *minutus*, *minor*, Russian *malo*, Mongol *baga*.

Smell, 味 wei, mi, "odour," Persian *bui*.

Sot, 醉 tsui, tsut, sot, "become intoxicated."

Sound, 全 t'siuen, zien, "sound," "whole," "all," Latin *sanus*, German *gesund*.

Sound (of voice), sheng, shang, Sanscrit *śramana*, "hearer," Latin *sonitus*.

Split, 別 pie, pit, "to separate."

Spoke (of a wheel), 輻 fu, pok.

Spread, 播 po, pat, "scatter," Latin *pateo*, "lie open," German *breit*, English *broad*, Mongol *badaraho*, "spread."

Stand, stood, 踏 ta, dat, "tread upon," Japanese *tatta*, "stand," Tamil *tan*, "stand," Latin *sto*.

Step, 踏 t'a, dap, "to step," Russian *stupat*.

Stick, 觸 c'hu, t'ok, "pierce," Latin *stigo*, German *stechen*.

Straight, 直 chï, dik, Tamil takudi, "right," Latin rectus, Greek δίκαιος, "just."

Strike, 打 ta, tang, Mongol tugsehu, "beat," Hebrew חקע, "struck."

Strong, 壯 chwang, tong.

Suck, 嗽 su, tso, sok, Latin sugo.

Suet, 脺 su, sot, "fat about the entrails."

Tablet, 札 and 劄 cha, tap, "bamboo or wooden tablets."

Take off, 摘 che, tak.

Take on the person, 載 tai, tak.

Tap, tapestry, 插 c'ha, t'ap, "pierce," "prick," "embroider," German teppich, French tapis, English tap a tree or a barrel.

That, the, this, 第 ti, di, "this," 這 che, te, "this."

Through, 透 t'eu, t'ok, "thorough."

Throw, 投 t'eu, du, dut, 丟 tieu, to.

To, 到 tau, to.

Tongue, 嘗 c'hang, dung, "to taste," Latin lingo, lingua.

Trickle, 滴 ti, tik.

Turn, 轉 chwen, tun.

Vain (that which is empty and unsubstantial), 煙 yen, in, "smoke," 雲 yun, on, "cloud," Latin vanus, anima, English vanish.

Wash, 浴 yü, yok, Mongol ogahu.

We, 予 yü, wu, "I."

When, where, which, who, 何 ho, ga, "what?" 幾 ki, ka, "how many?"

Wicked, 惡 ngo, ak.
Wind, 彎 wan, "a bending," "to bend."
Wish, 欲 yü, yok, Latin volo.
Word, 曰 yue, wat, "say," German wort.
Yoke (that which connects), 約 yo, yak, "agree," "agreement," Latin jugum, jungo, Greek ζεῦγος.

This vocabulary of 153 words is taken almost exclusively from the Saxon part of the English language. The few words of Latin origin which occur might as well be placed in a Latin list, but as they form part and parcel of our English tongue they have also a right to be here.[1]

The old pronunciation of the Chinese words is indispensable in the comparison, and has been inserted in one or two forms.

Most of the words are such as belong to the pith and marrow of language, and are not unlikely to be really primeval.

A considerable difference in meaning, such as occurs, for example, under the words "vain," "shed," "leaf," "shoot," is not a fatal objection to the identification of the words, because of the great lapse of time since the ancestors of the Chinese and English spoke a common language.

The great advantage of the comparison of roots of

---

[1] For further examples, see Professor Haldeman's Relations between the Chinese and Indo-European Languages, p. 13, and Chalmers's Origin of the Chinese.

the European stock with those of the Chinese lies in the fact of the great antiquity of both. By lists such as those compiled by Eichhoff in his work on Comparative Grammar, English words are carried back to a period about two thousand years before the Christian era, because the Hindoo family cannot well have entered the Indian peninsula later, and the identification of the English and Sanscrit vocabularies is well established. But the Chinese vocabulary can be traced by the aid derived from the phonetic elements of the characters to a time equally ancient. During the lapse of four or five millenniums, the roots must be expected to appear not without some considerable modifications in the sense. When they are verbs in China, they may be nouns in England, and *vice versâ*. The existence of these differences thus adds increased certainty to the identification.

CHAPTER XIV.

CONCLUSION. — PRIMEVAL ARYAN CIVILIZATION AS KNOWN FROM LANGUAGE.—THE COMMON CIVILIZATION OF ARYANS AND CHINESE MAY BE KNOWN FROM LANGUAGE IN THE SAME WAY.—ACTIVITY OF THE THIRD MILLENNIUM B.C.—ETHNOLOGY OF GENESIS X. COMPARED WITH THE MODERN DISTRIBUTION OF RACES.— CHARACTERISTICS OF FAMILIES: THE CHINESE, ORDER; THE SEMITIC, LIFE; THE HIMALAIC, QUIETNESS; THE TURANIAN, EXTENSION; THE MALAYO-POLYNESIAN, SOFTNESS; THE INDO-EUROPEAN, ELEVATION; ALL OF ONE BLOOD.—PROOF FROM POLYNESIAN AND AMERICAN TRADITIONS.—RÉSUMÉ.—DUTY OF CHRISTIANS TO ASIA.

SUFFICIENT proof has already been given that a vocabulary of common words is just as possible for Europe and Eastern Asia as for Europe and India. If language proves that the English race is akin to the Hindoo, it also shows that it is akin to the Chinese. Philologists have shown that historical data may be recovered from the common vocabulary of the Indo-European family. Before their separation into Hindoo and Persian, Goth and Sclave, Greek and Latin, the Aryan race had towns and fortified places, reared cattle and ploughed the ground. They possessed as domestic animals the horse, swine, ox, dog, sheep, and goat;[1]

[1] Whitney's Lectures on Language; Max Müller's Lectures, first course, p. 223.

they built ships; they wove cloth; they lived in houses; they mined the earth for metals; they counted to a hundred; they recognized the social duties and the family bonds.

Similar results flow, as shown in the last chapter, from an examination of the European and Chinese common vocabulary. We find there words used in the west for the horse, ox, dog, and domestic fowl. The boat was known, but not the ship. Weaving was practised, and was called by the same name by the Chinese as by the Latins. Wheels and carts were in use. Corn was ground with mill-stones. Wooden bowls were employed for holding food. The processes of sowing and reaping were known by the same simple names. The same is true of some useful vegetable productions. The Arabic word for flax, *kuttan*, is like the Chinese *kot*. The old Chinese had three words for houses of different sizes, corresponding to the European οἶκος, cot, and shed.

If a complete comparative vocabulary were drawn up for each division of the Indo-European family, including the Celtic, Lithuanian, and Armenian, we should be in possession of all the important words in the primitive language spoken at the time when in the earth "there was one language and one speech." Roots which have survived the destroying effects of time through four thousand years may be assumed to have lived through the preceding period without much difficulty. The vitality of roots is most remarkable, and nothing brings it more vividly into view than the fact of their contemporaneous existence through so many ages at the extreme ends of Europe and Asia. Perhaps five hundred roots would satisfy the wants of the first men.

The activity of the language-forming faculty was at its maximum during the period when the distribution of nations took place. At B.C. 2000 most of the races were settled in the regions they now occupy. Since that time the language-forming faculty has limited itself to the evolution of new languages out of old ones. Before that epoch the formation of the families took place, and for this result a space of 1500 years is not too much.

During the 1500 years which seem to have intervened between the Deluge and the final settlement of the races, bands of colonists were traversing every region of the vast inheritance assigned by Providence to the human family. The energy and enterprise revealed in the mighty emigrations of those times, were paralleled by an intense intellectual activity, which rapidly and unconsciously traced the outline of the linguistic systems which have ever since prevailed in the two continents of Europe and Asia. What are now families were then languages, and they were cognate to one another as branches from the same stock.

This time of busy activity is described in the tenth

and eleventh chapters of the Book of Genesis, which constitute the most valuable record we possess for primeval ethnology. Independent investigation leads us to the same period, described in the Bible as that "when the earth was divided." The Confusion of Tongues at Babel marks the time when the families of language now existing became separated. Patient inquiry leads to the support of the Scriptural statement, and throws light upon it. It seems to refer specially to the separation of the Semites, Turanians, Indo-Europeans, and a part of the Himalaic race, for the rest of the families had probably already left the Mesopotamian region.

The object of the compiler of the tenth chapter was ethnological as well as genealogical, for Mizraim's seven sons are rather, as the plural termination indicates, seven races, and Canaan is said to be the father of eleven races.

As Cush had an eastern and western branch, so other races, usually located in the west, may also have an eastern habitat. The name Bod, common to several races in Eastern Asia, ought, as already said in a former chapter, to be compared with Phut, the name of the third son of Ham.

The Confusion of Tongues was followed by the domination of the Semite language, from Elam in Western Persia to Lydia in Asia Minor, and from Assyria to Sheba and Ophir in the south of the Arabian peninsula. Striking traces of Semite influence are found in the Zend, the Persian, and all the Himalaic languages.

The race of Ham extended into Africa. It fringed the sea-coast from Arabia Felix to the Indus, following the line of Cushite settlements. It then seems to have spread eastward, including the area of the Bod stock and that of China.

Modern research finds no place for the Turanians or the Malayo-Polynesians among the names of the descendants of the sons of Noah.[1] If they are to be included in the range of the tenth chapter of Genesis, it must be without the light of race names. The Scripture record is silent. To the inspired writers "they are the nations that sat in darkness" and "the uttermost parts of the earth." The links of connexion are lost, and they have created no ancient literature that might have served as a guide.

The linguistic proof, however, remains to show that they are of the common human stock. The Turanians are most nearly connected with the Japhetic languages, as the Himalaic and Malayo-Polynesian are with the Semitic.

Thus we seem to have the Japhetic influence in the northern half of Eastern Asia, as that of Shem and Ham in the southern half. In the Pacific Ocean, Japan

[1] The word *Mongol* may be compared with *Magog*, and *Togarmah* with the Turks and Tungus. The race name of the Japanese is *Wo*, which, as not having a consonant in it, is most nearly like Javan.

represents Japheth, and the Polynesian Archipelago, with Australasia, combine to spread Semite principles of language.

On the American continent, Turanian and Polynesian linguistic principles meet in the various Indian languages. New combinations are formed. But the peculiarities of the languages have not been found sufficiently distinctive to form a thoroughly satisfactory division into families. Yet it has been generally agreed to classify them as northern, central, and southern.

The characteristics of the six families of languages reviewed in the preceding chapters are, in the Chinese *order*, in the Semitic *life*, in the Himalaic *quietness*, in the Turanian *extension*, in the Malayo-Polynesian *softness*, and in the Indo-European *elevation*.

The love of order shown by the Chinese in their political and social sphere is found also in their language. The musical effect of the tones on the ear is parallel to the rigid laws of arrangement in their syntax. Antiquity prevails over novelty, and monosyllabism has retained its empire among them, through a conservative principle, which has thus, happily for science, secured to us a copy more like the original mother of languages than can be found in any other land. The accuracy of the Chinese picture of that lost tongue, which it is the highest duty of philology to restore, is in proportion to the restraining force which among the Chinese has always hindered development. That restraint has been caused partly by a feeling of art, which pleased itself with simple triumphs and the retention of the antique; and partly from want of the poetic impulse, which in more western regions has had so powerful an influence on the advance of language.

The principle of *life* characterizes remarkably the Semitic languages. The Koran and the Bible are replete with poetic expression. The people among whom these books originated were accustomed to look on the world with the poet's eye. This impulse was imparted to them by their possession of early revelation; and its effect was to modify, first, their language, and afterwards their literature, by rapid transitions, personifications, and the breaking up of natural order, so as to place them in complete contrast to the linguistic and literary development of Eastern Asia. The poetic spirit of the Semites probably originated the Indo-European mythology, as it did the more imaginative part of the Indo-European languages. Where the distinctions of gender are found in nouns, there will also be found male and female divinities with names and genealogies. The same feeling for personification, perhaps, has impressed on the Hamitic languages and systems of thought whatever features they possess of a kindred kind. The Hamites were a materialistic race, working patiently at trades and land cultivation. They were farmers and artificers, and they appear to have originated writing. With such tastes they would not create the mythology which prevailed in Babylon and Egypt. Semite influence may be pointed to as a more likely source of their religious ideas, as it would be also of much of their grammar.

The Himalaic peoples from Tibet to Cochin-China are characterized in their language, and in their history, by nothing so much as *quietness*. They have founded no institutions, originated no arts. They have received without giving. Their religion came from India and is Indo-European. Their arts were borrowed from China. The Tibetians have taken some elements in their language from the Semites, others from the Turanians, and others, again, from the Chinese. The Himalaic race are more thoroughly Buddhist than any other linguistic family. A contemplative religion, opposed to activity, pleased them because it agreed with their natural disposition. Its effect on them has been to confirm them in their quiet ways of thinking. They can never produce any impress on history till they abandon this inactive and gentle religion.

The Turanian race has played in the world a much more important part than those who reside east and north of the Himalayan Mountains. In the fifth century, the Huns under Attila were named "The scourge of God"; and in the thirteenth century, the

Mongols were the conquerors of all Asia and the dread of all Europe. Occupying Siberia, North Europe, Japan, Tartary, and South India, they won for themselves a good title to the name of Japheth "*the extender.*" In harmony with this name are the characteristics of their language. They founded the polysyllable and the most widely used system in the world of cases, tenses, and moods. They thus added immensely to the progress of language, by the simple process of appending syllables to roots by agglutination. The language-forming faculty then applied itself to the crystallization of these polysyllabic forms into the grammatical paradigms which belong to the several languages respectively of the Turanian and Indo-European stocks.

The characteristic of the Malayo-Polynesian languages is *softness*. The primitive monosyllable became a dissyllable by the enervating effect of climate. The initial consonant formed the first syllable and the final the second. Agglutination proceeded on the same principle to work out the Oceanic polysyllable. Everything favoured an easy pronunciation adapted to a race accustomed to lassitude and contented to deteriorate. A people having a very soft language can never elevate themselves unless under new conditions, such as the introduction of Christianity.

The last of the series, the Indo-European, is remarkable for *elevation*. This system is built on those that went before, and in many respects combines and perfects their peculiar excellences. The topmost branches of the tree of language, those that spread widest and aspire highest, are the Indo-European. It is this race that has led the mind of the world in science and philosophy, and its language constitutes the most fitting vehicle for the transmission of scientific and philosophic thought. The monosyllabic languages are the lower branches, thick and of great length, but with no bend upwards. The dissyllabic modes of human speech are higher and are turned heavenwards. The earlier polysyllabic languages have a vast extension, but not much upward curvature. The chief beauty of the tree is in its higher foliage. Here are seen the greatest variety of picturesque effects, the most vigorous growth, the most elegant forms, the most imposing altitude. All the branches, however, upper or lower, proceed from one trunk.

"God hath made of one blood all nations of men for to dwell on all the face of the earth." When the European goes into the other continents of the world, as traveller, colonist, missionary, and civilizer, he meets everywhere with men of the same race. "But what have we in common with the Turanians, with Chinese, and Samoyedes? Very little it may seem: and yet it is not very little, for it is our common humanity. It is not the yellow skin, or the high cheek-bones, that make the man. Nay, if we look but steadily into those black Chinese eyes, we shall find that there, too, there is a soul that responds to a soul, and that the God whom they *mean* is the same God whom we *mean*, however helpless their utterance, however imperfect their worship."[1] Language proves them to be one with ourselves. The black, the yellow, the copper-coloured, and the brown races come of one stock. If the yellow and the white can by linguistic proofs be shown to be one, the presumption will be strong that the same is true of all. The evidence is more accessible in the case of the yellow race than of the rest, because they have an ancient literature and a writing by means of ideographic signs, of which the phonetic values are known. With the less civilized races we have not this advantage. Their languages are perpetually changing, and we cannot recover their ancient forms. But if the differences between a white and a yellow skin, an upright and a receding forehead, a Caucasian and a Mongolian head, a large blue eye, set deep, and a small black eye, set on the surface, are not conclusive against consanguinity, so neither must it be allowed that a black or red skin, proves descent from a different Adam.

If Adam were the progenitor of Caucasians only, as held by M'Causland,[2] we should not find European roots existing in abundance in the Chinese vocabulary.

[1] Max Müller, Lectures on the Science of Religion.

[2] Adam and the Adamites, 1864. Dr. M'Causland has felt strongly the force of the stone hatchet argument. But the right way to proceed is rather to make mutual concessions in chronology.

Nor should we meet the old type of the Aryan pronouns and the Aryan system of accidence in Turanian languages still spoken in Tartary and Siberia.

If the Polynesians were not of Asiatic origin, we should not find proofs of their syllabic system being based upon an old Asiatic syllabary and their laws of syntax all formed on Asiatic models. Man cannot retain his civilization and morality when isolated—he will cease to practise old arts, he will forget facts once familiar to him, his religious ideas will become dim, his range of thought will in each successive century grow more limited, and he will fall into habits which are immoral and debasing. That the Polynesians are now inferior to the Japanese and Chinese is the effect of their distant wanderings, and is an argument for the propriety of offering to them early the blessings of religious and moral teaching, with instruction in the arts of civilized man.

The religion of the Polynesians is more like that of the Brahmans than of the Buddhists, and there were probably communicated to them, in early times, from India, some features of the Hindoo faith. Who can Tiki be but Śakra? What can be the paradise of Tiki, as believed in by the Samoans, but the thirty-third heaven of Śakra? At any rate ś is changed into *t* quite commonly in the cognate languages spoken on the Birman peninsula. Yet the Samoan belief in a Supreme God, called *Tangoloa* reminds us strongly of the Mongol and Turkish faith in Tengri, and that of the Chinese in Tien. The addition of the two consonants *g*, *r*, is Turanian, and it was apparently from the Turanians, therefore, that faith in the Supreme Being under this name was derived. The worship of ancestors, common in the South Seas, would be learned from the Chinese; while the human sacrifices, which also existed among them to a frightful extent,[1] must be viewed as Turanian,—for in some parts of India the aborigines are, under British eyes, only beginning to allow this practice to fall into desuetude,—or they are Semitic, and are of the same origin as the sacrifices to Moloch condemned in the Old Testament.

Let the reader now recall the successive steps of this investigation from the commencement. The old institutions of China were shown to be like those of the renowned cities of ancient Mesopotamia. It was stated that the remarkable similarity in arts, usages, and ideas, existing among the races that lived near the Yellow River, the Euphrates, and the Nile, indicated that they sprang from a common source.

After briefly glancing at the geographical areas of the families of languages spoken in Asia, a sketch was drawn of their most general features, as constituting a rough picture of the world's primeval language. The roots are recoverable in a monosyllabic form. They were chiefly imitations of natural sounds, and were

[1] Williams's Missionary Enterprizes.

increased by the aid of the principle of the association of ideas. Special divine aid was afforded to primeval man in the task of forming for himself a language.

In the chapter on the Chinese language, after it had been shown that the conditions of the situation would be best suited by supposing the Chinese to have left Western Asia about 5,000 years ago, and yet subsequently to the Deluge of Noah, the mode of recovering the primeval Chinese syllabary from the phonetic element of the characters was described. The syntax, so accordant with nature and innocent of inversions, was seen to be of the most primeval type.

The next step in the progress of language was taken in the formation of the Semitic language. The people who used Semite speech added a consonant to the root, introduced prefixes to mark conjugations and moods, invented a plural and dual number, originated genders among nouns not properly masculine or feminine, and revolutionized the syntax.

In speaking of the languages used in the region south of China, it was seen that while their tones, their syllabaries, and their vocabulary, connect them closely with China, their syntax links them remarkably with the Semitic type. While this is the case with the Siamese, the Cochin-Chinese, and the Miau aborigines in China itself, some still more striking Semitic characteristics belong to the Tibetan language. Though its tones, roots, and radical syllabary show it to be akin to the Chinese, and its syntax and case suffixes prove its relationship to the Turanian type, its mode of conjugating verbs and its consonantal prefixes are Semite, and seem to point for their origin to a time earlier than the Aryan occupation of India and Persia, which drove the Semites and Turanians from their neighbourhood on the west and south.

The Japanese received special attention as the oldest of the polysyllabic languages in Asia, and it was shown how case particles grew into existence by agglutination, the syllables made use of for this purpose being words existing as separate roots in Chinese and other languages.

The second division of the polysyllabic Turanian system was described as the Dravidian. The growth of the verb by agglutination was here traced, and a growing resemblance in vocabulary and grammar to the western type found to be perceptible.

The greatest likeness and nearest kinship between the Indo-European languages and the threefold Turanian type was proved to exist in the Tartar, of which Mongol was taken as the best representative. Here it was shown that the pronouns and substantive verbs, declension of nouns, and verb conjugation of western speech, rest chiefly upon the Tartar branch of the Turanian family as their source and foundation.

The Malays and Polynesians have a syllabary and vocabulary which was evidently once continental. The

Malay and Siamese are specially connected with each other, while Chinese influence in the principles prevailing in the Polynesian languages is very perceptible. These islanders retain traces of a lost civilization, which comes more prominently to view on the American continent. Language and religious beliefs alike point to Southern Asia as the source from which came the tribes that inhabit Australia, Polynesia, and the civilized portion of the American tribes.

The sudden expansion of language observable in Sanscrit, as compared with the preceding systems, indicates the commencement of a new era of development, characterized by unparalleled richness of forms. This new advance proceeds on principles already existing in older systems. In introducing gender in nouns, and sex in mythology, Semitic example was followed. So, also, the prefix of sibilants in the root and the insertion of r and l after the initial of the primeval syllable seem to have come from the same source. But in all the newer portions of the Sanscrit grammatical formation we find laws prevailing which also characterize Turanian languages. Case suffixes, the verb, and the syntax, bear united testimony to this statement. But there is a more highly wrought appearance in the forms. Agglutination has become inflexion. Root and suffix are fused into a closer union. The advance in analytical acuteness, which was after a few centuries to culminate in the creation of

Hindoo philosophy, is first seen in the minute subdivisions of the verb paradigms. The adjective was now for the first time declined like the substantive, and the relative pronoun began to exert some of that power which it has more fully assumed in the European languages.

When the speech of ancient and modern Europe was brought under our review, it was found, as in Sanscrit, that the principles of older languages were working underneath the surface. But they appeared in new combinations suited to the mental conditions of the successive races who have in that favoured continent wrought out such a marvellous history in the political, social, and intellectual sphere. Greece, happily placed in the vicinity of the ancient empires, was able early to derive from them the seeds of progress. Carefully nurturing these, she was seen to develope with astonishing rapidity those creations in poetry, science, history, and philosophy, which the world will never cease to admire. A language and literature so beautiful and complete as the Greek could never have originated but from the happy combination of fruitful principles, derived from the pre-existing systems of language and thought. The Latin, the Teutonic, and the Sclavonic forms of language were each modified by special elements, contributed in varied proportion from the same sources.

In all these languages, early changes foreshadowed

later ones, and new phenomena exemplify over again what took place long ago. When we say, "Alfred the Great," we use a French idiom, dating from the Norman Conquest; and among our Saxon idioms, old and new, forming the major part of the language, Turanian modes of expression may be pointed out, which at some distant time, when our ancestors lived near the Caspian, found their way into colloquial use in some similar manner. For the English, "and came before him," the Anglo-Saxon Gospels have, in Mark vi. 33, "and him beforan comon." These words are exactly in the order of Manchu and Mongol syntax.

How great are the linguistic accessions to European speech received from far Asia has been shown by examples of common words. They are enough to make plain that the vocabularies of the east and west are essentially the same. This identity dates from a time previous to the settlement of the Chinese in China and the Mongols in Mongolia. Philology may here safely take her stand, and add a chapter of illustration to the sacred record, where it treats of the division of the earth and the planting of nations.

It is the duty, as it is the destiny, of the nations of Europe to give back to the east the treasure of heavenly light which they once received from it. To Asia they owe the first impulses to thought, the earliest lessons in the arts, the invention of writing, and the priceless deposit of divine revelation. "Freely ye have received," says the Saviour, "freely give." Their higher mental elevation and their richer stores of knowledge fit them to be the instructors of the old world; and to this undertaking Divine Providence is leading them by unmistakable signs. England has received the rule of India for this purpose, that she may become the teacher and evangelizer of India. Commerce and war have opened the gates of China, that Christian truth may enter them. All new facts, therefore, should be welcome that tend to show that the Chinese are one with us in origin, and that their history, their institutions, their language even, derive their source, as ours do, from Western Asia. Let the kindly sympathy of the west for the east be the more called forth as the proofs of common brotherhood are accumulated.

THE END.

STEPHEN AUSTIN AND SONS, PRINTERS, HERTFORD.

www.ingramcontent.com/pod-product-compliance
Lightning Source LLC
Chambersburg PA
CBHW020545300426
44111CB00008B/797